D0619670

Human Resource Strategies for the High Growth Entrepreneurial Firm

WITHDRAWN
UTSA LIBRARIES

a volume in
Research in Human Resource Management

Series Editors:
Rodger Griffeth, *Georgia State University*

Reserarch in
Human Resource Management

Rodger Griffeth, Series Editor

Human Resource Management in Virtual Organizations (2002)
edited by Robert L. Heneman and David B. Greenberger

Innovative Theory and Empirical Research on Employee Turnover (2002)
edited by Rodger Griffeth and Peter Hom

IT Workers Human Capital Issues in a Knowledge Based Environment (2005)
edited by Rodger Griffeth

Human Resource Strategies for the High Growth Entrepreneurial Firm

edited by

Judith W. Tansky
Ohio State University

and

Robert L. Heneman
Ohio State University

INFORMATION AGE
PUBLISHING

Greenwich, Connecticut • www.infoagepub.com

Library of Congress Cataloging-in-Publication Data

Human resource strategies for the high growth entrepreneurial firm /
edited
by Judith W. Tansky and Robert L. Heneman.
    p. cm. — (Research in human resource management)
 Includes bibliographical references.
 ISBN 1-93068-14-4 (pbk.) — ISBN 1-930608-15-2 (hardcover)
 1. Entrepreneurship 2. Small business—Personnel management.
I. Tansky, Judith W. II. Heneman, Robert L. III. Series.
 HF5549.H84 2006
 658.3'01—dc22

                     2006014586

ISBN 13: 978-1-930608-14-6 (pbk.)
        978-1-930608-15-3 (hardcover)
ISBN 10: 1-930608-14-4 (pbk.)
        1-930608-15-2 (hardcover)

Copyright © 2006 IAP–Information Age Publishing, Inc.

All rights reserved. No part of this publication may be reproduced, stored in a
retrieval system, or transmitted, in any form or by any means, electronic, mechanical,
photocopying, microfilming, recording or otherwise, without written permission
from the publisher.

Printed in the United States of America

Library
University of Texas
at San Antonio

With love,
To my best supporters
Tom, Katie, Nate, and my parents
—JWT

To all my brothers for their guidance
Herbert G. Heneman III, John A. Fossum, and Mark Younghans
—RLH

CONTENTS

ACKNOWLEDGMENT

This book is the result of an invitational conference that was held at The Ohio State University, Fisher College of Business, in 2003. The conference was funded by a grant from Ewing Marion Kauffman Foundation. The grant was to study the issue of Human Resource Management in small and entrepreneurial firms and to encourage academic research in this area of intersection between human resources and entrepreneurship. The chapters for this book were, with the exception of one, written by academics attending the conference. The chapters were blind reviewed for acceptance.

We wish to thank Ewing Marion Kauffman Foundation for the opportunity to host this conference and encourage research in this area of human resource management and entrepreneurship.

The views expressed in this book are those of the authors and do not necessarily reflect the views of The Kauffman Foundation.

HR IN HIGH GROWTH ENTREPRENEURIAL FIRMS

Judith W. Tansky and Robert L. Heneman

In 1959, Penrose argued that managing human resources is a critical variable in the growth of emerging firms. Since that time we have seen an extensive stream of research in the area of Human Resource Management, as well as in the field of Entrepreneurship, but we have seen little research that focuses on HR in small and entrepreneurial firms. In fact, we (Heneman, Tansky, & Camp, 2000) reviewed the academic and practitioner literature from 1984 to 1999 and found a total of 17 empirical articles that examined human resource management in SMEs (small and medium sized enterprises). Since our call for more research (Heneman et al., 2000), we have seen growth in the area but as noted by Shane and Venkataraman (2000) we still need models and frameworks to organize and direct theory development as well as empirical studies.

We know that small firms as well as entrepreneurial ventures are important to the economy. In 2003, 99.7% of the 5.7 million companies in the United States that had employees had fewer than 500 employees (United States Small Business Administration Office of Advocacy [USSBA], 2003). Brush, Greene, and Hart (2001) argued that the development and composition of initial resources are vital to the success of a new venture. In

Human Resource Strategies for the High Growth Entrepreneurial Firm, xi–xx
Copyright © 2006 by Information Age Publishing
All rights of reproduction in any form reserved.

fact, Brush et al. (2001) point out that ineffective management, human failings, or the inability of the firm to attract and maintain qualified personnel, all contribute to the failure of new ventures every year.

In our special issue of *Human Resource Management* (Heneman & Tansky, 2003), we argued that few of our existing human resource management theories apply to small and entrepreneurial firms (Heneman & Tansky, 2002). In this book, we continue our quest for the development of the science of human resource management in small and entrepreneurial firms. The starting point for the normal development of science is to describe the phenomenon in question. This requires descriptive surveys of practices and cases that illustrate the practices. The next step in the development of science is to develop frameworks and taxonomies to categorize and organize the variables identified by observation. These taxonomies help to synthesize the observations so that testable hypotheses can be created using theory as the guide. Although we are still in the early stages of developing science in the area of human resources in small and entrepreneurial firms, the content of this book illustrates the progress that has been made.

The first three chapters focus on conceptual frameworks and theories to give us a better understanding of entrepreneurial firms.

In the first chapter, Alvarez and Molloy argue that human resource practices differ in entrepreneurial and established firms because entrepreneurial firms operate under conditions of uncertainty. They argue the objective of human resource management is to maximize firm performance (Noe, Hollenbeck, Gerhart, & Wright, 2006). Firm performance is defined by comparing the value that a firm creates using its productive resources with the value that those resources would generate in the next best alternative investment. Entrepreneurial firms operate under conditions of uncertainty because firm performance is both unknown and unknowable. Thus, the uncertain conditions of entrepreneurial firms are in contrast to the risk condition of established firms. The authors draw on both economic literature and entrepreneurship literature to support the above conclusion.

They also question the use of transactions-cost theory to address the issue of the exercising managerial control in a way that ensures the efficient operation of a firm since the theory requires the manager to have certain information that is not available in the entrepreneurial firm. Alvarez and Molloy pose the following questions: What happens to the owner's ability to exercise managerial control when the required information to exercise control does not exist? When the value of specific investments is not known? When the type and level of commitments required are not known? "In these uncertain settings, how can the owner efficiently monitor and control an exchange?"

Alvarez and Molloy conclude their chapter by positing that we must identify why differences exist between human resource management in established firms and in entrepreneurial firms and use this information to aid both theoretical and descriptive research.

In their chapter entitled "Toward an understanding of strategic human resource management in entrepreneurial firms: Opportunities for research and action," Goswami, McMahan, and Wright examine in detail the issues involved in defining small business, small and medium size companies, and entrepreneurial firms. They argue that although small businesses play a major role in the economy, it is the entrepreneurial firms that become high-growth firms. Thus, their discussion of strategic human resource management in entrepreneurial firms is limited to privately held, small, high growth firms started by an individual entrepreneur, perhaps with the support of some other entrepreneurs, family or venture capitalists but without the sponsorship of an existing corporation. A review of the literature emphasizes that we have limited knowledge about the extent to which existing HRM theories extend to smaller entrepreneurial firms. Their conclusions agree with those of Cardon and Stevens (2004) that we need to understand three fundamental aspects of HRM in the context of small organizations: retention and ongoing employee issues, integration and interactions of HR practices, and the evaluation of HR practices within evolving organization.

Thus, Goswami et al. build their case for developing a model of strategic HR in entrepreneurial firms. After a discussion of Strategic Human Resource Management with an emphasis on the resource-based view (RBV) of the firm, a conceptual model and propositions that can be tested are presented. Deviating from the traditional HR functional approach, the authors argue that people management practices including leadership, communication, and work design combined with an understanding of multiple practices beyond the traditional HR practices have the potential to impact employees and thus their competencies, cognitions and attitudes. This relationship will be moderated by the firm's access to people expertise. Employee competencies, cognition and behaviors will lead to a knowledge climate which in turn will lead to entrepreneurial performance including such outcomes as higher sales, increased new product development, creating more core competencies, enhancing employee capabilities and creation of additional competitive advantage. The authors conclude that they are offering a starting point for studying the role of people in entrepreneurial firms. They appear to recognize the importance of the actual people involved in the firm as opposed to the human resource functional areas often studied in large firms.

In his chapter, "Human capital management practices and performance in small and medium sized enterprises: A conceptual framework,"

Hayton next presents a conceptual framework for understanding the contribution of Human Capital Management to entrepreneurial firm performance. Human Capital Management (HCM) represents an important feedback mechanism for the HRM system. HCM includes the use of human capital measurement techniques as well as human resource information management strategies. The author argues that HCM is a form of strategic resource according to RBV or resource-based theory of the firm also discussed by Goswami et al.

Hayton's model depicts HCM sophistication as a predictor of (1) HR System internal consistency, (2) HR System external fit, (3) HR System resource flexibility, and (4) HR System coordination flexibility. HR System resource flexibility is the capability to sustain elevated rates of broadly targeted product creation (Sanchez, 1995, p. 135) and is consistent with the concept of sustained regeneration. HR System coordination flexibility is associated with redefining strategic goals, reconfiguring the chains of resources for achieving the goals, and deploying resources. These variables in turn influence entrepreneurial performance. This relationship between entrepreneurial performance and the predictors of entrepreneurial performance are established and moderated by the environmental complexity and dynamics.

The next five chapters focus on what are traditionally considered functional areas of Human Resource Management and who performs the duties of human resource management.

Cardon and Tolchinsky offer a discussion of SMEs and the alternative means of staffing that can be employed including permanent employees, contingent labor, and outsourcing of staffing to a PEO. They acknowledge the lack of managerial capability in the area of human resources in most small or start-up companies. A model for determination of whether to use the traditional permanent employee, contingent workers or a PEO is tied to the speed of growth of the organization and the mental model or type of company the founder is trying to create. Using the work of Baron and Hannan (2002), the authors argue that mental models include images of the culture, espoused values, structures (hierarchy of lack of hierarchy and levels of decision authority throughout the organization), rules and procedures of lack thereof, interdependencies among the various members of the SME, and compensation.

Mental models are culturally dependent if the leaders' mental model is based on specific ways of acting, behaving and performing duties and responsibilities that define the organization I unique ways. The culturally dependent mental models require a very good fit between the organization and its members (traditional employees or employees hired by the PEO). Culturally independent firms change cultural factors more easily. They do not have a strong identifiable culture. Cardon and Tolchinsky recommend that culturally dependent, fast growth companies should hire direct (traditional) employees or use PEOs. Culturally dependent, slow growth companies should hire direct or use contingent workers. Culturally independent, fast growth organizations should use PEOs or contingent workers while culturally independent companies can use all three. These authors call for more research in how small firms make staffing and other HR decisions. Specific research questions raised include: How do concerns for the legitimacy of SMEs as viable employers impact a firm's need to utilize alternative staffing sources? If individuals are attracted by the more relaxed innovative cultures of SMEs, but concerned about stability and legitimacy or the organization would they be more likely to take assignments in SMEs though labor brokers such as PEOs and consulting firms? Cardon and Tolchinsky encourage scholarly inquiry into the HR decision-making processes of SME leaders and specifically their use and implementation of nontraditional staffing approaches.

Next, Barber confirms that although hiring and retaining qualified employees is one of the greatest difficulties that small firms encounter, the vast majority of published studies focus on large firms. Thus, what do we know about recruitment in small firms? Barber concludes that small and large firms do indeed differ in their recruitment practices. Therefore, concerns about generalizing from a literature dominated by large firms appear to be valid. She also raises the issue that her chapter does not differentiate between small firms and start-ups even though we need to understand the differences between these two groups.

Based on research, there is support that indicates that recruitment practices used by large firms are more formal and costly than those used by small firms. Evidence also suggests that small firms are more concerned with person-organization fit rather than person-job fit.

This chapter raises some very interesting topics for future research. Do small firms consider personal qualities such as integrity and conscientiousness more important than ability, work experience and credentials? Do small firms offer different opportunities to applicants and if so how does that affect the attractiveness of the job? For small firms, is smallness a liability or a strength and how does that affect the firm's ability to attract and retain employees? Should small firms mimic the recruitment practices of large firms? Do small firms define recruitment effectiveness differently than large firms and if so does that influence any comparison of recruitment effectiveness? Barber does an excellent job accomplishing her goals of (1) encouraging research that will improve our ability to provide useful advice to small firms, and (2) to encourage researchers to use the differences between large and small firms as a means of extending our understanding of a variety of recruitment issues.

Cardy and Miller next discuss the issue of performance management. After a discussion of the traditional performance management system found in large organizations and based on research, the authors discuss performance management in small and high growth companies. They emphasize the importance of performance in small and high growth companies and the fact that a poor performance has much more impact on the firm. Cardy and Miller assume that work processes are less established in small and high growth firms, that agility and adaptability are competitive advantages, that bureaucracy does not exist and is not desired and that staffing may be inadequate and employees may need to take on a variety of duties. Thus, workers need a breadth of capabilities to perform effectively in the small and/or growing firm. In fact, the dynamic, unstructured environment requires personal characteristics such as interpersonal skills and values.

The importance of performance leads to a need for a system that focuses on an administrative purpose where decisions are made about employees based upon their performance. At the same time the loss of an employee can be devastating to a small or growing company. Thus, retention can be helped by providing feedback and growth opportunities for workers. This relationship has been established based on research and is often part of the developmental approach to performance management. Thus, small and growing firms probably need to focus on administrative and developmental purposes to maximize performance and retention.

The authors emphasize that a task-based system is probably too narrow and that roles are more important in a dynamic organization. Thus, job analysis which is the basis for the HR system in large organizations may be irrelevant for the small firm. The basis for performance may focus on the roles the person plays in the organization and how effectively these roles are performed. These ideas provide a basis for research questions in the area of performance management for the small and/or growing firm.

One of the functional areas of HR that has been researched in large firms is the area of compensation and reward systems. Balkin and Swift offer eight research propositions predicting relationships between selected pay strategies and the stage of growth of new ventures. The issues focus on the distribution of equity among members of the team of founders, the design of the pay package for key employees who are non-founders, and the compensation strategy for employee groups who are hired as the company grows.

This chapter provides a good review of the life cycle and growth models of development and their importance in the study of small and entrepreneurial firms. The authors provide arguments and research to support their propositions which could lead to interesting research. The team of founders will receive equal amounts of equity. When there are differences in levels of commitment, contributed capital, or skill between the founders, the amount of equity will be proportion to the value of the input of each founder. For key employees who are nonfounders the amount of equity will be small than that allocated to the founders. The variable pay component for the key nonfounders will be emphasized during launch of the firm.

During growth, broad employee groups will be hired with the person as the basis of pay for determining base salaries. External pay equity will be emphasized so that the firm can attract people with the right skills and fit to the organization. Variable pay will represent a substantial portion of total pay. A longtime orientation for pay incentives will be adopted during the growth stage. Balkin and Smith do a good job of laying out the differences between large firms and small, growing firms.

Klaas, McClendon, Gainey, and Yang introduce the concept of the PEO (Professional Employer Organization) as a means of helping SMEs deal with the effective management of human resources. Klaas et al. identify some of the questions raised by the PEO as well as what future research would be beneficial. They argue that variability exists between SMEs and their use of PEOs. For smaller SMEs, the decision is between an informal, ad-hoc approach to HR or reliance on a third-party vendor. For the largest SMEs, the choice is between reliance on a third-party vendor (similar to outsourcing) and in-house HR. A thorough discussion of the benefits and threats of PEOs and their different relationships (transactional or strategic) with the organization are discussed. The authors offer prescriptive information based on research for SMEs when selecting and managing a PEO relationship. Future research directions are presented.

The next two chapters focus on specific types of firms. Belman and Kossek focus on the self-employed truck driver owner-operators while Mayson and Barrett point out the issues faced by small companies in Australia where small is defined as less than 20 rather than less than 500.

Bellman and Kossek provide a case for defining or redefining entrepreneurship and self-employment due to employment relations moving toward greater subcontracting and more contingent employment. They then argue that truck driver owner-operators are a form of small-scale entrepreneur. Bellman and Kossek hypothesize that owner-operators should, on average, be better rewarded than employees doing similar work, that their work effort defined as hours worked and miles driven will be higher than employees, and that they will have more control over their work. Owner-operators will be more diverse because the employment relationships will be attractive to minorities and less subject to discrimination. Last, older owner-operators should perform better than younger owner-operators because they have accumulated more physical and human capital.

Owner-operators are not more economically successful but their working conditions are considerably better than similar drivers. Evidence suggests that they may choose their owner-operator status because of the superior working conditions, the ability to have greater control over their working lives, and possibly to improve their longevity in their chosen profession. Future research might look at outcomes other than wealth as motivators for individuals pursuing self-employment or even entrepreneurship. The authors argue that they have demonstrated the importance of future research in entrepreneurship to draw from human resource management and organizational behavior.

Mayson and Barrett focus on HRM practices in growing small firms in Australia. They present a review of the literature that supports their argument that growing small firms should exhibit greater formalization in their HRM practices than nongrowing small firms. Small firms in Australia are defined as firms with less than 20 people. The sample is 600 small CPA firms in Australia. Forty-nine percent of the firms employed only one or two people in total. Ninety-eight firms were categorized as growing firms because they had hired a full or part-time staff member in the last twelve months. Growing small firms were significantly different from nongrowing firms in that they have a list of skills and qualifications being sought when they hire, they have a written job description for the position being filled, and they are more likely to get outside help with recruitment. Significant differences also existed in that growing firms were more likely to: (1) offer bonuses or incentives to reward performance, (2) pay for off-site training or work-related education, (3) offer salary increases to reward performance, (4) have an incentive scheme, (5) offer job-sharing or part-time work, (6) offer addition time off to reward performance, (6) offer promotions to reward performance, (7) offer special training or conference to reward performance, (8) have a succession plan, and (9) have an employee share plan. The results show that growing small firms are more likely to exhibit more formalized HRM practices.

In the final chapter, Klaas and Klimchak stress the important role that the management of human resources plays within the entrepreneurial firm. They then argue that this book is premised on the assumption that context matters. They call for researchers to develop a conceptual framework for identifying the organizational pathologies to which small and medium enterprises are likely to be susceptible. Then it is possible to think about HR systems that might lead to competitive advantage.

Klaas and Klimchak also present arguments for the following types of research: (1) the need to examine the impact of employee relations norms within entrepreneurial firms; (2) the issue of understanding when investing in HR is most likely to generate benefits; (3) the need to examine how industry and occupational characteristics affect the need for human resources in entrepreneurial firms; (4) the need to examine how financial stability affects the utility of investing in HR; (5) the role of the CEO/owner in the development of HR practices, and (6) the variation in the investment in HR among entrepreneurial firms.

This volume not only illustrates the research that is being done in the area of human resources in entrepreneurial firms but it raises many issues that exemplify the complexity of the topic. It is not a case of small versus large firms. There are small established firms, small start-up firms and small high growth firms. As pointed out by Alvarez and Molloy these firms differ with established firms dealing with risk while high growth firms deal with uncertainty. These firms vary in ownership based on family ownership, ownership by founder, or some type of privately held stock ownership. These firms also vary based on how they handle people issues: structure versus lack of structure; the traditional HR functional approach versus the use of people management practices; person-job fit versus person-organization fit; ability and work experience versus integrity and conscientiousness; work processes and bureaucracy versus agility and adaptability; tasks versus roles; in-house professionals versus reliance on third-party vendors; traditional pay versus variable pay; short-term orientation of incentives versus long-term orientation of incentives; and many more.

We challenge you to pursue this stream of research and to help not only develop theory and conceptual models and pursue empirical research but to also disseminate your information in a way that will help practitioners and owners in all the small and high growth firms.

REFERENCES

Baron, J. N., & Hannan, M. T. (2002). Organizational blueprints for success in high-tech start-ups; Lessons from the Stanford project on emerging companies. *California Management Review, 44*(3), 8-36.

Brush, C. G., Greene, P. G., & Hart, M. M. (2001). From initial idea to unique advantage: The entrepreneurial challenge of constructing a resource base. *Academy of Management Executive, 15*(1), 64-80.

Cardon, M. S., & Stevens, C. E. (2004). Managing human resources in small organizations: What do we know? *Human Resource Management Review, 14*, 295-323.

Heneman, R. L., & Tansky, J. W. (2003). Introduction to the special issue on human resource management in SMEs: A call for more research. *Human Resource Management, 42*(4), 299-302.

Heneman, R. L., & Tansky, J. W. (2002). Human resource management models for entrepreneurial opportunity. In J. A. Katz & T. M. Welbourne (Eds.), *Manag-*

ing people in entrepreneurial oganizations: Learning from the merger of entrepreneurship and human resource management (pp. 54-81). Boston: JAI Press.

Heneman, R.L., Tansky, J.W., & Camp, S.M . (2000). Human resource management practices in small and medium size enterprises: Unanswered questions and future research perspectives. *Entrepreneurship: Theory and Practice, 25*(1), 11-26.

Noe, R., Hollenbeck, J., Gerhart, B., & Wright, P. (2006). *Human resource management: Gaining a competitive advantage* (5th ed.). New York: McGraw Hill Irwin.

Penrose, E.T. (1959). *The theory of the growth of the firm.* Oxford: Blackwell.

Sanchez. R. (1995). Strategic flexibility in product competition. *Strategic Management Journal, 16,* 135-159.

Shane, S., & Venkataraman, S. (2000). The promise of entrepreneurship as a field of study. *Academy of Management Review, 25,* 217-226.

United States Small Business Administration Office of Advocacy (USSBA). (2003). *Statistics about business size (Including small businesses) from the U.S. Census Bureau.* www.sba.gov.

CHAPTER 1

WHY HUMAN RESOURCE MANAGEMENT DIFFERS IN ENTREPRENEURIAL AND ESTABLISHED FIRMS

Theoretical Foundations

Sharon A. Alvarez and Janice C. Molloy

Although there has been recognition that human resource management practices in entrepreneurial firms are fundamentally different from those in established firms, there is limited understanding as to *why* human resource management practices differ in entrepreneurial and established firms. More specifically, the chapter suggests that unlike established firms, entrepreneurial firms operate under conditions of *uncertainty*. The implications of these uncertain conditions are discussed. The objective of the chapter is to stimulate research and discussion regarding *why* human resource management differs in entrepreneurial and established firms. To provide a starting point for such discussion, the chapter draws on the entrepreneurship and economics literatures to begin to articulate a theoretical basis for potential differences in human resource management.

Human Resource Strategies for the High Growth Entrepreneurial Firm, 1–12
Copyright © 2006 by Information Age Publishing
All rights of reproduction in any form reserved.

1

INTRODUCTION

The human resource management literature has noted that the human resource management practices in entrepreneurial firms are fundamentally different from those in established firms. However, human resource management in entrepreneurial firms has been under-researched; the vast majority of manuscripts in leading outlets for human resource management research focus solely on established firms (Williamson, 2000). Given the prominent role of entrepreneurial firms in the economy there have been calls for research on human resource management in entrepreneurial settings (Heneman, Tansky & Camp, 2000; Tansky & Heneman, 2003). Heneman et al.'s (2000) and Cardon and Stevens' (2004) comprehensive reviews describe the human resource management practices in such settings and provide a strong foundation for future research.

What remains unclear, however, is *why* human resource management practices differ in entrepreneurial and established firms. That is, although attributes such as firm size and age have been used to identify and categorize firms likely having significantly different approaches to human resource management, there is currently no theoretical explanation as to why the differences exist. This chapter draws on the entrepreneurship and economics literatures to articulate a theoretical basis for differences in human resource management in entrepreneurial vs. established firms.

More specifically, the chapter suggests such differences are based on the underlying conditions in which firms are organized. That is, unlike established firms, entrepreneurial firms operate under conditions of uncertainty—conditions in which that which constitutes firm performance is not only *unknown*, but also *unknowable* (Alvarez & Barney, 2005). In turn, such uncertainty limits the information on which decision-makers typically rely as human resource management decisions are made. Moreover, the uncertainty associated with entrepreneurial settings also influences the efficacy of traditional hierarchy-based governance systems. As these hierarchy-based governance systems are the focus of transactions-cost economics, the extent to which transactions-cost economics theories explain variation in human resource management practices is unclear.

The objective of the chapter is to stimulate research and discussion regarding *why* human resource management differs in entrepreneurial and established firms. Toward this end, the chapter first discusses the underlying conditions in which entrepreneurial and established firms are organized. Next, transactions-cost economics is described and the implications of uncertainty for transactions-cost economics applications are defined. The chapter concludes with a summary of considerations for future research.

DIFFERENCES BETWEEN
ENTREPRENEURIAL AND ESTABLISHED FIRMS

The objective of human resource management is to maximize firm performance (Noe, Hollenbeck, Gerhart, & Wright, 2006). As firm performance is based on the notion that a firm is a bundle of productive resources that are coordinated to obtain economic advantages (Barney, 2002), it is possible to define firm performance by comparing the value that a firm creates using its productive resources with the value that those resources would generate in the next best alternative investment. Thus, in order to determine firm performance, the expected cash flow of the resources invested in the firm—as well as their alternative investment value—needs to be calculated.

However, entrepreneurs face an unusual challenge in that their firms specialize in pursuing new, untried market opportunities (Schumpeter, 1934; Shane & Venkataraman, 2000). In other words, as stated above, entrepreneurial firms operate under conditions of uncertainty, in which firm performance is both unknown and unknowable. In this present discussion, such *uncertain* conditions are said to contrast with conditions of *risk*—which are the conditions in which established firms are said to operate. This distinction is discussed in more detail below.

Risk Verses Uncertainty

Much of the business strategy and entrepreneurship literatures use the terms "risk" and "uncertainty" as if they were synonyms (e.g., Shane, 2003); therefore, it is not surprising that the human resource management literature does not distinguish between these concepts either. However, there is a long tradition in economics that does distinguish between these concepts (Knight, 1921); moreover, there is growing agreement that one of the most important differences between nonentrepreneurial and entrepreneurial decision-making is that the former takes place under conditions of risk, while the latter takes place under conditions of uncertainty (Alvarez & Barney, 2005; Alvarez & Busenitz, 2001; Loasby, 2002).

Risky investments. The decision to exploit a market opportunity is defined as risky when two conditions exist: first, when all possible future outcomes of exploiting that market opportunity are known at the time the decision is made and, second, when the probability of each of these outcomes occurring is also known when the decision is made (Wald, 1950). The outcomes of risky decisions are governed by well-defined probability distributions, which have three characteristics (Triola, 2003): (a) all possible future outcomes are known, (b) the probability of any one of these outcomes occurring is less than or equal to one, but greater than zero, and (c) the probability of any these outcomes occurring sums to one.

Making risky investment decisions is analogous to rolling a die known to have six sides and known to be fair and balanced. The outcome of rolling this die is not certain; however, it is risky in that the full range of possible outcomes is known, and the probability of each outcome occurring (1/6) is also known. This makes it possible to calculate a probability distribution that describes the possible outcomes from rolling this die.

Most economic and financial models of business decision-making are applicable to risky decisions (Brealey & Myers, 1988; Cyert & DeGroot, 1987). For example, to calculate the present value of a new investment, both the possible outcomes associated with this investment and the probability of these outcomes must be known. These concepts are reflected in the net cash flow an investment is expected to generate (i.e., possible investment outcomes) and the discount rate applied to that projected net cash flow (i.e., one minus the likelihood that this outcome will occur). As long as the discounted present value of the cash flows generated by a risky investment is positive, there is an economic incentive to make the investment (Brealey & Myers, 1988).

Uncertain investments.   The decision to invest in a market opportunity is uncertain when the possible outcomes of this decision and the probabilities associated with each outcome are not known when the decision is made (Knight, 1921). In these situations, decision-makers are often unaware of their ignorance of possible future outcomes (Shackle, 1972, 1979). Making uncertain investment decisions is also analogous to rolling a die. However, in the uncertain case, the number of sides on the die—is it two, three, four, eight, or an infinite number of sides?—and whether or not the die is balanced and fair—is not known when the die is rolled. Indeed, in these settings, decision-makers may think they are "rolling dice" only to discover later that they are actually playing games with much less favorable odds, but larger payoffs.

Research investments in the drug Viagra turned out to be uncertain in this sense. Pfizer originally invested in Viagra as a cardiovascular drug. This investment decision was based on Pfizer's knowledge about Viagra's mechanism of action. Unfortunately, Viagra did not have the cardiovascular effects that Pfizer expected. However, during its evaluation, Pfizer became aware that Viagra had some wholly unexpected side effects—including the potential for treating male impotency. This outcome of the drug's development was not known at the time the decision was made to invest in the drug. Certainly the probability that Viagra might turn out to be a blockbuster treatment for male impotency could not have been known when Pfizer was examining its efficacy as a cardiovascular drug.

Decision-makers' estimates and uncertain opportunities.   Before discussing the ability of individuals to coordinate human resources under conditions of uncertainty vs. risk, additional comments about these two concepts are required.

Theoretically, some wonder whether uncertainty actually exists. In particular, some have hypothesized that decision-makers always possess their own individual estimate of the probability distribution of outcomes associated with a decision they are making (Rossi & Allenby, 2003). If this is the case, individuals are never uncertain of these estimates. Rather, because they always know the mean and variance of the probability distributions they envision, individuals' decisions with respect to such distributions will always be characterized in their minds by risk and not uncertainty.

However, the fact that a person may have such an estimated probability distribution in his or her own mind, does not suggest that there is a valid reason to believe that distribution corresponds to the actual distribution of outcomes associated with the decision (Kahneman & Tversky, 1972). Therefore, if the only probability distribution of decision outcomes that inform decision-makers is that which exists in the minds of the individuals, and if this distribution is not grounded in any empirical observations, then the conditions of uncertainty are present.

Whether or not a decision to invest in a market opportunity is risky or uncertain depends on the objective properties of that setting, not on the perceptions of decision-makers. Moreover, there is good reason to believe that many decision-makers will be systematically overconfident about their ability to anticipate the results of a decision (Kahneman & Tversky, 1972, 1973). Entrepreneurs have been shown to be particularly overconfident (Busenitz & Barney, 1997). Thus, from the point of view of these decision-makers, few decisions are either risky or uncertain. However, no matter how a decision-maker "feels" and no matter what he or she "believes" about the outcomes of a decision, if the outcomes of the decision are unknown, then the decision is either risky or uncertain. If prior empirical observations make it possible to estimate a probability distribution associated with a decision, then that decision is risky. If it is not possible to estimate such a probability distribution, that decision is uncertain.

Second, although it is clear why individuals would invest in risky market opportunities, some wonder why individuals would ever invest in uncertain market opportunities. After all, if so little is known about the potential of uncertain market opportunities to generate economic value at the time investment in these opportunities is required, why would anyone invest in such opportunities?

Several explanations for why people might invest in uncertain opportunities have been proposed in the literature (Casson, 2003; Kirzner, 1973; Rumelt, 1987). First, as was shown initially by Knight (1921), the economic returns available to those who invest in uncertain market opportunities that end up being valuable will, in general, be much greater than the returns associated with risky market opportunities. Second, although a market opportunity may objectively be uncertain, decision-makers may believe that it is risky, or even *certain*, and thus may make investment decisions on that basis. Third, as noted by Rumelt (1987, p. 156), "if it can be modeled it is too late to make money." The following section discusses the implications of uncertainty for transactions-cost economics, an economic theory which underlies many human resource management practices in established firm settings.

TRANSACTIONS-COST ECONOMICS AND UNCERTAINTY

As noted earlier, the objective of human resource management is to support and enable firm performance, and for entrepreneurial firms, firm performance is both unknown and unknowable. According to transactions-cost economics, however, it is precisely this firm performance information that is needed in order to make human resource coordination and management decisions that in turn support future performance. This section describes transactions-cost theory and its implications for entrepreneurial settings.

Transactions-cost theories of the firm focus on the role of hierarchical governance in reducing the threat of opportunism due to transaction-specific investment in economic exchanges (Williamson, 1985). The central prediction of transactions-cost economics is that economic actors will adopt hierarchical forms of governance (i.e., a firm) when the threat of opportunism due to transaction-specific investment is very high.

Transactions-cost theory is based on the seminal insight of Coase (1937) that there is a cost associated with using markets to govern certain economic exchanges. This theory begins with the observation that individuals will often find it in their self-interest to make specific investments to complete particular economic exchanges. However, making specific investments in a transaction increases the threat of opportunism—in particular, the threat that the party that makes these investments will not receive appropriate compensation for doing so (Williamson, 1975, 1985). Indeed, the inability to receive appropriate compensation for making specific investments can be so significant that individuals will not make these investments in the first place (Klein, Crawford, & Alchian, 1978).

Transactions-cost theory addresses this issue by bringing problematic exchanges within the boundaries of a firm so that a manager can monitor and control the behavior of all parties to such exchanges. The ability to exercise managerial control in a way that ensures the efficient operation of a firm, in turn, requires "the manager" to have the information required to value the specific investments made by parties to an exchange; determine whether or not parties to an exchange are fulfilling their obligations; determine how the profits generated by an exchange should be fairly distributed among parties to that exchange; and so forth. Indeed, the reason that the firm is thought to be able to control threats of opportunism in an exchange is that this form of governance makes it possible for those exercising managerial control to have sufficient information to manage an exchange efficiently (Williamson, 1975, 1985).

But what happens to the ability to exercise managerial control when the information required to exercise control does not exist—when the value of specific investments is not known, when the level and type of commitments required to complete an exchange are not known, and when the possible economic outcomes of an exchange are not known? In these uncertain settings, how can "the manager" efficiently monitor and control an exchange? More broadly, if it is difficult to efficiently exercise managerial control under conditions of uncertainty, on what basis then does an entrepreneur coordinate resources—including human resources—in these settings? Such important questions as "What resources should be coordinated? "Who should exercise managerial control in the coordination and assembly process?" "On what basis should that control be exercised?" and "Who should receive the residual benefits of engaging in the coordination and assembly of resources?" are all problematic under conditions of uncertainty.

The assertion that managerial control is difficult to exercise under uncertainty may seem ironic to many transactions-cost theorists, since some very influential transactions-cost theorists assign a central role to uncertainty in their theory (e.g., Williamson, 1975, 1985). However, the uncertainty that is part of transactions-cost economics is not uncertainty about the economic value associated with the exploitation of particular market opportunities. Rather, uncertainty in transaction-cost economics has to do with the inability to anticipate whether or not an exchange partner will behave opportunistically, along with all the different ways the partner may behave opportunistically. Although transactions-cost theory clearly incorporates what might be called behavioral uncertainty into its theoretical framework, it is less obvious that it incorporates uncertainty about the economic value that might be created by investing in a given market opportunity.

Indeed, some transactions-cost theorists acknowledge that transactions-cost theory takes the economic gains from an exchange as given, and instead focuses on how firms are used to allocate these gains to the parties involved (Riordan & Williamson, 1985; Williamson, 1985). However, although entrepreneurs clearly must concern themselves with threats of opportunism in any exchanges they engage in, they also face a prior uncertainty—uncertainty about the value these exchanges create in the first place.

Empirically, it may be that behavioral uncertainty and uncertainty about the value that might be created by exploiting a new market opportunity are correlated. However, that correlation will not always be high. For example, two individuals who trust each other completely and thus face very little behavioral uncertainty may nevertheless face substantial uncertainty with respect to the economic value their joint investments may create. This lack of distinction between behavioral uncertainty and uncertainty about future outcomes of economic exchanges may be one reason why empirical tests of transactions-cost theory routinely support the theory's central prediction about the relationship between transaction-specific investment and firms, but generate less consistent support for the theory's predictions about uncertainty and firms (Mahoney & Pandian, 1992; Walker & Weber, 1984).

More fundamentally, from the point of view of entrepreneurs contemplating whether or not they should use a firm to exploit a new market opportunity, transactions-cost economics can be helpful in deciding whether or not to use firms to respond to possible opportunism. However, it has little to say about whether or not to use such governance in order to exploit opportunities whose value is not currently known, even probabilistically.

DISCUSSION AND FUTURE RESEARCH

The intent of this chapter was to provide a starting point for investigations and theoretical developments that can explain why human resource management differs in entrepreneurial and established settings. Given the critical role human resource management likely plays in the survival of entrepreneurial firms, an understanding of the underlying conditions that account for such differences is important.

This chapter suggested that one primary explanation for the fundamental differences in human resource management approaches within entrepreneurial and established firms concerns the role of uncertainty in entrepreneurial settings. Unlike established firms, entrepreneurial firms operate under conditions in which firm performance outcomes are both unknown and unknowable, yet our current understanding of managerial decision-making (both human resource management decision-making and decision-making related to all other resource coordination issues) is based on the assumption that these courses of action have well-defined probability distributions.

This chapter also noted that, given the uncertain context for human resource decisions in many entrepreneurial firms, hierarchy-based governance structures grounded in transactions-cost economics may have limited efficacy in entrepreneurial settings. Take, for instance, the design and administration of compensation programs. To illustrate the implications of transactions-cost theory, consider the hypothetical development of a compensation portfolio for a marketing vice president. In an established firm, information regarding both potential individual and firm performance outcomes would be utilized in this process. Specifically, a list of potential individual outcomes would be created. Then, based upon marketing research or the prior experience of the firm or competitors, a list of mutually exclusive and collectively exhaustive potential firm performance outcomes would be created. Using this probability distribution, sensitivity analysis regarding potential firm and individual outcomes would be conducted. Finally, economic theory related to risk premiums and uncertainty avoidance would be applied to design a compensation portfolio which optimized firm performance.

In contrast, in entrepreneurial settings, not only are potential individual and firm performance outcomes unknown, but there is not the benefit of prior experience or marketing research to inform the compensation portfolio decision. Furthermore, in such uncertain settings, the product or service that the firm will ultimately market may not have been discovered or created at the time the compensation portfolio is created. This lack of information on both the firm's and applicant's parts fundamentally changes the negotiation dynamics. That is, the information asymmetries typically underlying employment negotiations in established firms are greatly diminished in entrepreneurial firms. In entrepreneurial settings neither party is privy to potential individual and firm performance outcomes, and both parties are likely aware of this information symmetry. Such a scenario is uncharacteristic of established firm contexts.

This example suggests that each area of human resource management—and each phase of the employment life-cycle, from initial attraction through turnover—is likely impacted by the unique characteristics of either the entrepreneurial or the established firm. The means by which entrepreneurs make human resource and other resource coordination decisions within uncertain settings—along with the underlying differences in entrepreneurial- and established-firm human resource management processes and practices—provide an intriguing and fertile domain for future human resource management research.

Moreover, to extend Barber's (2006) observations on recruitment, perhaps the underlying dynamics of human resource management in entrepreneurial and established firms are so different that research specific to entrepreneurial settings is warranted for each human resource management practice area (including human resource planning, recruitment, selection, training and development, compensation, performance management, and employee relations). For instance, contemporary performance management systems are informed by the hierarchical definitions of strategy (Barney, 2002; Williamson, 1975), which are grounded in transactions-cost economics and related management-by-objectives principles. Given that in entrepreneurial settings meaningful firm performance objectives do not exist, it is not likely that meaningful individual performance objectives and incentives can be created using practices, policies, and decision-making processes designed for established firm settings.

There are innumerable examples showing that human resource management in entrepreneurial contexts differs from human resource management in established firm contexts. Identification of *why* such differences exist will aid both theoretical and descriptive research. When such theoretical accounts are created and integrated with descriptive and empirical research, a rich understanding of the role of human resource management in the performance and survival of entrepreneurial firms will result.

AUTHOR NOTE

Correspondence concerning this manuscript should be addressed to Sharon A. Alvarez, Department of Management and Human Resources, Fisher College of Business, The Ohio State University, 2100 Neil Avenue, Columbus, OH 43210-1144. Email: alvarez_42@cob.osu.edu; phone: 614-688-8289.

REFERENCES

Alvarez, S., & Barney, J. (2005). How do entrepreneurs organize firms under conditions of uncertainty? *Journal of Management, 31*(5) 776-773.

Alvarez, S., & Busenitz, L. (2001). The entrepreneurship of resource-based theory. *Journal of Management, 27*(6), 755-775.

Barber, A. (2006). Recruitment in entrepreneurial firms. In J. Tansky & R. Heneman (Eds.), *Human resource strategies for high-growth entrepreneurial firms: Research in human resource management.* Greenwich, CT: Information Age.

Barney, J. (2002). *Gaining and sustaining competitive advantage.* Upper Saddle River, NJ: Prentice-Hall.

Brealey, R., & Myers, S. (1988). *Principles of corporate finance.* New York: McGraw-Hill.

Busenitz, L., & Barney, J. (1997). Differences between entrepreneurs and managers in large organizations: Biases and heuristics in strategic decision-making. *Journal of Business Venturing, 12*, 9-30.

Cardon, M., & Stevens, C. (2004). Managing human resources in small organizations: What do we know? *Human Resource Management Review, 14*(3), 295-323.

Casson, M. (2003). *The entrepreneur: An economic theory* (2nd ed.). Cheltenham: Edward Elgar.

Coase, R. (1937). The nature of the firm. *Economica, 4*, 386-405.

Cyert, R., & DeGroot, M. (1987). *Bayesian analysis and uncertainty in economic theory.* Totowa, NJ: Rowman & Littlefield.

Heneman, R., Tansky, J., & Camp, S. (2000). Human resource management practices in small and medium-sized enterprises: Unanswered questions and future research perspectives. *Entrepreneurship: Theory & Practice, 25*(1), 11-26.

Kahneman, D., & Tversky, T. (1972). Subjective probability: A judgment of representativeness. *Cognitive Psychology, 3*, 430-454.

Kahneman, D., & Tversky, T. (1973). On the psychology of prediction. *Psychological Review, 80*, 237-251.

Kirzner, I. (1973). *Competition and entrepreneurship.* Chicago and London: University of Chicago Press.

Klein, B., Crawford, R., & Alchian, A. (1978). Vertical integration, appropriable rents, and the competitive contracting process. *Journal of Law & Economics, 21*(2), 297-327.

Knight, F. (1921). Cost of production and price over long and short periods. *Journal of Political Economy, 29*, 304-335.

Loasby, B. (2002). The organizational basis of cognition and the cognitive basis of organization. In M. Augier & J. G. March (Eds.), *The economics of choice, change and organization: Essays in memory of Richard M. Cyert* (pp. 84-102). Cheltenham: Edward Elgar.

Mahoney, J., & Pandian, J. (1992). The resource-based view within the conversation of strategic management. *Strategic Management Journal, 13*(5), 363-381.

Noe, R., Hollenbeck, J., Gerhart, B., & Wright, P. (2006). *Human resource management: Gaining a competitive advantage* (5th ed.). New York: McGraw Hill Irwin.

Riordan, M., & Williamson, O. (1985). Asset specificity and economic organization. *International Journal of Industrial Organization, 3*, 365-378.

Rossi, P., & Allenby, G. (2003). Bayesian statistics and marketing. *Marketing Science, 22*(3), 304-328.

Rumelt, R. (1987). Theory, strategy and entrepreneurship. In D. J. Teece (Ed.), *The competitive strategic challenge: Strategies for industrial innovation and renewal* (pp. 137-158). Cambridge, MA: Ballinger.

Schumpeter, J. (1934). *Theory of economic development: An inquiry into profits, capital, credit, interest and the business cycle.* Cambridge: Harvard University Press.

Shackle, G. (1972). *Epistemics and economics.* Cambridge: Cambridge University Press.

Shackle, G. (1979). *Imagination and the nature of choice.* Edinburgh: Edinburgh University Press.

Shane, S. (2003). *A general theory of entrepreneurship: The individual-opportunity nexus.* Northampton, MA: Edward Elgar.

Shane, S., & Venkataraman, S. (2000). The promise of entrepreneurship as a field of research. *Academy of Management Review, 25*(1), 217-226.

Tansky, J., & Heneman, R. (2003). Introduction to the special issue on human resource management in SMEs: A call for more research. *Human Resource Management, 42*(4), 299-303.

Triola, M. (2003). *Elementary statistics* (9th ed.). Boston: Addison Wesley.

Wald, A. (1950). *Statistical decision functions*. New York: John Wiley.

Walker, G., & Weber, D. (1984). A transaction cost approach to make or buy decisions. *Administrative Science Quarterly, 29*, 373-91.

Williamson, I. (2000). Employer legitimacy and recruitment success in small businesses. *Entrepreneurship: Theory & Practice, 25*(1), 27-42.

Williamson, O. (1975). *Markets and hierarchies: Analysis and antitrust implications*. New York: Free Press.

Williamson, O. (1985). *The economic institutions of capitalism*. New York: Free Press.

CHAPTER 2

TOWARD AN UNDERSTANDING OF STRATEGIC HUMAN RESOURCE MANAGEMENT IN ENTREPRENEURIAL FIRMS

Opportunities for Research and Action

Roshni M. Goswami, Gary C. McMahan, and Patrick M. Wright

This chapter provides a framework to comprehend the impact of strategic human resource management in entrepreneurial organizations. As entrepreneurial firms face a multitude of challenges in today's rapidly changing economy, the chapter deviates from the often followed functional approach and takes a strategic approach to managing human resources in private entrepreneurial firms. In doing so, the chapter conducts an extensive review of literature from the fields of strategic human resource management and entrepreneurship and tries to elucidate the underlying mechanisms of the HR practices—firm performance relationship in an entrepreneurial con-

Human Resource Strategies for the High Growth Entrepreneurial Firm, 13–50
Copyright © 2006 by Information Age Publishing
All rights of reproduction in any form reserved.

text. In this regard, the importance of people management practices, employee competencies and behaviors, knowledge climate and entrepreneurial sophistication are highlighted, and the chapter endeavors to provide a preliminary framework that has the potential to provide direction for further research and knowledge creation.

INTRODUCTION

The forces of globalization including global market opportunities, rapidly changing technology, outsourcing and declining trade and investment barriers have transformed the US economy. At this point in time, more than 70%s of workers in the United States are employed in the service sector and there is a general consensus among people that the economy has moved to information, service and intellectual capital jobs (Ulrich, 1999). The term "knowledge economy" has been frequently used to describe the current business environment. The knowledge economy places a huge responsibility on HR professionals to integrate HR into the overall corporate strategy such that HR can be viewed as a strategic partner. The knowledge economy, characterized by the widespread presence of companies that rely on knowledge-based strategies to build competitive advantage, provides an opportunity for the HR function to fundamentally change its existing role inside corporations and become true value-adding strategic partners (Lawler & Mohrman, 2003; McMahan, Lawler, & Mohrman, 1996).

Since intellectual capital is a primary important source of competitive advantage in the knowledge economy, people management has become an integral part of corporate strategy.

There is growing evidence that HR practices play a critical role in creating competitive advantage in companies and influencing organizational performance, and organizations which deploy good people management practices reap the benefits (Thite, 2004). Thus, the field of strategic human resource management, which makes evident the role of human resource practices in creating competitive advantage and enhancing organizational performance, seems to be in the unique position of having the capacity to provide guidance and direction for research to unravel the strategic role of people in organizations in this new knowledge economy.

The structural shift toward the knowledge economy has been accompanied by a growing importance of small businesses and entrepreneurial companies. The United States Small Business Administration estimates that in 2003, there were about 23.7 million businesses in the United States and small firms with less than 500 employees represent 99.7% of these businesses. They employ half of all private sector employees and generate 60 to 80% of the net new jobs added annually to the economy (United States Small Business Administration Office of Advocacy, 2003). The recent Global Entrepreneurship Monitor survey, funded by the Ewing Marion Kauffman Foundation reported that in 2003, about 11 out of every 100 working adults in the United States were involved in some form of entrepreneurial activity, either starting a business or playing a lead role in one less than three and a half years old (Ewing Marion Kauffman Foundation, 2003). Another report concluded that entrepreneurship is a widespread activity in the United States and about 6.2 in every 100 U.S. adults 18 years and older are engaged in trying to start new firms. Thus, approximately 10.1 million adults in the United States are attempting to create a new business at any one time. The 10.1 million people involved in startup activities represent about 5.6 million potential new businesses (Reynolds, Carter, Gartner, Greene & Cox, 2004). Many posit that new ventures are the main source of new jobs in the economy and today they create seven of ten jobs in this country (Baldwin, 2004).

In addition, it is argued that new firms are essential to the U.S. economy since they are the engines of innovation and have the ability to smooth the exigencies of the business cycle (Schramm, 2004). Further, research indicates that entrepreneurial firms positively impact economic growth and "variations in rates of entrepreneurship may account for as much as one-third of the variation in economic growth" (Ewing Marion Kauffman Foundation, 1999, p. 3). A recent report by the National Governors Association (NGA) stated that entrepreneurship is a key determinant of economic growth and nearly 70% of economic growth can be attributed to entrepreneurial activity. They went on to elaborate that entrepreneurial companies are the primary drivers of growth and innovation and these new, fast growth companies (sales growth of at least 20% each year for four straight years) comprise about 350,000 firms out of a total of six million U.S. businesses with employees. These firms created about two-thirds of new jobs between 1993 and 1996. Further, about 35% of the companies on the Fortune 500 list are displaced every three or four years by more rapidly expanding firms (National Governor's Association Center for Best Practices, 2004). These new ventures have been credited with improving choices for consumers by developing new products and services, stimulating competition among existing companies (both large and small) thereby improving product quality and reducing price to benefit consumers, accelerating the advancement and diffusion of new technologies and improving the quality of life. A Kaufmann Center report on entrepreneurship stated that "Entrepreneurs contribute to economic and social well-being by (1) Developing and commercializing innovative products and services that improve our quality of life and improve our position in the global economy, (2) Generating new industries and firms to replace those that have run their course, (3) Creating employment opportunities, (4) Creating wealth that is reinvested in new economic enterprises and, through philanthropy, in communities" (Kayne, 1999, p. 1).

Organizational researchers have recognized the critical role of new ventures and increasingly entrepreneurship research has gained prominence in the management field. Extensive theoretical and empirical research has been conducted in the entrepreneurship arena to provide comprehensive frameworks and understand the various entrepreneurial processes, behaviors and outcomes (Cooper & Gason, 1992). One area that has not received adequate attention is the role of human resources (HR) in entrepreneurial organizations. Two recent reviews of the literature concluded that there was a scarcity of theory and research in this area. Further, the existing research was incoherent (Cardon & Stevens, 2004; Heneman, Tansky & Camp, 2000). Thus, there appears an urgent need to develop models and frameworks to organize and comprehend the purpose and the impact of human resource management (HRM) in entrepreneurial firms.

The knowledge economy and the continual emergence of entrepreneurial organizations provide the perfect platform to integrate research on the strategic human resource perspective and entrepreneurship, such that we can begin to understand the various human resource processes and outcomes in entrepreneurial organizations. This chapter attempts to do just that. In this chapter, we try to provide a framework that can help us begin the process of understanding the strategic role of human resource management in entrepreneurial organizations. Thus, the purpose of the chapter is to analyze and assimilate research from the field of strategic human resource management and entrepreneurial studies such that we can move toward establishing a model of strategic human resource management in entrepreneurial organizations. We begin by addressing some definitional issues in entrepreneurship research. This is followed by a brief discussion of the important characteristics of entrepreneurial firms, wherein we highlight some specific challenges they face in today's rapidly changing business environment. Next, we provide an overview of existing human resource management research conducted in the context of small businesses and entrepreneurial firms. We then review some important theoretical concepts in the area of strategic human resource management. Finally, we attempt to synthesize the research on strategic human resource management and entrepreneurship in an effort to develop a model which provides us with a starting point in our endeavor to understand the importance of strategic human resource management in entrepreneurial firms.

DEFINING ENTREPRENEURIAL FIRMS

Entrepreneurial activity arises due to an imbalance between the potentiality of something new and its realization that is the creation of an exploited opportunity where none existed previously, by one or more individuals. This recognition and pursuit of opportunity give rise to entrepreneurship (Stevenson & Jarillo, 1990). Entrepreneurship has been defined as an attempt to create value by an individual or individuals (a) through the recognition of significant (generally innovative) business opportunity, (b) through the drive to manage risk-taking appropriate to that project, and (c) through the exercise of communication and management skills necessary to mobilize rapidly the human, physical and financial resources that will bring the project to fruition (Kao & Stevenson, 1985). The Kauffman Center provided the following definition of entrepreneurship: "Entrepreneurship is the ability to amass the necessary resources to capitalize on new business opportunities. The term is frequently used to refer to the rapid growth of new and innovative businesses and is associated with individuals who create or seize business opportunities and pursue them without regard for resources under their control. They build something from practically nothing and usually reinvest earnings to expand their enterprise or to create new enterprises. Other words that characterize entrepreneurship include innovative, creative, dynamic, risk-tolerant, flexible and growth-oriented" (Kayne, 1999, p. 3). Thus, the field of entrepreneurship involves "the study of sources of opportunities; the processes of discovery, evaluation and exploitation of opportunities; and the set of individuals who discover, evaluate and exploit them" (Shane & Venkataraman, 2000, p. 218).

An entrepreneur has been defined as someone who uses innovation to destroy existing economic order by introducing new products and services, by creating new forms of organization and by exploiting new raw materials (Schumpeter, 1934). Others define an entrepreneur as "one who organizes, manages, and assumes the risks of a business or enterprise. While an entrepreneur can be a small business person, not all small businesspersons are entrepreneurs" (Kentucky Office for the New Economy, 2002, p. 42).

When it comes to defining an entrepreneurial firm, there is little agreement among entrepreneurship researchers. As a result, they have conceptualized the entrepreneurial firm in multiple ways ranging from a high-growth firm to an owner managed business to a founder run business (Daily, McDougall, Covin, & Dalton, 2002). Entrepreneurial firms have often been defined in various ways based on their size, growth rate and origin. Additionally, there has been considerable debate on the issue of differences between a small business and an entrepreneurial firm. The

Kauffman center points out that entrepreneurship is independent of size. Several firms that meet the Small Business Administration's criteria for small or medium sized enterprises (SME) are very entrepreneurial in nature. They state that the differences between a small business and an entrepreneurial firm lie more in the desired outcome. They argue that small businesses play a very important role in the overall economy and through these small businesses we obtain many basic products and services (e.g., gasoline for automobiles, accounting services). In addition, many small business owners demonstrate entrepreneurial qualities as they attend to product demand and customer satisfaction. However, they stress that entrepreneurship focuses on individuals who blend innovation with sound business practices to commercialize new products and services that result in high-growth firms (Kayne, 1999).

The Kentucky Innovation Commission states that entrepreneurial enterprises focus on new and innovative products and/or processes. They are growth-oriented and aggressively strive to capture market share. They may begin as small businesses but often grow to be large firms, bringing wealth to their communities. Entrepreneurs frequently reinvest earnings to expand their original enterprise or to create new ventures (Kentucky Office for the New Economy, 2002). The National Commission on Entrepreneurship (NCOE) defines entrepreneurs as leaders of small companies that are based on innovation and are designed to grow quickly—often at an annual rate of 15-20%. Small business researcher David Birch categorized high growth entrepreneurial firms as "gazelles." These firms grow at least 20% per year over a period of five years. These firms are distinguished from the majority of small businesses whose main objective is usually to provide employment and income for the owner and the owner's family (Birch, 1987). To sum it up, there seems to be some consensus about the difference between entrepreneurial firms and small businesses and many researchers agree that entrepreneurial firms are small high growth companies.

Regarding the issue of origin, the concept of independent entrepreneurship has been defined as "the process whereby an individual or group of individuals, acting independently of any association with an existing organization creates a new organization" (Sharma & Chrisman, 1999, p. 18). Brazeal and Herbert (1999) explicitly distinguish between (individual) entrepreneurship and corporate entrepreneurship. They define corporate entrepreneurship as a business setting where "individual or group entrepreneurship is fostered within a pre-existing organizational setting, which provides support for the development and exploitation of one or more innovations deemed strategically and financially consistent with the supporting organization's mission" and their conception of (individual) entrepreneurship is "that of the individual, independent entrepreneur who assumes financial and other risks in order to exploit a new idea or product possibility; he or she may be supported by another, perhaps a venture capitalist or a family member, but the risks of failure uniquely devolve upon the entrepreneur" (1999, p. 40). Additionally, in the realm of independent/individual entrepreneurship, the venture capital (VC) literature which has extensively studied the VC-entrepreneur relationship makes a distinction between VC-backed and non-VC-backed firms (Cyr, Johnson, & Welbourne, 2000).

The diversity in the way entrepreneurial firms have been characterized makes it important for us to clarify our definition of the entrepreneurial firm. We build on the distinction made by previous research in the context of individual/independent entrepreneurship and focus on two kinds of entrepreneurial firms: one with access to extensive VC and/or investment backing which we refer to as the Professional Management Model of Entrepreneurship (PME) and the other that does not initially receive extensive VC and/or investment backing and is founder-managed which we refer to the Garage Model of Entrepreneurship (GME). It is important to note here that the term "Professionally Managed Firm" has been used in the entrepreneurship literature before, however our conception of the Professional Management Model of Entrepreneurship is novel. For example, Willard, Krueger, and Feeser (1992) compared a group of publicly owned, founder managed high growth firms with a group of similar but "professionally managed firms." They tested the hypothesis that professionally managed, rapidly growing firms would outperform similar firms headed by the founder CEO. They collected data on entrepreneurial firms and examined whether or not a/the founder of the firm was also CEO. They presumed that a firm not managed by the founder was headed by professional managers and they categorized these firms as "professionally managed firms." We conceptualize the PME to include venture capitalists. Many startup firms receive private funding from investors and venture capitalists. Recently, a survey of the 100 fastest growing new entrepreneurial businesses in the United States reported that 31 firms received startup capital from private investors ("Entrepreneur and D&B's," 2004). The firm following the PME is a venture capital-investor-backed, private startup that has access and the influence of the venture capitalists/investors and their strategic, technical, managerial and financial resources. Thus, in the PME, we focus on firms started by individual entrepreneurs with the help of venture capital and/or investor funding. An example of this would be Zhone Technologies, a telecommunications equipment startup firm that received $500 million in venture capital financing from several different venture capital firms and its founders and board members at inception (Weinberg, 2000).

The GME includes privately held startup firms that are primarily managed by the individual entrepreneur, in some cases with members of his/her family or a group of entrepreneurs who started the firm without extensive, initial venture capital funding. Recent research studying the 100 fastest growing new entrepreneurial businesses in the United States, documented that many firms obtained their startup capital from the entrepreneur's savings and personal funds, friends and family, bank loans, line of credit and credit cards (Entrepreneur, 2004). We use the term "garage" since it is well documented that many well-known firms like Apple, Disney, Dell, and Hewlett Packard were started by entrepreneurs acting on their creative ideas in their garage (or in Dell's case, a college dorm room). Hence, the garage has achieved iconic startup status in U.S. business history and is reflective of the potential of creative ideas, innovation and ingenuity of individual entrepreneurs in America. Thus, our primary focus in this chapter is limited to privately held, small, high growth firms started by an individual entrepreneur, perhaps with the support of some other entrepreneurs, family or venture capitalists but without any sponsorship from an existing corporation.

DISTINGUISHING CHARACTERISTICS
OF ENTREPRENEURIAL FIRMS

From the research evidence presented in the preceding section, we argue that a significant proportion of entrepreneurship research categorizes entrepreneurial firms as small, high growth companies. A fair amount of research over the last few decades has outlined the various problems faced by fast growing companies. Kotter and Sathe (1978) examined 12 high growth companies and identified common problems of human resource management and the solutions implemented by some of the more successful firms to deal with them. Their model pointed out that in a situation of rapid growth, important decisions have to be made quickly, job demands expand continually, there are significant recruiting and training needs, resources are scarce, constant change is inevitable and the environment is full of uncertainty and ambiguity due to constantly changing employees, job demands, structures, systems, products and markets. These characteristics of rapid growth companies lead to a variety of human resource problems leading to adverse consequences. For example, due to constant resource scarcity, frequently changing job roles, employee's inability to grow and change as quickly as their jobs, and the rapid speed of decision making needed, employees feel tremendous pressure and experience stress leading to unmet career expectations, frustration, burn out or turnover. In addition, the firm's formal and informal structures have difficulty coping with the demands placed on them which leads to slow and often ineffective decision making.

Hambrick and Crozier (1985) focused on the people, processes and structures of 30 rapid-growth firms and described four key challenges faced by high growth firms. These were the challenges of (1) instant size, (2) sense of infallibility, (3) internal turmoil and frenzy and (4) extraordinary resource needs. High growth firms face instant size and often double and triple in size very quickly. This creates problems of lack of cohesion among employees, disaffection, disorientation, inadequate skills and inadequate systems. Another problem facing high-growth firms is the fact that they often think of themselves as infallible even under conditions of rapid technological or market change. The success that they experience leads them to believe that their strategies and behaviors are infallible. High growth firms tend to experience a great deal on internal turmoil. There is a constant stream of new employees, people who do not know each other and who do not know the company. Decision making may slow down considerable due to turf battles between employees and a huge increase in the amount of information that needs to be processed. The stress that accompanies rapid business growth also leads to burn out among employees. Rapid-growth firms have extraordinary resource needs and are often strapped for cash in spite of profits. This is because to keep up with the pace of growth they constantly need funds for new machinery, equipment, talent, etc. Siegel, Siegel, and MacMillan (1993) compared small, young companies with larger, mature companies and found that small growth companies ran leaner organizations with fewer managers, slimmer payrolls (as a percentage of sales), and more productive use of assets.

It is widely acknowledged that innovation and creativity are important characteristics of entrepreneurship (Drucker, 1985; Olson, 1985; Timmons, 1978). Brazeal and Herbert (1999) highlight the central roles played by change, innovation and creativity in the entrepreneurial process. They suggest that "entrepreneurship is enabled by (a) the current or potential existence of something new (an innovation), (b) which may have been developed by new ways of looking at old problems (creativity), (c) or the lessened capability of prior processes or solutions to respond effectively to new problem parameters brought on by new or emerging external conditions (environmental change), (d) which can supplant or be complementary to existing processes or solutions (a change), (e) when championed by one or more invested individuals (the innovator)" (1999, p. 34). Additionally, they point out that entrepreneurial organizations should have strategic intentions of developing, nurturing, and maintaining entrepreneurially oriented individuals and innovation-generating processes and an internal environment of creativity.

Using the resource-based view, Rangone (1999) conducted empirical research based on 14 case studies of small to medium sized enterprises (SME) and produced a model of an SME's sustainable competitive advantage based on three capabilities: innovation capability, production capability and market management capability. Innovation capability comprised a company's ability to develop new products and processes, achieve superior technological and/or management performance. Chandler and Hanks (1994) examined the market attractiveness, resource-based capabilities, venture strategies and venture performance of 800 startup manufacturing firms. A significant finding was that startup manufacturing companies who reported having superior resource capabilities in the form of innovative employees had higher levels of performance.

Collins and Clark (2003) conducted a field study to examine the social networks of top management teams (TMT) of 73 high-growth, high technology firms and their impact on firm performance. They specifically studied the relationships between a set of network-building HR practices, aspects of internal and external networks of TMT's and firm performance. The findings indicated that top manager's social networks are important for firm performance. Strong and diverse TMT external networks resulted in higher sales growth and stock price. Additionally, they found that large and diverse internal TMT networks were related to firm performance. The results suggested that a high level of connectedness internally allows a TMT to recognize where information is located within the firm and the information needs of various organizational units. Thus, the TMT's internal networks facilitate the exchange of information within the firm and this in turn equips them better to seek the relevant information from their external networks. Overall, the study concluded that both external and internal networks serve as important informational resources for high tech firms.

The discussion presented above highlights the fact that entrepreneurial firms face a variety of challenges associated with their rapid rate of growth. They often operate in an environment of resource scarcity and with a lean organizational structure. It is important for them to create an environment that promotes creativity, innovation and information exchange. This kind of an environment will allow them to develop resources and capabilities which can in turn provide them with sustainable competitive advantage. They especially need to focus on their HR structures and systems in order to deal with the issues of employee stress and burnout.

EXISTING LITERATURE OF HRM
IN ENTREPRENEURIAL FIRMS

Researchers in the field of human resource management have primarily focused on larger firms and we have limited knowledge about the extent to which existing HRM theories extend to smaller entrepreneurial firms. Heneman et al. (2000), conducted qualitative research to identify the areas of unanswered questions that existed between the current literature on HR practices in small and medium sized enterprises (SME) and the human resource issues that were perceived to be important by the entrepreneurial leaders of SME's. They surveyed 173 CEO/founders who headed small, fast growth firms. The results of this extensive qualitative survey indicated that HRM issues were of significant professional and personal concern to these entrepreneurs and they were interested in getting new information about these topics. Growth oriented CEO's were especially concerned about the competencies of their employees and matching these competencies with organizational, rather than job requirements. Further, the data indicated that CEO/Founders viewed compensation in a very broad context. They viewed compensation to include not just money but other dimensions like recognition, quality of life, learning and psychological characteristics of work. Additionally, the researchers reviewed 129 articles published between 1984 and 1999 that dealt with HRM issues in SME's. They found that only 17 studies used hypothesis testing and staffing and compensation were the issues most frequently addressed by researchers in the context of SME's. Other issues examined were general human resource practices in small firms, training, motivation, labor relations and certain HR related aspects of business strategy.

Rogg, Schmidt, Shull, and Schmitt (2001) investigated the relationship between human resource practices, organizational climate and customer satisfaction using data from 351 small businesses. The results provided evidence for the hypothesis that human resource practices influence organizational climate which in turn influences customer satisfaction. Johnson and Cyr (2001) conducted a study to specifically investigate a climate for human resources in entrepreneurial firms and collected data from employees and supervisors at three entrepreneurial software firms. They suggested that, frequently entrepreneurial firms do not have the resources to establish formal HR departments, so these firms can manage their employees by establishing a climate for valuing human resources. They argued that entrepreneurial firms can promote and maintain desired employee behaviors by letting employees know that they are valued and important to the success of the company. Their results suggested some support for this argument and provided initial support for the importance of a climate for valuing human resources. Heneman and Tansky (2002) reviewed existing human resource management models to assess whether they have any relevance to the management of human resources in entrepreneurial firms. They concluded that traditional HRM models in and of themselves have limited relevance to entrepreneurial firms and they need to be supplemented with new models and frameworks. Their article integrated existing HRM theories to provide a new, comprehensive framework for evaluating HRM in entrepreneurial firms.

Vogus and Welbourne (2003) examined HR practices and mindful processes in reliability seeking organizations using data from 184 small initial public offering (IPO) software firms. They presented arguments to highlight the fact that in many industries like the software industry or in an early stage of an organizational life cycle (e.g., IPO), firms are faced with a complex, rapidly changing environment and often they are tight coupled to this high-hazard environment. To combat this uncertainty, these firms use HR practices to remain flexible and capture information so that they can achieve maximum innovation. They concluded that the software entrepreneurial firms which used HR practices like skilled temporary employees, positive employee relations and emphasized on training achieved higher rates of innovation. The higher levels of innovation led to improved financial performance in the form of higher stock prices. In a followup to their study conducted in 1990, Hornsby and Kuratko (2003) examined HRM practices in 262 small businesses. The small firms were divided into three categories based on size where the first category included firms that had between one and fifty employees, the second category consisted of companies that had between 51 and 100 employees and the third category included companies with between 101 and 150 employees. The survey gathered data on the company's line of business, size, number of years in existence, absence or presence of an HRM department and HRM practices in five major areas including job analysis and description, recruiting and selection, training, performance appraisal and compensation. The research indicated that surprisingly fewer of the firms had a formal human resource department compared to the 1990 study. The greatest issue of concern to firms in all three categories was the availability of workers and benefits. The results of this study indicated little advancement in the human resource functions of smaller firms. It suggested that during the past decade, HR practices in smaller ventures of all sizes have generally stagnated and even appear to have regressed in some areas.

Kaman, McCarthy, Gulbro, and Tucker (2001) examined the use of two types of HRM practices namely bureaucratic HRM practices and high commitment HRM practices in 283 service firms with 100 or fewer employees. They concluded that larger firms, which had between 49-100 employees used bureaucratic practices to a higher extent. These larger firms also had more concerns about attracting and motivating workers, higher rates of absenteeism and more cases of employment litigation. Secondly, they found that use of high commitment HRM practices was not related to the size of the organization. These high commitment HRM practices were found to be related to lower turnover rates, less litigation and fewer concerns about motivating workers. Finally, they reported that even after removing the effects of organizational size, an emphasis on bureaucratic practices lead to more problems with employee motivation and higher absenteeism. Overall, their study indicated that bureaucratic practices increased with firm size, but high commitment practices had the most positive effect on firm performance.

Zenger and Lazzarini (2004) surveyed 352 electrical engineers from both small and large high technology firms in the Silicon Valley and Boston-Route 128 areas to explore the hypothesis that small companies, unlike large firms have the ability to attract top engineering talent and motivate high effort by crafting effective incentive-intensive employment contracts. The results indicated that, in general measures of ability were more related to pay in small than in large firms. Small firms also rewarded performance more aggressively such that engineers perceived a stronger pay-performance relationship, whereas larger firms aggressively rewarded seniority. It also appeared that small firms aggressively rewarded enhanced ability, effort and performance by aggressively compensating those who had attended elite educational institutions and had completed master's degrees. Additionally, engineers in larger firms reported greater use of rules, procedures and restrictions of behavior than engineers in smaller firms. Interestingly, in small firms which linked individual pay more closely to overall firm performance, engineers reported that colleagues were more actively involved in hiring decisions, more aggressive in removing low performers and more engaged in enforcing the norms of high performance. With regard to incentives and compensation structure, larger firms use merit pay to a greater extent. The small firms were more likely to have employees with considerable equity stakes and substantial percentage of their compensation explicitly paid as a variable bonus. The results also indicated that more talented engineers were attracted by these kinds of aggressive incentive plans.

Recently, Cardon and Stevens (2004) conducted a comprehensive review of extant research on managing people within small and emerging ventures and evaluated 37 articles published between 1984 and 2004. They used a functional HR framework to explore the existing research on HRM in small and emerging organizations. The review found that scholars had addressed the issues of staffing, compensation, training, performance management, organizational change and labor relations in the context of small firms. Recruiting and staffing were the most widely researched topics followed by compensation whereas, the issues of performance management and labor relations received very little attention. The researchers concluded that there was a need to understand three fundamental aspects of HRM in the context of small organizations, namely retention and ongoing employee issues, integration and interactions of HR practices, and the evaluation of HR practices within evolving organizations. Thus, the above discussion draws attention to the fact that overall, existing HRM research has emphasized a functional, traditional, or much more "micro" approach when conducting research in the context of small firms.

TOWARD A MODEL OF STRATEGIC HR
IN ENTREPRENEURIAL FIRMS

In this section we start with a brief review of the SHRM literature followed by the introduction and explanation of the model of SHRM in entrepreneurial firms. Strategic Human Resource Management has been defined as "the pattern of planned human resource deployments and activities intended to enable a firm to achieve its goals" (Wright & McMahan, 1992, p. 298). Two ideas are central to SHRM; the first being that an organization's human resources are of vital strategic importance such that the skills, behaviors and interactions of employees have the potential to provide the foundation for formulating strategy as well as the means for implementing a strategy. Secondly, an organization's HR practices are of critical importance in the development of the strategic capability of its human resources pool (Colbert, 2004). The field of Strategic Human Resource Management has been a setting for very vibrant research for two decades. The evolution of SHRM began with researchers trying to unearth the link between business strategy and human resources (Devanna, Fombrum, & Tichy, 1984). Ever since, a large number of empirical studies have been conducted to gain an understanding of the relationship between HR practices, strategy and firm performance (Wright & Boswell, 2002). Additionally, at various points researchers have reviewed the state of theoretical development in SHRM to resolve theoretical and definitional differences and to provide a forum for understanding the advancements in the field and assess the direction for future research (Legnick-Hall & Legnick-Hall 1988; McMahan, Virick, & Wright, 1999; Wright & McMahan, 1992).

Wright and McMahan (1992) assessed the state of theoretical development in SHRM and reviewed six theoretical perspectives (behavioral perspective, cybernetic models, agency/transaction costs, resource based, power/resource dependence and institutional) that had been used by researchers to understand and elaborate on the strategic role of human resource management in organizations. In a subsequent review, McMahan, Virick, and Wright (1999) reviewed the reactive theories (behavioral perspective, cybernetic systems, agency/transaction cost theory, resource-based view) and proactive theories (resource dependence, institutional theory) along with some additional theories including population ecology, strategic reference points, human capital theory and a Foucaldian approach. Interestingly, the authors noted that the most popular theoretical framework for examining SHRM was the resource-based view. Consistent with this observation, other researchers have argued that the SHRM literature has drawn increasingly from the resource-based view of strategy leading to extensive investigations about whether human resources can be a source of competitive advantage for the firm (Kamoche, 1996).

The resource-based view (RBV) unlike some environmentally focused strategic management paradigms (Porter, 1980, 1985) is firm focused and originated in the writings of Penrose (1959), Wernerfelt (1984), Prahalad and Hamel (1990), and Barney (1991). The central themes of this theory are the concepts of resources, competitive advantage and sustained competitive advantage. Barney defined resources to include "all assets, capabilities, organizational processes, firm attributes, information, knowledge, etc., controlled by a firm that enable the firm to conceive of and implement strategies that improve its efficiency and effectiveness" (1991, p. 101). According to Barney, the three basic types of resources are physical capital resources, human capital resources and organizational capital resources. Physical capital resources include such things as the firm's plant, equipment and finances. Human Capital resources include such things as the skills, experience, judgment and intelligence of the firm's employees. Organizational capital resources consist of such things as the firm's structure, planning, controlling and coordinating systems. The RBV states that these resources as the sources of competitive advantage. Competitive advantage is defined as taking place "when a firm is implementing a value creating strategy not simultaneously being implemented by any current or potential competitors" (Barney, 1991, p. 102). The resource-based view argues that competitive advantage exists under situations of resource heterogeneity and resource immobility wherein resources vary across firms and competing firms are unable obtain resources from other firms or resource markets. Within the resource-based view sustained competitive advantage exists only when other firms are unable to duplicate the benefits of a competitive advantage. Thus, for a resource to provide sustained competitive advantage, it must possess the following four attributes: (1) the resource must add value to the firm, (2) the resource must be unique or rare, (3) the resource must be inimitable, and (4) the resource cannot be substituted with another resource by competing firms (Barney, 1991).

The RBV emphasizes internal resources of the firm and as a result has gained enormous popularity in the SHRM literature. The RBV concepts applied in the context of human resources argues that the skills, knowledge, behavior of employees, or organizational resources like control systems, routines and learning mechanisms—that are products of complex social structures and social relationships within a firm, are built over time making them difficult to understand and imitate due to the complexity and causal ambiguity (Wright & McMahan, 1992). Thus, RBV has been applied by SHRM researchers to argue that an organization's employees (i.e., human resources) can be a source of competitive advantage. The company's human resources if properly utilized is a resource that adds value to the firm, is inimitable due to its complexity and causal ambiguity, is rare and is nonsubstitutable (Wright, McMahan, & McWilliams, 1994).

Entrepreneurship researchers have also made the connection between entrepreneurship and resource-based theory (Chandler & Hanks, 1994). They have attempted to show how the resource-based view can be a very helpful exploration instrument for questioning and better comprehension of entrepreneurship related phenomena. Additionally, their research arguably extended the boundaries of the resource-based view in that their research has tried to unravel how new resources come into existence and how employees sometimes personify bundles of heterogeneous resources that allow them to create new entrepreneurial opportunities and sustain exiting ones (Alvarez & Busenitz, 2001). Further, HR researchers have pointed out that the resource-based view adds value to all phases of entrepreneurship and can provide valuable insight in the study of human resources in entrepreneurial organizations (Heneman & Tansky, 2002). Consistent with these opinions, we use the resource-based view as a base to develop our model for strategic human resource management in an entrepreneurial firm.

SHRM researchers have increasingly used the resource-based view to explicate the role of human resources management in firm performance (Wright, Dunford, & Snell, 2001) It has been suggested that systems of HR practices can be sources of sustained competitive advantage due to the fact that these systems of practices are often unique, causally ambiguous and inimitable (Lado & Wilson, 1994). Further, organizational scholars have pointed out that HR practices can be a source of sustained competitive advantage when they support and develop the resources and competencies that add value to the firm (Wright, Smart, & McMahan, 1995). Thus, it is important for SHRM researchers to analyze the business environment of a firm and identify the crucial resources needed for successful firm performance and then identify the HR practices that can develop and support these critical resources (Wright et al., 2001).

Conceptual Model of Strategic Human Resource Management in Entrepreneurial Firms

Entrepreneurial firms provide a very important and fascinating context for studying the effect of HR practices on firm performance. As highlighted in the preceding sections, these firms play a significant role in today's knowledge economy. They exist in a highly competitive and dynamic environment characterized by rapid growth, a continually changing business environment and uncertainty. This requires the firms to create a climate that fosters learning, creativity and innovation. Additionally, these small high growth firms usually operate with very limited number of employees and scarce resources. This creates a need for maximum efficiency and high productivity from every employee. Thus, it is evident that small, high growth firms which are heavily dependent on their limited number of employees for their success especially need to focus on HR practices that can enhance the competencies of their most critical resource, their employees. It is important to understand how entrepreneurial companies can enhance worker effectiveness by adopting human resource practices and initiatives. Enhanced worker effectiveness positively effects organizational processes like innovation, worker motivation, etc., leading to subsequent higher organizational performance (Ciaverella, 2003).

Our basic conceptual model of strategic HRM processes in entrepreneurial firms is presented in Figure 2.1.

This model posits that in an entrepreneurial environment, certain types of people management practices will develop important employee competencies and lead employees to exhibit certain desired behaviors. These desirable employee behavior patterns in turn create an environment conducive to the development and flow of knowledge. Ultimately, this knowledge climate leads to enhanced organizational performance for the entrepreneurial firm. Thus, this model aims to explore the employee behaviors and outcomes occurring in the "black box" between human resource activities and indicators of firm performance (Becker & Gerhart, 1996). The model clarifies the mechanism though which HR practices in an entrepreneurial setting can develop critical employee competencies and create a favorable organizational climate for improved firm performance.

Additionally, we propose that certain firm characteristics like the presence or absence of VC's will moderate this relationship between people

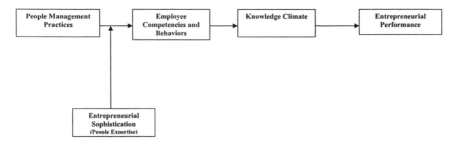

Figure 2.1.   Basic Conceptual Model.

management practices and employee behaviors and outcomes. Research conducted to examine the effect of VC's on human resources states that VC backing will have an effect on the firms overall human resource strategy and VC backed entrepreneurial firms have a more sophisticated and comprehensive HR strategy as compared to non VC backed entrepreneurial firms (Cyr et al., 2000). Consistent with this line of research, we propose that this concept of entrepreneurial sophistication (people expertise) will play an important role in the execution of the firm's HR strategy, thereby impacting the resulting employee behaviors and outcomes.

Expanded Model of Strategic Human Resource Management in Entrepreneurial Firms

The proposed expanded model of strategic human resource management in entrepreneurial firms is presented in Figure 2.2. In the following few sections, we elaborate on the concepts and processes outlined in this model.

Impact of People Management Practices on Employee Competencies and Behaviors in Entrepreneurial Firms

HRM researchers have increasingly tried to explain the various intermediate processes which are at play in the HR practices—firm performance relationship. It is well documented in RBV-based SHRM research that human resource practices can create competitive advantages and have a significant impact on firm performance (Bae & Lawler, 2000; Guthrie, 2001; Huselid, 1995). Specifically, there is consensus that a number of HR systems can be used to develop the competencies of employees as well as create and sustain competitive advantages stemming from these employee capabilities. The High Performance Work System (HPWS) and

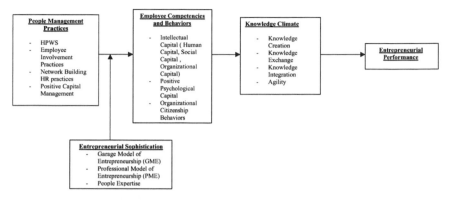

Figure 2.2.   Expanded Model.

Employee Involvement (EI) approach are two prominent theories in this area.

Becker and Huselid (1998) clarified that a HPWS treats systems for managing people as investments, rather than costs that need to be minimized. HPWS generally refer to a set of distinct but interrelated HR practices that can be combined together for employee selection, training and development, retention and motivation such that employees develop superior abilities and competencies including effective skills and behaviors. HPWS lead to higher employee motivation, enhanced communication and greater application of employee efforts toward work related objectives. HPWS and the resulting employee outputs and behaviors lead to higher firm performance and the creation of sustainable competitive advantage for the firm (Guthrie, 2001; Huselid, 1995). Additionally, HPWS develops and brings about optimal use of intellectual capital (Becker & Huselid, 1998). Intellectual capital consists of human capital, social capital and organizational capital. Intellectual capital represents the entire scope of a firm's potentially useful knowledge, skills and information (Snell, Lepak, & Youndt, 1999). Human capital consists of the knowledge, skills and abilities of employees. Employees own their human capital and can deploy it for various productive organizational functions (Becker, 1964; Schultz, 1961). Social capital is embedded in the structure of relations between actors and among actors, and represents knowledge flows among individuals within a network (Burt, 1997). Social capital facilitates productive activity (Coleman, 1988) and emphasizes a wide variety of specific benefits that flow from the trust, reciprocity, information and cooperation associated with social networks. Defined as "the sum of actual and potential resources embedded within, available through, and derived from the network of relationships possessed by individual or social units" (Nahapiet & Ghoshal, 1998, p. 243), social capital creates value for the people linked by the social ties created by these networks (Putnam, 1995). Organizational capital comprises institutionalized knowledge that is codified in databases, cultures, patents, manuals, political structures etc. It represents the knowledge base left behind and preserved when employees quit (Snell et al., 1999).

Lawler (1986, 1992, 1996) conceptualized the idea of employee empowerment in organizations and argued that organizations must equip employees with the skills and resources they need to make and implement effective decisions. He suggested that a company's HR practices should be structured in a way that promotes distribution of power and business information, creates rewards based on incentives linked to organizational performance, and helps employees develop the skills and knowledge needed for decision making. Thus, central to this employee involvement (EI) model are the four organizational processes namely power, information, knowledge and rewards. Power is concerned with the decision making processes in the organization and Lawler's model proposes that employees should be given more leeway in making decisions and participative decision-making should be encouraged. This will lead to higher motivation, greater job satisfaction and improved decision-making, coordination and communication. Information refers to sharing communication with respect to business performance, plans and goals. Sharing information with employees can lead to higher levels of power and knowledge in the firm accompanied by better decisions and, cooperation between employees and suggestions from employees on how to structure the work processes more effectively. Knowledge refers to the knowledge, skills and abilities of employees in the organization. EI systems are designed to provide training targeted toward developing the skills of employees so that they can perform their jobs effectively. Rewards are structured to elicit employee actions and behaviors that will enhance organizational performance and are tied to organizational performance. This kind of a reward system increases employee motivation and empowerment.

In addition to focusing on effective sets of HR practices, researchers in SHRM have increasingly argued for integrating relationships and development of networks into the HR systems of a firm to achieve superior firm performance. For example, Uhl-Bien, Graen, and Scandura (2000) argued the importance of building a relationship based HR architecture through strategic human resources management. They suggested that relationship based HR architectures would (1) provide a structure to form relationships, (2) build high quality relationships, (3) increase employee interaction in an organization thereby promoting network exchange, and (4) create a culture based on mutual trust, respect and obligation. This kind of relationship-based architecture involves formulating HR practices which enhance and reward effective relationship development. They argued that since today's organizations face many external challenges and demands, effective work relationships and networks within the organization will generate social capital thereby leading them to produce superior products and services, and be more flexible in adapting to the rapid changes in the environment. Evans and Davis (2004) argued that HPWS may be configured in a relationship based human resources architecture leading to the creation of an empowered relational structure, high quality relationships and shared mental models. This results in the development of social capital in the form of internal firm networks and organizational citizenship behaviors (OCB) within the company. OCB's are employee work behavior such as helping others, staying late or working weekends, performing at levels that surpass enforceable organizational standards, tolerating impositions or inconveniences on the job and assuming an active role in company affairs (Bolino, Turnley, & Niehoff, 2004). It should be noted that a review of the research indicates that some other terms for domains of behavior that overlap with OCB include *prosocial organizational behavior* (Brief & Motowidlo, 1986; George, 1990, 1991; George & Bettenhausen, 1990; O'Reilly & Chatman, 1986), *organizational spontaneity* (George & Brief, 1992; George & Jones, 1997), and *extra role behavior* (Van Dyne, Cummings, & McLean Parks, 1995; Wright, George, Farnsworth, & McMahan, 1993).

Bolino and Turnley (2003) suggested that companies can use certain HR practices like team training to elicit cooperation and OCB's from employees. It is important to note that social capital and OCB's appear to have a mutually reinforcing relationship. Research indicates that OCB's contribute to the creation of social capital and social capital in turn stimulates additional citizenship behaviors (Bolino, Turnley, & Bloodgood, 2002).

Wright et al. (2001) reviewed the conceptual developments in the field of SHRM and argued that the people management system in a company can create competitive advantage by developing the human capital pool and eliciting desired employee behaviors like discretionary OCB's. Further, their integrated model explained that people management systems can create value by developing the stock of intellectual capital (also referred to as the stock of knowledge) in firms. They elaborated that the term people management practices is used to highlight the importance of understanding multiple practices (rather than single practices) that impact employees as well as to go beyond the realm of HR practices and include relevant practices like leadership, communication, work design, etc., that have the potential to impact employees and develop their competencies, cognitions and attitudes.

From the discussions above, we can conclude that previous models of SHRM have underscored the importance of specific sets of HR practices like HPWS and EI systems and their crucial role in developing important employee competencies like intellectual capital. Recently, entrepreneurship researchers have begun to recognize the importance of HPWS and EI systems in the context of entrepreneurial firms. Way (2002) examined the impact of HPWS on firm performance in small businesses in the United States and categorized HPWS to include HR practices in the area of staffing, compensation, flexible job teamwork, assignments, teamwork, training and communication. The sample comprised 446 U.S. firms with less than 100 employees. The empirical results indicated that in small firms, HPWS are associated with lower employee turnover and higher employee productivity. Thus, he concluded that HPWS enhance the ability of small firms to select, develop, retain and motivate a competent work force which produces superior employee outputs. Researchers have proposed that entrepreneurial firms can implement employee involvement systems more easily when compared to larger firms since they begin with an informal structure and communication system (Hyman & Mason, 1995; Lawler, 1992). Ciaverella (2003) argued that organizations should implement EI initiatives from the introduction stage of a new venture and this will lead these new firms to have significantly longer periods of growth, higher morale and higher levels of organizational performance. Thus, researchers agree HPWS/EI programs can play a very important role in developing the skills and competencies of the workforce in an entrepreneurial firm.

We integrate this existing research in SHRM and entrepreneurship and propose that in entrepreneurial companies certain kinds of relationship based HR systems like HPWS and EI systems will impact the competencies and abilities of their workforce and lead to certain favorable outcomes and behaviors. We use the term people management practices to encompass HPWS, EI approaches along with other types of HR practices like positive capital management and network building HR practices. This is consistent with Wright et al. (2001) and their conceptualization of people management practices. Both HPWS and EI programs comprise sets of multiple HR practices and apart from including traditional HR functions like staffing, compensation, etc., they also address issues of communication, work design etc. Thus, we argue that in an entrepreneurial setting, people management practices will develop and augment the intellectual capital of workers and lead employees to exhibit desired behaviors like OCB's and formation of more internal networks. Specifically, we propose that:

Proposition 1: People Management practices like HPWS and EI systems will generate higher levels of intellectual capital (higher levels of human capital, social capital, and organizational capital) in an entrepreneurial firm.

Proposition 2: People Management practices like HPWS and EI systems will lead to the development and use of OCB's by employees in an entrepreneurial firm.

The propositions presented above highlight the unique operating environment of entrepreneurial firms. As highlighted in preceding sections, entrepreneurial firms often face resource scarcity and operate with a lean organizational structure. These small, high growth firms are constantly faced with the challenge of how to do more with less, which makes managing the human resource component very important. Higher levels of intellectual capital translate into higher levels of human capital, social capital and organizational capital all of which lead to higher employee productivity. Additionally, select people management practices like team training will develop a cooperative spirit between employees and lead them to engage in OCB's.

In addition to developing internal networks within the firm, entrepreneurial firms need to develop external networks to get access to valuable and timely information. It is necessary for them to form alliances and partnerships with customers, suppliers distributors, firms with complementary resources, other firms in the same industry etc. External networks can be useful because they provide the opportunity to learn new capabilities and can provide information that will help entrepreneurial firms identify potential opportunities (Anand & Khanna, 2000; Cooper, 2001; Hitt, Ireland, & Lee, 2000). Entrepreneurial firms often have limited resources and external networks enable entrepreneurial firms to compete effectively without actually owing all the resources they need. Research suggests that new start up firms improve their chances of survival and success by establishing alliances and developing them into an effective network (Baum, Calabrese, & Silverman, 2000; Cooper 2001; Dubini & Aldrich, 1991; Starr & MacMillan, 1990). Thus an external network enhances the intellectual capital of employees by adding to the social capital component. Researchers have found that certain types of HR practices provide incentives to employees in order to motivate them to develop valuable external networks. Collins and Clark (2003) argued that specific network-building HR practices like training, performance assessment and rewards designed to help and encourage top managers to build relationships with both external and internal actors will help build valuable top management team (TMT) networks. Their results indicated that network building HR practices played an important role in building up valuable TMT networks and ultimately improved the financial performance of the firm reflected through sales growth and better stock performance.

Using this perspective we suggest that it would be valuable for entrepreneurial firms to use network building HR practices and motivate not only top managers but all employees to establish alliances and relationships that can provide the entrepreneurial firm with valuable resources. Hence, the following:

> **Proposition 3:**   People Management Practices like network building HR practices will lead to employees developing more external networks consequently enhancing the firms stock of intellectual capital.

Recently, scholars have suggested that we need to look beyond human capital, social capital, and organizational capital and explore the notion of positive psychological capital (PPC) which can also be a source of competitive advantage in firms (Luthans & Youssef, 2004). PPC lies beyond human and social capital and addresses the issue of "who you are," rather than "what you are" (human capital) and "who you know" (social capital). Like other forms of capital, (PPC) is made up of certain components which are unique and measurable and have the potential to impact performance. The dimensions of PPC include efficacy/confidence, hope, optimism and resiliency. Thus, PPC is inherent in an individual and represents positively oriented human resource strengths and psychological capacities that can be measured, developed and managed for effective performance.

Luthans, Luthans, & Luthans (2004) suggests that higher levels of an employee's PPC can contribute to higher productivity, better customer service, more employment retention and overall higher job performance. Additionally, the elements of PPC are state like variables (as opposed to being traits, dispositional factors etc.) that can be developed with employees through workplace interventions and proactive management. Therefore, Luthans, et al. (2004) argues that certain HR strategies like specific kinds of training (interactive, activity-based training), risk focused strategies, asset focus strategies and process focused strategies can be developed to enhance manager's and employee's confidence, hope, optimism and resiliency. Thus, this type of Positive Capital Management (PCM) will lead to enhanced levels of hope, optimism, resiliency and confidence resulting in better employee performance and can be a source of competitive advantage for firms.

The concepts of PPC and PCM are particularly important in an entrepreneurial environment and can be usefully applied to an entrepreneurial enterprise. As discussed earlier, employees in entrepreneurial firms operate in a highly pressurized environment stemming from rapid growth rates, constantly changing business environment, resource scarcity, internal turmoil and the like. Very often, this constant pressure leads to high levels of stress, employee turnover and burnout. People Management Practices like PCM strategies can help employees develop higher levels of PPC thereby instilling in them more hope, optimism, confidence and resilience all of which will enable them to manage their stress levels more effectively and alleviate burnout. We argue that people management practices like PCM strategies are especially well suited for entrepreneurial firms and therefore we propose the following:

Proposition 4:   People Management practices like PCM will generate higher levels of positive psychological capital among the employees of an entrepreneurial firm.

Effect of Employee Competencies and Behaviors on the Knowledge Climate

SHRM researchers have reiterated the positive relationship between the components of intellectual capital and a firm's knowledge management environment. It is well documented that higher levels of human capital enhances knowledge creation in a firm. Social capital represents the internal and external networks established by the firm's employees and these networks facilitate information exchange and knowledge transfer thereby promoting knowledge exchange. Overall, researchers state that human capital and social capital are the primary elements of knowledge creation in organizations (Argyris & Schon, 1978; Nonaka, 1991; Senge, 1990). The knowledge created and exchanged through human capital and social capital can be institutionalized and codified through processes, databases, culture, routines, patents, etc., and this gives rise to organizational capital which integrates and preserves the firm's knowledge base (Snell et al., 1999).

Evans and Davis (2004) presented comprehensive arguments to highlight the positive impact of social capital and OCB's on the creation and transfer of knowledge within a firm. Wright et al. (2001) suggested that a firms stock of intellectual capital represents its stock of knowledge. Their model proposed that a firm's stock of intellectual capital (comprising human, social and organization capital) will facilitate knowledge creation, knowledge transfer and knowledge integration. Thus, prior research has established employee competencies like intellectual capital and employee behaviors like OCB's will interact and foster an environment of knowledge creation, exchange and integration. We draw on this stream of research to suggest that in an entrepreneurial setting, employee competencies created as a result of people management practices will result in the creation of an organizational climate that promotes knowledge creation, exchange and integration. Hence, we propose the following:

Proposition 5:   Higher levels of intellectual capital will lead to greater knowledge creation, knowledge exchange, and knowledge integration in an entrepreneurial firm.

Another concept that has been used to analyze firms in a rapidly changing environment is the concept of organizational agility (OA) (Dyer & Shafer, 1999). Advocates of OA have cited examples of agile organizations to include companies like Texas Instruments, Nike, 3M etc. and also smaller computer companies. In a fiercely competitive and rapidly changing environment agile organizations (AO) are able to identify sources of competitive advantage repeatedly by being the first to recognize threats and opportunities and by being able to deal with threats and exploit opportunities much more efficiently than current and potential competitors. AO's aim to foster organizational competencies like reading the market, mobilizing rapid response, and embedding organizational learning.

Dyer and Shafer (1999) point out that employees of AO's need to be business driven, focused, generative, adaptive and values driven and these personal attributes will lead them to exhibit initiative, spontaneously collaborate, be innovated and adjust quickly to the rapidly changing environment. They further outline a variety of personal competencies that employees need to cultivate in order to embody the successful personal attributes in an AO. Among other things these personal competencies include being fast learners, team players, comfortable with oneself, emphatic and resilient. The research on AO can be extended to include entrepreneurial firms since they face similar competitive and rapidly changing environments as outlined in the discussion earlier. Agile organizations can identify opportunities and threats very quickly and effectively neutralize threats and exploit opportunities, therefore entrepreneurial firms should strive to acquire these capabilities since this will enable them to effectively deal with their own ambiguous and high growth environment. Thus, we suggest that entrepreneurial firms should strive to be agile organizations. Additionally, we integrate the concept of PPC with organizational agility. If employees possess higher levels of PPC, they will develop and embody personal competencies like confidence and resiliency necessary to develop organizational agility. Therefore, we propose the following:

Proposition 6:   Higher levels of PPC among employees will enable entrepreneurial firms to enhance organizational agility.

Impact of the Knowledge Climate on Entrepreneurial Firm Performance

In a comprehensive review of governance and strategic leadership in entrepreneurial firms, Daily et al. (2002) concluded that there is a lack of consistency about what constitutes entrepreneurial firm performance. Researchers have suggested that sales growth is perhaps the most important indicator of entrepreneurial firm performance, but Daily et al. (2002) presented four distinct but not mutually exclusive performance categories. These categories included financial performance of the firm, the performance of the firm at the initial public offering, the growth of the firm and the survival of the firm. Cooper, Gascon, and Woo (1994) operationalized firm performance with three mutually exclusive categories, namely failure, marginal survival (survival with low growth), and growth. Entrepreneurial performance has been refereed to as the ability to innovate, accept risk, and identify and exploit entrepreneurial opportunities (Hayton, 2003). Way (2002) used workforce turnover and labor productivity to measure small firm performance. Thus, it is evident that firm performance can be composed of several different dimensions.

Knowledge is viewed as critical firm specific critical resource (Hitt, Ireland, Camp, & Sexton, 2001). Grant (1996) proposes that knowledge is a firm's most crucial competitive resource. Research indicates that an organization which fosters knowledge creation, knowledge exchange and knowledge integration will improve organizational performance by affecting some specific dimensions of firm performance. Wright et al. (2001) argue that the flow of knowledge through creation, transfer and integration in a way that is inimitable, valuable, rare and organized creates core competencies for the firm which in turn leads to higher firm performance. Knowledge exchange and knowledge creation are fostered through the social capital generated by an employee's participation in both internal and external networks. Evans and Davis (2004) suggest that employee's social capital and OCB's promote information sharing and cooperative behavior within the company leading to knowledge creation and knowledge exchange which in turn contributes to high performance sustainability. Hitt, Bierman, Shimizu, and Kochhar (2001) found that the transfer of knowledge within a firm builds employee capabilities and contributes to higher firm performance. Knowledge is viewed as an especially critical asset for entrepreneurial firms. Yli-Renko, Autio, and Sapienza (2001) found that small, high technology firms acquired knowledge through the knowledge exchange process in their interactions with key customers. This knowledge acquired through external networks led to higher levels of knowledge exploitation and was positively related to new product development, technological distinctiveness, and sales cost efficiency. Hence, it can be concluded that in entrepreneurial firms, knowledge can be created though enhanced levels of human capital, exchanged and used fruitfully though social networks and social capital and preserved and integrated through organizational capital. This knowledge will in turn contribute to improved firm performance through higher sales, increased new product development, creating core competencies, enhancing employee capabilities and creation of additional competitive advantages. Thus, we propose:

> **Proposition 7:**   Greater knowledge exchange, transfer, and integration will lead to improved entrepreneurial firm performance.

As previously discussed, if firms foster organizational agility, they can adapt to rapid changes in the environment, spot new opportunities and threats and exploit new opportunities to create competitive advantages repeatedly. These characteristics of agile organizations will lead them to adjust their product or service offerings, improve decision making and critical business processes, and ultimately lead to improved firm performance. Hence we propose that these same advantages will accrue to entrepreneurial firms if they strive to foster organizational agility. Hence the following proposition:

> **Proposition 8:**   Entrepreneurial firms that attempt to foster organizational ability will develop unique capabilities to adjust rapidly and effectively react to their ambiguous and uncertain business environment resulting in improved firm performance.

The Moderating Role of Entrepreneurial Sophistication as People Expertise

Organizational researchers have often focused on the importance of venture capitalists in entrepreneurial firms. It is commonly believed that VC's closely monitor the operations of the businesses they finance and undertake certain activities including mentoring, strategic advice, monitoring, corporate governance, professionalization of the company and recruitment of senior management all of which benefit the entrepreneurial firm (Hellman & Puri, 2000). Researchers agree that VC's influence the human resource structure and functions in the company. For example, Bygrave and Timmons (1992) suggested that VC backed companies nurture talented employees and they allow employees to use their creativity to achieve business objectives. VC's also play an important role in identifying and recruiting top executives and members of the top management team (Tybjee & Bruno, 1984). Recent empirical studies have investigated the relationship between VC's and their impact on the human resources structure. Cyr et al. (2000) examined whether or not VC backing will affect the probability that IPO firms will report having a vice president (VP) of human resources. Additionally, they also examined the combined effect of being VC backed and having a VP of human resources on firm performance. The results of their study indicated that VC's do influence the human resources approach of the firms they finance. VC backed firms were more likely to have VP's of human resources than non VC backed firms. Additionally, they reported that VC backed firms will probably not have another member of the top management team (like the CFO or VP of administration) dealing with HR responsibilities. They suggested that this result indicates that VC's prefer a top management team member to be solely responsible for HR and not be involved in other administrative functions. The researchers highlight the fact that from the SHRM point of view this result is significant because in such a situation the HR executive will be completely focused on HR activities and will be in a position to add maximum value by addressing people related issues and incorporating those issues into the overall strategy formulation for the firm.

Hellman and Puri (2004) analyzed a sample of 173 private startup companies located in California's Silicon Valley region to examine whether VC's play any role in the professionalization of these firms. They first examined whether VC's provided any support to build up the internal organization of the firm by analyzing a variety of evidence like recruitment processes, the overall HR policies, adoption of stock plans, and the hiring of a VP of marketing and sales. The results indicated that for each of these dimensions, VC backed entrepreneurial firms were more likely and/or faster to professionalize along these dimensions. Specifically, VC financing was related to recruiting in that VC backed firms made greater use of business and personal contacts for recruiting employees. Additionally, the results indicated that they played an influential role in the formulation of HR policies. VC backed firms were more likely to adopt stock option plans and had a higher probability of appointing an outsider to the position of CEO. Overall, their results indicated that the effect of venture capital is more evident when the companies are still private.

The research evidence presented above indicates that VC backed firms have a higher probability of pursuing a more sophisticated and focused HR strategy and having a more expert approach to managing human resources. VC backed firms will have a higher chance of having dedicated HR professionals at various levels to formulate and implement strategic HR policies. Drawing on this research, we can conclude that private entrepreneurial firms following the PME will have a more sophisticated and focused HR strategy than the firms following the GME. Entrepreneurial firms following the GME are more likely to be managed by the founder and have less HR expertise to articulate a formal HR strategy. This absence or presence of people expertise will play an important role in determining what HR practices and policies are implemented in the firm and as a result will impact the development employee competencies. For example, firms following the PME have a dedicated HR executive directing and formulating HR practices and HR policies and are more likely to implement strategic people management practices like HPWS and EI systems leading to the development of specific employee competencies like higher levels of intellectual capital and positive psychological capital. Thus, the presence of VC's will promote entrepreneurial sophistication of the firm such that these firms will have greater access to people expertise and thereby influence the implementation of strategic HRM practices. Hence, we explicate the moderating role of entrepreneurial people sophistication as follows:

Proposition 9:   There is a moderating effect of entrepreneurial sophistication on the relationship between people management practices and employee competencies and behaviors; such that the strategic people management practices implemented by HR professionals in firms following the PME will strengthen the positive relationship between people management practices and the development of employee competencies and behaviors.

CONTRIBUTIONS AND LIMITATIONS

The arguments presented above emphasize the importance of strategic human resource management in the context of entrepreneurial firms. This paper deviates from the often followed functional approach and takes a strategic human resource approach to managing HR in entrepreneurial firms. First, the chapter attempts to envision a direction for

SHRM in entrepreneurial firms and provide a preliminary framework that has the potential to provide direction for further research. Secondly, the underlying mechanisms of the HR practices—firm performance relationship in an entrepreneurial setting are explicated. In doing so, we try to clarify the ambiguous definition of entrepreneurial firms and in the interest of clarity and parsimony, the focus is on analyzing the SHRM processes in privately owned entrepreneurial firms. In addition, the impact of venture capital investments on HR strategies is highlighted. Finally, the role of Positive Psychological Capital and Positive Psychological Capital Management (or simply positive capital management—PCM) in an entrepreneurial firm is emphasized. Further, the importance of network building HR practices in an entrepreneurial environment is highlighted and the importance of external networks is addressed. Finally, the importance of the people expertise is discussed as a moderating influence on the ability to achieve the intended benefits from strategic people management practices.

It is however important to note that this paper is not meant to be a normative or a complete comprehensive model and has certain limitations. The majority of research investigating HR and entrepreneurial firms has used a functional approach to HRM. This paper aims to provide a framework that we can use to start integrating the various concepts. Using this framework, we can move toward developing more sophisticated and encompassing models of SHRM in entrepreneurial firms. This model begins to "scratch the surface" of the black box in the HR practices-firm performance relationship in entrepreneurial firms. It does not consider all stages in the life cycle of an entrepreneurial firm. Additionally, the model does not consider IPO entrepreneurial firms as the focus is limited to private firms. Finally, the chapter should serve as a starting point for studying the role of people in entrepreneurial firms and in analyzing the strategic role of HR in these firms. In our opinion, entrepreneurial firms are truly people dependent for both survival and success.

REFERENCES

Alvarez, S. A., & Busenitz, L. W. (2001). The entrepreneurship of resource-based theory. *Journal of Management, 27*, 755-775.

Anand, B. N., & Khanna T. (2000). Do firms learn to create value? The case of alliances? *Strategic Management Journal* [Special Issue], *21*(3), 295–315.

Argyris, C., & Schon, D. (1978). *Organizational learning: A theory of action perspective*. Reading, MA: Addison-Wesley.

Bae, J., & Lawler, J. J. (2000). Organizational and HRM strategies in Korea: Impact on firm performance in an emerging economy. *Academy of Management Journal, 43*(3), 502-517.

Baldwin, W. (2004). In praise of job killers. *Forbes*. Retrieved October 1, 2005, from http://www.forbes.com/free_forbes/2004/1101/022.html.

Barney, J. (1991). Firm resources and sustained competitive advantage. *Journal of Management, 17*, 99-120.

Baum, J. A. C., Calabrese, T., & Silverman, B. S. (2000). Don't go it alone: Alliance network composition and startups' performance in Canadian biotechnology. *Strategic Management Journal* [Summer Special Issue], *21*(3), 267–294.

Becker, G. S. (1964). *Human capital*. New York: National Bureau of Economic Research.

Becker, B. E., & Gerhart, B. (1996). The impact of human resource management on organizational performance: Progress and prospects. *Academy of Management Journal, 39*(4), 779-801.

Becker, B. E., & Huselid, M. A. (1998). High performance work systems and firm performance: A synthesis of research and managerial implications. In K. M. Rowland & G. R. Ferris (Eds.), *Research in personnel and human resource management* (Vol. 16, pp. 53-101. Greenwich, CT: JAI Press.

Birch, D. (1987). *Job creation in America*. New York: The Free Press.

Brazeal, D. V., & Herbert, T. (1999). The genesis of entrepreneurship. *Entrepreneurship: Theory & Practice, 23*(3), 29-45.

Brief, A. P., & Motowidlo, S. J. (1986). Prosocial organizational behaviors. *Academy of Management Review, 11*, 710–725.

Bolino, M. C., Turnley, W. H., & Bloodgood, J. M. (2002). Citizenship behavior and the creation of social capital in organizations. *Academy of Management Review, 27*(4), 505-522.

Bolino, M. C., & Turnley, W. H. (2003). Going the extra mile: Cultivating and managing employee citizenship behavior. *Academy of Management Executive, 17*(3), 60-71.

Bolino, M. C., Turnley, W. H., & Niehoff, B. P. (2004). The other side of the story: Reexamining prevailing assumptions about organizational citizenship behavior. *Human Resource Management Review, 14*, 229-246.

Burt, R. S. (1997). The contingent value of social capital. *Administrative Science Quarterly, 42*(2), 339-365.

Bygrave, W. D., & Timmons, J. A. (1992). *Venture capital at the crossroads*. Boston: Harvard Business School Press.

Cardon, M. S., & Stevens, C. E. (2004). Managing human resources in small organizations: What do we know? *Human Resource Management Review, 14*, 295-323.

Chandler, G. N., & Hanks, S. H. (1994). Market attractiveness, resource based capabilities, venture strategies and venture performance. *Journal of Business Venturing, 9*, 331-349.

Ciaverella, M. A. (2003). The adoption of high involvement practices and progresses in emergent and developing firms: A descriptive and prescriptive approach. *Human Resource Management, 42*(4), 337-356.

Colbert, B. A. (2004). The complex resource based view: Implications for theory and practice in strategic human resource management. *Academy of Management Review, 29*(3), 341-358.

Coleman, J. S. (1988). Social capital in the creation of human capital. *American Journal of Sociology, 94*, 95-120.

Collins, C. J., & Clark, K. D. (2003). Strategic human resource practices, top management team social networks and firm performance: The role of human resource practices in creating organizational competitive advantage. *Academy of Management Journal, 46*, 740-751.

Cooper, A. C., & Gascon, F. J. G. (1992). Entrepreneurs, processes of founding and new firm performance. In D. L. Sexton & J. D. Kasarda (Eds.), *The state of the art of entrepreneurship* (pp. 301-340). Boston, MA: PWS Kent.

Cooper, A. C., Gascon, F. J. G., & Woo, C. Y. (1994). Initial human and financial capital as predictors of new venture performance. *Journal of Business Venturing, 9*, 371-395.

Cooper, A. C. (2001). Networks, alliances, and entrepreneurship. In M. A. Hitt, R. D. Ireland, S. M. Camp, & D. L. Sexton (Eds.), *Strategic entrepreneurship: Creating a new integrated mindset*. Oxford, England: Blackwell.

Cyr, L. A., Johnson, D. E., & Welbourne, T. M. (2000). Human resources in initial public offering firms: Do venture capitalists make a difference? *Entrepreneurship: Theory & Practice, 25*, 77-91.

Daily, C. M., McDougall, P. P., Covin, J. G., & Dalton, D. R. (2002). Governance and strategic leadership in entrepreneurial firms. *Journal of Management, 28*(3), 387-412.

Devanna, M. A., Fombrum, C. J., & Tichy, N. M. (1984). A framework for strategic human resource management. In *Strategic human resource management* (chap. 3, pp. 33-51). New York: Wiley.

Drucker, P. (1985). *Innovation and entrepreneurship*. New York: Harper and Row.

Dubini, P., & Aldrich, H. E. (1991). Personal and extended networks are central to entrepreneurial process. *Journal of Business Venturing, 6*, 305–313.

Dyer, L., & Shafer, R. A. (1999). From human resource strategy to organizational effectiveness: Lessons from research on organizational agility. In P. Wright, L. Dyer, J. W. Boudreau, & G. T. Milkovich (Eds.), *Strategic human resources management in the twenty-first century*, Supp. 4, *Research in personnel and human resource management*. Stamford, CT: JAI Press.

Entrepreneur and D&B's 10th Annual 2004 Hot 100: The fastest growing new entrepreneurial businesses in America. (2004). Retrieved September 1, 2005, from http://www.entrepreneur.com/hot100/0,6524,,00.html

Evans, R. & Davis, W. D. (2004). High performance work systems: The role of social capital and organizational citizenship behavior. Paper presented at the Academy of Management Annual Meeting, New Orleans, LA.

Ewing Marion Kaufmann Foundation. (1999). *Global entrepreneurship monitor 1999 global report*. Kansas City, MO: Author.

Ewing Marion Kaufmann Foundation. (2003). *Global entrepreneurship monitor 2003 global report*. Kansas City, MO: Author.

George, J. M. (1990). Personality, affect, and behavior in groups. *Journal of Applied Psychology, 75*, 107-116.

George, J. (1991). State or trait: Effects of positive mood on prosocial behaviors at work. *Journal of Applied Psychology, 76*, 299-307.

George, J. M., & Bettenhausen, K. (1990). Understanding prosocial behavior, sales performance, and turnover: A group-level analysis in a service context. *Journal of Applied Psychology, 75*, 698-709.

George, J. M., & Brief, A. P. (1992). Feeling good-doing good: A conceptual analysis of the mood at work-organizational spontaneity relationship. *Psychological Bulletin, 112*, 310-329.

George, J. M., & Jones, G. R. (1997). Organizational spontaneity in context. *Human Performance, 10*, 153-170.

Grant, R. M. (1996). Toward a knowledge-based theory of the firm. *Strategic Management Journal* [Winter Special Issue], *17*, 109–122.

Guthrie, J. P. (2001). High-involvement work practices, turnover, and productivity: Evidence from New Zealand. *Academy of Management Journal, 44*(1), 180-190.

Hambrick, D. C., & Crozier, L. M. (1985). Stumblers and stars in the management of rapid growth. *Journal of Business Venturing, 1*, 31-45.

Hayton, J. C. (2003). Strategic human capital management in SME's: An empirical study of entrepreneurial performance. *Human Resource Management Review, 42*(4), 375-391.

Hellman, T., & Puri, M. (2000). The interaction between product market and financing strategy: The role of venture capital. *The Review of Financial Studies, 13*(4), 959-984.

Hellman, T., & Puri, M. (2004). Venture capital and the professionalization of start-up firms: Empirical evidence. *The Journal of Finance, 57*(1), 169-197.

Heneman, R. L., & Tansky, J. W. (2002). Human resource management models for entrepreneurial opportunity: Existing knowledge and new directions. In J. Katz & T. M. Welbourne (Eds.), *Managing people in entrepreneurial organizations* (Vol. 5, pp. 55-82). Amsterdam: JAI Press.

Heneman, R. L., Tansky, J. W., & Camp, S. M. (2000). Human resource management practices in small and medium-sized enterprises: Unanswered questions and future research perspectives. *Entrepreneurship: Theory & Practice, 25*(1), 11-26.

Hitt, M. A., Ireland, R. D., & Lee, H. (2000). Technological learning, knowledge management, firm growth and performance. *Journal of Engineering and Technology Management, 17*, 231– 246.

Hitt, M. A., Ireland, R. D., Camp, S. M., & Sexton, D. L. (2001). Strategic entrepreneurship: Entrepreneurial strategies for wealth creation. *Strategic Management Journal, 22*, 479-491.

Hitt, M. A., Bierman, L., Shimizu, K., & Kochhar, R. (2001). Direct and moderating effects of human capital on strategy and performance in professional service firms: A resource based perspective. *Academy of Management Journal, 44*, 13-28.

Hornsby, J. S., & Kuratko, D. F. (2003). Human resource management in U.S. small businesses: A replication and extension. *Journal of Developmental Entrepreneurship, 8*(1), 73-92.

Huselid, M. A. (1995). The impact of human resource management practices on turnover, productivity, and corporate financial performance. *Academy of Management Journal, 38*, 635-672

Hyman, J., & Mason, R. (1995). *Managing employee involvement and participation*. Thousand Oaks, CA: Sage.

Johnson, D. E., & Cyr, L. A. (2001). *Exploring the relationship between climate for valuing human resources and employee performance in entrepreneurial firms*. Poster session at Babson XXVIII. Working paper.

Kaman, V., McCarthy, A. M., Gulbro, R. D., & Tucker, M. L. (2001). Bureaucratic and high commitment human resource practices in small service firms. *Human Resource Planning, 35*, 33-44.

Kamoche, K. (1996). Strategic human resource management within a resource-capability view of the firm. *Journal of Management Studies, 33*(2), 213-233.

Kao, J. J., & Stevenson, H. H. (1985). *Entrepreneurship: What it is and how to teach it*. Cambridge, MA: Harvard Business School.

Kayne, J. (1999). *State entrepreneurship policies and programs*. Kansas City, MO: Ewing Marion Kaufmann Foundation.

Kentucky Office for the New Economy. (2002). *A strategic plan for the new economy*. Frankfort: Cabinet for Economic Development, Kentucky Innovation Commission.

Kotter, J., & Sathe, V. (1978). Problems of human resource management in rapidly growing companies. *California Management Review, 21*(2), 29-36.

Lado, A. A., & Wilson, M. C. (1994). Human resource systems and sustained-competitive advantage: A competency based perspective. *Academy of Management Review, 19*(4), 699-727.

Lawler, E. (1986). *High-involvement management: Participative strategies for improving organizational performance*. San Francisco: Jossey-Bass.

Lawler, E. (1992). *The ultimate advantage: Creating the high involvement organization*. San Francisco: Jossey-Bass.

Lawler, E. (1996). *From ground up: Six principles for creating the new logic organization*. San Francisco: Jossey-Bass.

Lawler, E. E., & Mohrman, S. A. (2003). HR as a strategic partner: What does it take to make it happen? *Human Resource Planning, 26*(3), 15-29.

Legnick-Hall, C. A., & Legnick-Hall, M. L. (1988). Strategic human resources management: A review of the literature and a proposed typology. *Academy of Management Review, 13*(3), 454-470.

Luthans, F., & Youssef, C. M. (2004). Human, social and now positive psychological capital management: Investing in people for competitive advantage. *Organizational Dynamics, 33*(2), 143-160.

Luthans, F., Luthans, K. W., & Luthans, B. C. (2004). Positive psychological capital: Beyond human and social capital. *Business Horizons, 47*(1), 45-50.

McMahan, G. C., Lawler, E. E., & Mohrman, S. A. (1996). *Human Resource Planning, 19*, 11-15.

McMahan, G. C., Virick, M., & Wright, P. M. (1999). Alternative theoretical perspectives for strategic human resource management revisited: Progress, problems, and prospects. In *Research in personnel and human resource management* (Suppl. 4, pp. 99-122). Stamford, CT: JAI Press.

Nahapiet, J., & Ghoshal, S. (1998). Social capital, intellectual capital and the organizational advantage. *Academy of Management Review, 23*, 242-266.

National Governor's Association Center for Best Practices. (2004). *A governor's guide to strengthening state entrepreneurship policy.* National Governor's Association, Washington, D. C.

Nonaka, I. (1991). The knowledge creating company. *Harvard Business Review, 6,* 96-104.

Olson, P. (1985). Entrepreneurship: Opportunistic decision makers. *Journal of Small Business Management, 11*(2), 25-31.

O'Reilly, C., & Chatman, J. (1986). Organizational commitment and psychological attachment: The effects of compliance, identification, and internalization on prosocial behavior. *Journal of Applied Psychology, 71*, 492-499.

Penrose, E. T. (1959). The theory of the growth of the firm. Oxford, United Kingdom: Basil Blackwell.

Porter, M. E. (1980). *Competitive strategy.* New York: Free Press.

Porter, M. E. (1985). *Competitive advantage: Creating and sustaining superior performance.* New York: Free Press.

Prahalad, C. K., & Hamel, G. (1990, May/June). The core competence of the corporation. *Harvard Business Review,* pp. 79-91.

Putnam, R. (1995). Bowling alone: America's declining social capital. *Journal of Democracy, 6,* 65-78.

Rangone, A. (1999). A resource based approach to strategy analysis in small-medium sized enterprises. *Small Business Economics, 12,* 233-248.

Reynolds, P. D., Carter, N. M., Gartner, W. B., Greene, P. G., & Cox, L. W. (2004). *The entrepreneur next door: Characteristics of individuals starting companies in America.* Kansas City, MO: Ewing Marion Kaufmann Foundation.

Rogg, K. L., Schmidt, D. B., Shull, C., & Schmitt, N. (2001). Human resource practices, organizational climate, and customer satisfaction. *Journal of Management, 27,* 431-449.

Schramm, C. J. (2004). Building entrepreneurial economies. *Foreign Affairs, 83*(4), 104-115.

Schumpeter, J. (1934). *The theory of economic development.* Cambridge, MA: Harvard University Press.

Schultz, T. (1961). Investment in human capital. *American Economic Review, 51*(1), 1-17.

Senge, P. M. (1990). *The fifth discipline: The art and practice of the learning organization.* New York: Doubleday.

Shane, S., & Venkataraman, S. (2000). The promise of entrepreneurship as a field of research. *Academy of Management Review, 25*(1), 217-226.

Sharma, P., & Chrisman, J. J. (1999). Toward a reconciliation of the definitional issues in the field of entrepreneurship. *Entrepreneurship: Theory & Practice, 23*(3), 11-27.

Siegel, R., Siegel, E., & MacMillan, I. C. (1993). Characteristics distinguishing high-growth ventures. *Journal of Business Venturing, 8,* 169-180.

Snell, S. A., Lepak, D. P., & Youndt, M. A. (1999). Managing the architecture of intellectual capital: Implications for strategic human resource management. In P. Wright, L. Dyer, J. W. Boudreau, & G. T. Milkovich (Eds.), *Strategic human resources management in the twenty-first century,* [Suppl. 4], *Research in personnel and human resource management.* Stamford, CT: JAI Press.

Starr J. A., & MacMillan I. C. (1990). Resource co-optation via social contracting: Rresource acquisition strategies for new ventures. *Strategic Management Journal* [Summer Special Issue], *11*, 79–92.

Stevenson, H. H., & Jarillo, M. J. (1990). A paradigm of entrepreneurship: Entrepreneurial management. *Strategic Management Journal, 11*, 17-27.

Thite, M. (2004). Strategic positioning of HRM in knowledge based organizations. *Learning Organization, 11*(1), 28-44.

Timmons, J. (1978). Characteristics and role demands of entrepreneurship. *American Journal of Small Business, 3*(1): 5-17.

Tybjee, T. T., & Bruno, A. V. (1984). A model of venture capital investment activity. *Management Science, 30*, 1051-1066.

Uhl-Bien, M., Graen, G. B., & Scandura, T. A. (2000). Implications of leader-member exchange (LMX) for strategic human resource management systems: Relationships as social capital for competitive advantage. In G. R. Ferris (Ed.), *Research in personnel and human resource management* (Vol. 18, pp. 187-185). Stamford, CT: JAI Press.

Ulrich, D. (1999). Integrating practice and theory: Towards a more unified view of HR. In P. Wright, L. Dyer, J. W. Boudreau, & G. T. Milkovich (Eds.), *Strategic human resources management in the twenty-first century*, [Suppl. 4], *Research in personnel and human resource management*. Stamford, CT: JAI Press.

United States Small Business Administration Office of Advocacy. (2003). *Characteristics of small business employers and owners.* Retrieved June 1, 2005, from www.sba.gov

Van Dyne, L., Cummings, L. L. & McLean Parks, J. M. (1995). Extra-role behaviors: In pursuit of construct and definitional clarity (A bridge over muddied waters). In L. L. Cummings & B. M. Staw (Eds.), *Research in organizational behavior* (Vol. 17, pp. 215-285). Greenwich, CT: JAI Press.

Vogus, T. J., & Welbourne, T. M. (2003). Structuring for high reliability: HR practices and mindful processes in reliability seeking organizations. *Journal of Organizational Behavior, 24*, 877-903.

Way, S. A. (2002). High performance work systems and intermediate indicators of firm performance within the US small business sector. *Journal of Management, 28*(6), 765-785.

Weinberg, N. (2000). Forget the garage. *Forbes, 165*(7), 54-56.

Wernerfelt, B. (1984). A resource-based view of the firm. *Strategic Management Journal, 5*(2), 171-180.

Willard, G. E., Krueger, D. A., & Feeser, H. R. (1992). In order to grow, must the founder go: A comparison of performance between founder and non-founder managed high-growth manufacturing firms. *Journal of Business Venturing, 7*, 181-194.

Wright, P. M., George, J. M., Farnsworth, R., & McMahan, G. M. (1993). Productivity and extra-role behavior: The effects of goals and incentives on spontaneous helping. *Journal of Applied Psychology, 78*(3), 374-381.

Wright, P. M., & McMahan, G. C., McWilliams, A. (1994). Human resources and sustained competitive advantage: A resource based perspective. *International Journal of Human Resource Management, 5*, 301-326.

Wright, P. M., Dunford, B. B., & Snell, S. A. (2001). Human resources and the resource based view of the firm. *Journal of Management, 27*, 701-721.

Wright, P. M., Smart, D., & McMahan, G. C. (1995). Matches between human resources and strategy among NCAA basketball teams. *Academy of Management Journal, 38*, 1052-1074.

Wright, P. M., & Boswell, W. R. (2002). Desegregating HRM: A review and synthesis of micro and macro human resource management research. *Journal of Management, 28*(3), 247-276.

Wright, P. M., & McMahan, G. C. (1992). Theoretical perspectives for strategic human resource management. *Journal of Management, 18*, 295-320.

Yli-Renko, H., Autio, E., & Sapienza, H. J. (2001). Social capital, knowledge acquisition, and knowledge exploitation in young technology based firms. *Strategic Management Journal, 22*, 587-613.

Zenger, T. R., & Lazzarini, S. G. (2004). Compensating for innovation: Do small firms offer high-powered incentives that lure talent and motivate effort? *Managerial and Decision Economics, 25*, 329-345.

CHAPTER 3

HUMAN CAPITAL MANAGEMENT PRACTICES AND PERFORMANCE IN SMALL AND MEDIUM SIZED ENTERPRISES

A Conceptual Framework

James C. Hayton

A conceptual framework for understanding the contribution of Human Capital Management (HCM) practices to HRM system characteristics and firm performance is presented. HCM practices serve as a feedback mechanism that has the potential to enhance HRM system fit and flexibility. It is suggested that sophisticated HCM practices are consistent with a strategic orientation toward HRM system control, in contrast to more simplistic practices which are more consistent with a financial control orientation. Since a strategic control orientation is supportive of an entrepreneurial orientation, it is anticipated that for SMEs operating in complex, dynamic and hostile technological and competitive environments, sophisticated HCM practices will contribute to innovation and ultimately financial performance.

Human Resource Strategies for the High Growth Entrepreneurial Firm, 51–68
Copyright © 2006 by Information Age Publishing
All rights of reproduction in any form reserved.

INTRODUCTION

It is now widely recognized that intangible assets, and in particular their human capital (e.g., Hitt, Bierman, Shimizu, & Kochhar, 2001), are an important source of sustained competitive advantage for firms operating in complex and dynamic competitive environments. In recent years there has been a rapid proliferation of studies seeking to explain the contributions that human resource management (HRM) makes to the achievement of organizational goals (e.g., Delery & Doty, 1996; Heneman & Tansky, 2002; Huselid, 1995). A significant contribution of this strategic perspective on HRM is the recognition of the importance of viewing HRM practices as a part of a coherent system with attributes, such as internal consistency and external fit, which are important determinants of organizational effectiveness.

While the importance of the HR system is widely acknowledged, a relatively recent addition to the HRM architecture has received very little research attention: human capital management (HCM). HCM refers to both human resource information management strategies and the use of human capital measurement techniques such as estimating human capital return on investment (e.g., Cascio, 1999; Becker, Huselid, & Ulrich, 2001; Fitz-Enz, 2001). HCM represents an important feedback mechanism for the HRM system (e.g., Kavanaugh, Gueutal, & Tannenbaum, 1990). In the broadest sense, as soon as a firm begins recording information on its employees, it is managing its human capital. However, HCM practices will tend to fall along a continuum from a simplistic cost focus, which examines historical data, to sophisticated, information technology-based methods, with an investment focused, which examine leading indicators that have been empirically linked to key measures of firm success (e.g., Becker et al., 2001; Rucci, Kirn, & Quinn, 1998).

The premise of this paper is that HCM represents an important strategy for firms seeking to leverage their human capital asset stocks. We define human capital in the traditional way: as the knowledge, skills, abilities and other characteristics of a firm's employees, at the level of the individual and the group. The latter acknowledge the salience of group characteristics such as diversity in education, age, and experience to organizational outcomes such as creativity (e.g., Bantel & Jackson, 1989).

In addition to ignoring recent developments in the practice of HRM, a second significant limitation within HRM research is that, with some exceptions (e.g., Chandler & McEvoy, 2000;), it has emphasized large, established firms. Scholars have noted that the field as a whole has tended to ignore a significant segment of the national economy: small and medium sized firms (e.g., Heneman, Tansky, & Camp, 2000). Yet, according to the U.S. Small Business Association, firms with fewer than 500 employees account for 99% of all employers and 39% of the gross national product (cited in Williamson, Cable, & Aldrich, 2002). While within smaller firms, HRM activities may be less formalized (Welbourne & Katz, 2002), they are not less significant to firm success (e.g., Welbourne & Cyr, 1999).

In this paper we address both of these limitations by examining the expected relationships between HCM practice and firm performance in small and medium sized enterprises. We will suggest that HCM represents a dynamic capability (Teece, Pisano, & Shuen, 1997). This means that the practice of HCM can contribute to an organization's ability to acquire and reconfigure resources. This further implies that HCM is a form of strategic resource according to the resource-based view (e.g., Barney, 1991). Such resources add value, yet are difficult to imitate, and embedded in complex ways within an organizations stock of tangible and intangible assets. Strategic resources, and HCM in particular, therefore is expected to contribute to firm performance and sustainable competitive advantage for SMEs. We focus the discussion on that segment of SMEs referred to as emerging or fast growth firms, which are frequently operating in the high technology sector of the economy. These firms face unique challenges stemming from the liability of newness (Stinchcomb, 1965) and the need to acquire and exploit resources in order to survive and prosper in dynamic, hypercompetitive environments.

HUMAN CAPITAL MANAGEMENT
THE MEASUREMENT PARADOX

The practice of measuring and valuing HRM practices and human capital assets has a long history, encompassing utility analysis (Boudreau, 1991, chap. 10; Brogden & Taylor, 1950), human resource accounting (e.g., Flamholtz, Searfoss, & Coff, 1988; Roslender, 1997), and more recently the strategic (return on investment) and balanced scorecard accounting techniques (Becker et al., 2001; see Cascio, 1999). Critics have noted the difficulty of placing a dollar value on the performance of individual employees (Scarpello & Theeke, 1989), and observed the perennial problem that what gets measured gets managed (Pfeffer, 1997). However, the increasing power of desktop computing coupled with powerful relational database software has made sophisticated human resource information systems (HRIS) readily available and cost effective for even small organizations. Typical criticisms such as those by Scarpello and Theeke (1989) and Pfeffer (1997) appear to ignore evidence that, when used as a part of a strategic decision making framework, HCM can contribute to HRM decision making effectiveness and support the strategic role of the HR function (e.g., Rucci et al., 1998).

HCM methods do vary in terms of their emphasis upon leading versus lagging indicators, and their emphasis upon human resource costs, versus human resource investments (e.g., Cascio, 1999). We propose that the distinction between historical, cost focused HCM techniques such as human resource accounting and future oriented, investment focused HCM techniques such as the balanced scorecard approach, parallels that between financial and strategic controls (Hitt, Hoskisson, Johnson, & Moesel, 1996). The focus of financial controls is upon goals, targets and performance quotas. For managers, success or failure is dependent upon how these predetermined goals are achieved. As a result, financial controls tend to promote a short-term orientation (Zahra, 1996) as well as greater rigidity and risk aversion in decision-making. For fast-growth companies facing uncertain and dynamic environments, this is expected to inhibit entrepreneurship and subsequent market and financial performance. In this paper, I use the terms entrepreneurship and entrepreneurial performance interchangeably. Entrepreneurial performance refers to the extent to which a firm is continually able to generate new products, identify and exploit new market opportunities, form partnerships and external ventures, and remake itself or adapt its strategies in the face of environmental or competitive pressure.

In contrast, strategic controls involve setting broader, open-ended goals, with a greater appreciation of the tasks, the risks involved, and the potential tradeoffs among the choices managers might make. Contrast, for example, the "strategic" goal of promoting employee satisfaction with the intent of enhancing the customer experience and ultimately firm performance, with the "financial" goal of minimizing total labor costs. Broad, flexible goals are particularly important for firms facing uncertain and dynamic market or technological environments, as the entrepreneurial orientation needed to succeed demands greater responsiveness (Zahra, 1996). Empirical evidence supports the proposition that an emphasis upon strategic controls is positively associated with higher levels of entrepreneurship (Barringer & Bluedorn, 1999; Zahra, 1996). Since entrepreneurship is a determinant of long run financial and market success for firms in dynamic and hostile environments (Zahra 1993; Zahra & Covin, 1995), strategic controls are also supportive of firm performance.

In this paper, we assume that HCM can take a variety of forms from relatively simplistic costing measures to more sophisticated ROI perspectives. While simplistic methods tend to be historical and emphasize HRM costs, sophisticated methods are future oriented, strategic in nature and emphasize returns on investments. Two examples of simplistic measures are cost-per-hire and unit-labor costs. Examples of more sophisticated

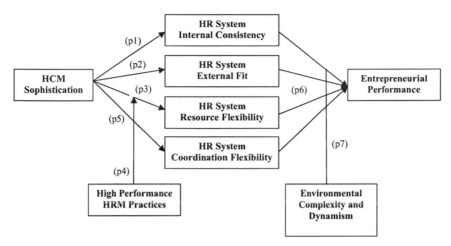

Figure 3.1.   Human capital management, system fit & flexibility, and firm performance in small and medium sized enterprises.

HCM metrics include return on investment indicators for HRM practices, and human capital value added. Therefore, we invoke the resource-based view of the firm to propose that the degree of sophistication of HCM practice is of significance for the performance of SMEs. The processes by which this is expected to occur are summarized in Figure 3.1, and described in the following sections.

THE RESOURCE-BASED VIEW: HRM AND FIRM PERFORMANCE

According to the RBV, sustained competitive advantage is derived from the control of scarce, valuable, inimitable and nontradable assets (Barney, 1991; Penrose, 1959; Peteraf, 1993; Wernerfelt, 1984). The RBV represents a configurational perspective on the relationship between HRM and firm performance (Heneman & Tansky, 2002) in that a firm's HRM practices must be both internally consistent and fit "externally" with the business strategy (Huselid, 1995; Wright & Snell, 1998). An HRM strategy that supports a firm's business strategy is very difficult to imitate due to a high degree of asset interdependency, causal ambiguity and substantial diseconomies resulting from time compression (Dierickz & Cool, 1989).

Furthermore, firms develop capabilities that facilitate the acquisition and transformation of resources (Teece et al., 1997). These dynamic capabilities also represent strategic "resources" that support sustained competitive advantage. The ability to identify, implement and sustain well fitting

HR practices adds value by aligning behaviors to organizational goals. This ability has been identified as scarce among practicing HR professionals (Huselid, Jackson, & Schuler, 1997). It is not readily imitated or traded as the specific linkages tend to be specific to an organization's unique context and history. Therefore, the ability to achieve fit is a dynamic capability (Teece et al., 1997) that supports sustainable competitive advantage (Wright & Snell, 1998).

HCM practices are feedback and control mechanisms that promote internal consistency and external fit in HRM systems. Internal consistency is facilitated by the processes of evaluating HR practices and their impact upon organizational goals. The process of evaluation and control makes explicit the intended effects of specific HRM practices, and therefore makes mismatches more apparent and observable. The process of achieving external congruence with business strategy is also facilitated by HCM, particularly when HCM is directed at the strategic decision making process (i.e., is "sophisticated"). Although it has typically been assumed that HR serves to implement a given business strategy (e.g., Jackson, Schuler, & Rivero, 1989), the firm's strategic choices should be driven by the resources and capabilities available to it (Capelli & Singh, 1992; Wright & Snell, 1998). Therefore, sophisticated HCM practices contribute to a "bottom up" approach to strategic decision making and thereby can be expected to achieve a closer fit between HRM and environmental demands.

HCM alters HR's relationship with the strategic management process in at least two ways. First, it offers a realtime check on effectiveness of HRM practices with respect to strategic goals (e.g., Rucci et al., 1998). Second, HCM reflects an active concern with linking HRM to the planning and decision making aspects of business strategy. This suggests the following propositions:

Proposition 1:   HCM sophistication is positively related to internal consistency of HRM practices.

Proposition 2:   HCM sophistication is positively related to external fit between HRM practices and business strategy.

HCM & HR SYSTEM FLEXIBILITY

Wright and Snell (1998) note three major assumptions with the traditional model of strategic HRM. First, it is assumed that HR decision makers are able to identify all behaviors needed to support a given strategy. This assumption fails when we examine fast growth firms and firms facing dynamic environments. The role behaviors required to compete in dynamic environments cannot be easily specified at the outset and are more likely to be revealed through a firm's interactions with its environment over time (e.g., Kanter, 1983). Second, it is assumed that the necessary HRM practices can be identified and controlled. However, if specific behaviors cannot be identified in advance, then the necessary practices are unlikely to be readily identifiable in dynamic environments. Only through monitoring, feedback, and adaptation will fit be achieved, and when the environment is changing, periods of system equilibrium are likely to be temporary. Third, the typical strategic HRM model has assumed a stable environment so that decision makers are able to carefully match practice to environmental demands. However, for new, fast growth, and entrepreneurial firms, environments are dynamic and hostile. Thus, while HR system fit is regarded as an important characteristic for all organizations, for entrepreneurial organizations, and new and emerging firms, flexibility is a second important system characteristic.

System flexibility allows adaptation over time as the environmental demands change, as new employee behaviors and their supporting HRM practices emerge in response to environmental triggers. The concept of strategic flexibility has been invoked in the context of new product development (e.g., Hitt, Keats, & DeMarie, 1998; Sanchez, 1995). Strategic flexibility involves the capability to "sustain elevated rates of broadly targeted product creation" (Sanchez, 1995, p. 135) and is consistent with the concept of sustained regeneration, the most frequently observed aspect of an entrepreneurial strategy (Covin & Miles, 1999). Thus strategic flexibility will be associated with higher levels of entrepreneurial performance—the ability to enter new markets and create technologies that are exploited for entrepreneurial profit.

Empirical studies have found that HR flexibility is positively associated with R&D concentration and coordination and consequently a firm's strategic position (Zhou & Özsomer, 1999). However, HR flexibility goes beyond functional flexibility (e.g., Friedrich, Kabst, Weber, & Rodehuth, 1998). Functional flexibility emphasizes the range of jobs that individual employees are capable of performing (e.g., Cordery, 1989). HR system flexibility refers to the range of contexts to which HR practices and architecture can be usefully applied and the speed at which they can be changed (Wright & Snell, 1998).

Flexibility within an HR system takes two forms: resource flexibility and coordination flexibility (Sanchez, 1995). Resource flexibility for human capital refers to the repertoire available to the organization—that is, the breadth of capabilities embedded in its human capital. Therefore, this resource flexibility encompasses functional flexibility (Friedrich et al., 1998). However, resource flexibility is also determined by the nature of

HR practices: that is, can specific practices such as job analysis and performance appraisal be applied even when strategic directions change, or do new practices have to be implemented?

Resource flexibility is greater when the range of uses to which it may be put is larger; when the costs of switching a resource from one use to another are lower; and when the time required for switching resources from one use to another is lower (Sanchez, 1995). HCM facilitates the identification of uses for which human capital is qualified, and increases the speed of the redeployment planning and implementation processes (e.g., Needy et al., 2002). This suggests the following proposition:

Proposition 3:   HCM enhances the resource flexibility of the HR system by reducing resource switching costs and the time required for switching resources to new applications.

Resource flexibility should be considered in the context of the flexibility of all other resources. That is, strategic flexibility is a function of the combined flexibility of a firm's interdependent resources (Sanchez, 1995). Therefore, in the presence of other flexible resources, the use of HCM is expected to enhance resource flexibility. Certain HR practices may either enhance or inhibit flexibility of a firm's human resources. For example, worker-based job analysis, and broad job descriptions with overlapping responsibilities and broadly defined responsibilities will enhance human resource flexibility. In contrast, task-based job analysis, and narrow, highly specific job descriptions will inhibit flexibility (e.g., Kanter, 1983). This suggests that the use of HCM in combination with HRM practices that promote human capital flexibility, will interact in positively influencing strategic flexibility and therefore entrepreneurial performance in SMEs. One characterization of HRM systems that are supportive of flexibility is the high performance work system (HPWS)(e.g., Huselid, 1995). The HPWS is a broad HR architecture which combines careful staffing activities with investments in employee skills and rewards based upon employee contributions. Within this broad architecture, employers may vary specific practices according to their business needs. Thus, the HPWS is an inherently flexible set of HRM practices. This leads to the following proposition:

Proposition 4:   HCM will interact positively with the presence of 'High Performance' HRM practices to positively influence resource flexibility in entrepreneurial small businesses.

The second aspect of flexibility is coordination flexibility (Sanchez, 1995). Coordination flexibility is associated with processes of (re)defining strategic goals, (re)configuring the chains of resources for achieving these goals, and (re)deploying resources in support of these goals (Sanchez, 1995). Typically, as organizations grow, they become increasingly rigid and bureaucratized. HRM may contribute to this process by establishing practices that become institutionalized and protected through the exercise of power and political processes. As the organization grows, the feedback process slows, and coordination flexibility consequently decreases. Much of modern management research is concerned with speeding information flows, restoring flexibility and revitalizing entrepreneurship within overly bureaucratic established organizations.

Coordination flexibility is a function of the speed at which a firm is able to reconfigure its resources to support new goals. The greater the sophistication of a firm's HCM strategy, the faster the flow of information. We propose that sophisticated HCM promotes HR system flexibility through three mechanisms: the creation of organizational slack; the promotion of decentralization, goal clarity and commitment to redefined goals; and by enhancing modularity in the HR system.

First, HCM contributes to strategic flexibility by contributing to organizational slack (Hitt et al., 1998). One way in which it achieves this, is by relieving the HR function of more traditional transactional activities (Ulrich, 1997), and facilitating a focus on strategic and change oriented activities. To the extent that it reflects a conscious effort to close the feedback loop with respect to HRM effectiveness, HCM also contributes to organizational learning, and therefore organizational, market or technological innovation (Garvin, 1993). Slack becomes more important when the rate of change—organization, technological, or market—is high (Lawson, 2001). Therefore, we believe that the slack generating effects of sophisticated HCM will contribute to the strategic flexibility of the firm.

Second, HCM contributes to flexibility through its capacity for clearly communicating goals and progress toward these goals. In its most sophisticated form, HCM promotes involvement of managers across functional boundaries in order to identify key strategic drivers (Becker et al., 2001; Rucci et al., 1998). When HCM is conducted in this inclusive "federalist" fashion (Davenport, Eccles, & Prusak, 1992), the various parties affected by a change are included in the change process. Involving stakeholders in the design process enhances perceptions of procedural justice and therefore builds buy-in and commitment (e.g., Kim & Mauborgne, 1997). Thus, through promoting attitudinal commitment, HCM contributes to overall system flexibility.

Furthermore, as HCM increases decentralization of information access, it will increase the flow of HRM information, speed decision-making and therefore enhance flexibility. Therefore, HCM will enhance coordination flexibility and support rapid feedback on the effectiveness of HR practices in relation to goals. Sanchez (1995) provides evidence that information technologies have the potential for enhancing coordination flexibility in the product creation process. As an information technology-based practice, HCM contributes to flexibility by facilitating the identification of appropriate strategies, and by providing much needed information concerning available human resources. Further, HCM increases the speed, accuracy and availability of relevant information, and thus accelerates the reconfiguration and redeployment of resources in pursuit of these goals.

Third, HCM contributes to resource flexibility by promoting a modular approach to the design and monitoring of HR practices (Sanchez & Mahoney, 1996). Modularity is a design strategy that intentionally creates independence among the components of a system. In product design these are components of the larger product. In organizational design these are departments or divisions. In the context of the HR system, the components are the individual practices such as performance appraisal and compensation.

Traditional design approaches involve high levels of coordination as each component is highly interdependent—outputs from one component become inputs for another. This requires tight coupling and high rates of information flow. Thus, complex, interdependent, tightly coupled systems place greater information processing demands upon decision makers. A modular system is one in which components are loosely coupled, facilitating design flexibility within those components. This independence is achieved by standardizing the interfaces between components. These interfaces do not change once specified. However, within each component there is complete freedom and independence in the design of the component providing it conforms to the interface specifications. Coordination is achieved purely through the component interface standards.

HCM provides a standardization of the interfaces among HR components. Within each component, the design is flexible. The interfaces in this case are the employee human capital specifications and the data that represents these employee specifications. An example of this is the use of competency modeling when using a balanced scorecard strategy (e.g., Becker et al., 2001; Kaplan & Norton, 1996). Using competencies as an organizing principle, different HRM practices can emphasize the acquisition or development of the needed competencies with a reduced need to refer back to the specific design of other practices or policies. Modularity enables variations in components to be made without necessitating redesign of an entire product or system. In the same sense, when designed according to modular principles, the HR system will be more flexible as each component may be redesigned without recourse to the entire system.

Flexibility also stems from the increased speed with which the HR system can respond to changing demands from the larger organizational system and the environment. Modularity also enhances the ability of the HR system to respond to unique situational demands, such as facilities located within distinct geographic labor markets, by offering alternative components that are each individually consistent with the system interface requirements. Thus customization of HRM practices to individuals and contexts, while maintaining strategic fit, becomes a practical and achievable goal. A specific example is the cafeteria benefits plan. Such a plan effectively allows employees to select from a range of components. The range offered each fits the overarching HR system goals, while responding to the demands of individual employees.

In a modular system, coordination becomes embedded in the specification of component outputs (Sanchez & Mahoney, 1996). In HRM this standardization is achieved through HCM, which specifies the information structure of the HR system. This embedded coordination speeds decision making and changes in system components by reducing the information flows across "components" of the system. As with organizational design, standardization reduces organizational complexity.

HCM in its highest form implies a sort of advanced *architectural knowledge* (Sanchez & Mahoney, 1996) of the HR system as a whole. According to this perspective, the firm has developed hypotheses concerning the HR factors driving strategic capabilities (e.g., Becker et al., 2001). This drives specification of information requirements and standardization of these interfaces. Organizational learning then occurs within each component, in parallel rather than sequentially, thus speeding the development process and enhancing flexibility.

A modular perspective may also increase flexibility at the level of the HR architecture. Having decoupled the components of the system from the HR architecture, it becomes easier to focus upon the architecture's purpose without consideration of individual component issues. Thus the system moves away from incremental changes driven by the short-term needs of specific component issues such as short-run labor market fluctuations and training needs, and toward consideration of the larger goals of the system as a whole. This reduces the problem of organizational myopia that is inherent in the learning process (March, 1991). This discussion suggests the following proposition:

Proposition 5: HCM enhances coordination flexibility of the HRM system through creation of slack resources, promoting decentralization, goal clarity and goal commitment, and by promoting modularity and embedded coordination.

In summary, achieving and maintaining fit between HR practices and firm strategic and operational goals is enhanced when information infrastructures are used to identify and monitor the achievement of these goals. Therefore we expect that sophistication with respect to HCM will be positively associated with resource flexibility when firms are facing high rates of change. Furthermore, to the extent that HCM facilitates decentralization and autonomy with respect to HR decision making (e.g., helping managers quickly access data on training needs and employee performance) this will increase responsiveness to new environmental demands, and therefore enhance the speed and accuracy of shifts in resource use.

FIT, FLEXIBILITY & FIRM PERFORMANCE

It has been argued that the internal consistency of a firm's HRM practices and external congruence with its business strategy are positively associated with firm performance. While the evidence is not incontrovertible (Wright, Gardner, Moynihan, Park, Gerhart, & Delery 2001), there is some empirical support for this perspective. Firm performance is a multidimensional construct frequently indicated by either market performance (sales) or financial performance (e.g., return on assets). A third measure of performance of relevance to entrepreneurial small businesses is their entrepreneurial or innovative performance. There is evidence that in the short-run (1-2 years) there is a weak or even negative association between entrepreneurship and firm financial performance (e.g., Zahra & Covin, 1995). However, over time this relationship becomes positive and significant. Therefore, we suggest the following proposition:

> **Proposition 6:**   HCM practices will be positively associated with firm entrepreneurial performance in the short run, and with market and financial performance in the long run.

As firms face increasing rates of change (internal or environmental) they also face ever increasing information processing demands. Sophisticated HCM enhances the ability of decision makers to consider multiple alternative strategic scenarios that are necessary when operating in dynamic environments (Eisenhardt, 1990). However, this implies that the impact of HCM will be moderated by the type of environment that an organization is operating in. Those firms interacting with information rich (complex), dynamic environments will face much greater demands for flexibility. Within this group of firms, those that develop capabilities for achieving and maintaining HRM system fit will obtain a source of sustainable competitive advantage. In contrast, while fit remains significant for firms in stable environments, flexibility is less of a challenge. This leads to the final proposition:

Proposition 7: The relationship between HCM and firm performance will be stronger for firms operating in dynamic environments than for firms operating in stable environments.

SUMMARY AND IMPLICATIONS FOR RESEARCH

In this paper, we have proposed a model of the relationships among HCM practices, HRM fit and flexibility and the entrepreneurial performance of small and medium sized firms. This contributes to a growing literature within the field that attends to the specific needs of SMEs, particularly those facing dynamic competitive environments. While the importance of HRM measurement and control has been repeatedly emphasized (e.g., Cascio, 1999), to our knowledge no theoretical explanation of its significance for firm performance has been offered.

We have suggested a theoretical explanation of the impact of HCM on firm performance by invoking the RBV. The model described here suggests that HCM is expected to support sustainable competitive advantage and firm performance by building a firm's dynamic capabilities with respect to HRM system fit and flexibility. The importance of the fit or consistency among HRM practices is well understood, as this promotes desired employee behaviors. External fit or strategic congruence has received mixed support, perhaps due to methodological difficulties associated with identifying fit itself as well as accurately measuring HRM practices (Wright et al., 2001). This model suggests that HCM contributes to the creation and maintenance of fit by providing timely and accurate feedback on the effectiveness of HRM practices. Furthermore, it is argued fit is not static but must be maintained over time, particularly for evolving organizations and those facing dynamic environments. Therefore HR system flexibility, the ability to redeploy and reconfigure human capital in response to changing environmental demands, becomes equally important for obtaining sustainable competitive advantage.

HCM is expected to contribute to these capabilities through multiple mechanisms. First by creating slack within the HRM function that can be applied to (re)deploying organizational resources in order to maintain fit in the face of a changing environment. Second, through its tendency to distribute information and responsibility for managing that information, HCM is expected to increase goal clarity and goal commitment as well as enhance responsiveness to new environmental conditions. Third, by requiring standardization of information gathering, we have argued that HCM increases the modularity of the HRM system's design, thereby increasing the coordination flexibility of the system.

We have also identified two important moderators or boundary conditions for these relationships. First, we have suggested that the impact of HCM upon flexibility will be positively enhanced when the rest of the HR system is also flexible. This follows Sanchez (1995) who argues that strategic flexibility is a function of the flexibility of all system components combined. We have suggested that high performance work systems are one example of a flexible HR architecture.

The second important moderator focuses on the association between HCM and firm performance. We have suggested that the significance of HCM for performance increases as the dynamism faced by firms increases. Therefore, we would expect to observe the strongest relationship with performance for fast growth or entrepreneurial firms operating in high technology environments.

This represents a first step in an attempt to understand the importance of HCM for the performance of firms. More empirical research is needed in the area of HCM as well as in the context of SMEs. There is clear evidence from the strategic management literature that managerial control practices are related to firm performance outcomes such as entrepreneurship. HCM represents a collection of control strategies applied specifically to the HRM function. While it is recognized that the use of "business intelligence" systems is increasing, and this practice is spreading rapidly from very large, to much smaller firms, very little is known about the performance impact of such practices. This is of great interest since investment decisions for complex technologies may be based more upon the fear of being left behind by competitors than by clear business need.

AUTHOR NOTE

Correspondence should be directed to the author at: Bocconi University—IOSI, Viale Isonzo 23, 20135 Milan, Italy, Phone: 39 02 5836 2628, Fax: 39 02 5826 2634, Email: jhayton@unibocconi.it

ACKNOWLEDGMENT

The author would like to thank the participants at the conference "Managing people in Small and Entrepreneurial companies: What are the Human Resource issues?" hosted by the Ohio State University, as well as the editors, and the anonymous reviewer for their insights and comments on earlier versions of this manuscript.

REFERENCES

Barney, J. (1991). Firm resources and sustained competitive advantage. *Journal of Management, 17*(1), 99-120.

Barringer, B. R, & Bluedorn, A. C. (1999). The relationship between corporate entrepreneurship and strategic management. *Strategic Management Journal, 20*(5), 421-444.

Bantel, K. A., & Jackson, S. E. (1989). Top management and innovations in banking: Does the composition of the top team make a difference? *Strategic Management Journal, 10,* 107-125.

Becker, B. E., Huselid, M. A., & Ulrich, D. (2001). *The HR scorecard: Linking people, strategy, and performance.* Boston: Harvard Business School Press.

Boudreau, J. W. (1991). Utility analysis for decisions in human resource management. In M. Dunnette & L. Hough (Eds.), *Handbook of industrial and organizational psychology* (2nd ed., Vol. 2., pp. 621-745).

Brogden, H. E., & Taylor, E. K. (1950). The dollar criterion: Applying the cost accounting concept to criterion selection. *Personnel Psychology 3,* 133-154.

Capelli, P., & Singh, H. (1992). Integrating human resource management. In P. Sherer, D. Lewin, & O. Mitchell (Eds.). *Research frontiers in industrial relations and human resource management* (pp. 165-192). Madison, WI: IRRA.

Cascio, W. F. (1999). *Costing human resources: The financial impact of behavior in organizations* (4th ed.). Cincinnati, OH: Southwestern.

Chandler, G. N., & McEvoy, G. M. (2000). Human resource management, TQM and firm performance in small and medium-size enterprises. *Entrepreneurship Theory and Practice, 25*(1), 43-57

Cordery, J. (1989). Multi-skilling: A discussion of proposed benefits of new approaches to labor flexibility within enterprises. *Personnel Review, 18*(3), 13-22.

Covin, J. G., & Miles, M. P. (1999). Corporate entrepreneurship and the pursuit of competitive advantage. *Entrepreneurship Theory and Practice, 23*(3), 47-63.

Davenport, T. H., Eccles, R. G., & Prusak, L. (1992, Fall). Information politics. *Sloan Management Review,* 53-65.

Delery, J. E., & Doty, D. H. (1996). Modes of theorizing in strategic human resource management: Test of universalistic, contingency and configurational performance patterns. *Academy of Management Journal, 39,* 802-825.

Dierickx, I. & Cool, K. (1989). Asset stock accumulation and sustainability of competitive advantage. *Management Science, 17,* 121-154.

Eisenhardt, K. M. (1990, Spring). Speed and strategic choice: How managers accelerate decision making. *California Management Review,* 39-50.

Flamholtz, E. G., Searfoss, D. G., & Coff, R. (1988). Developing human resource accounting as a decision support system. *Accounting Horizons 2,* 1-9.

Friedrich, A., Kabst, R., Weber, W., & Rodehuth, M. (1998). Functional flexibility: Merely reacting or acting strategically? *Employee Relations, 20*(5), 504.

Garvin, D. A. (1993, July-August). Building a learning organization. *Harvard Business Review,* 78-91.

Heneman, R. L., & Tansky, J. W. (2002). Human resource management models for entrepreneurial opportunity: Existing knowledge and new directions. In J. Katz & T. M. Welbourne (Eds.) *Managing people in entrepreneurial organizations: Learning from the merger of entrepreneurship and human resource management.* New York: JAI Press.

Heneman, R. L., Tansky, J. W., & Camp, S. M. (2000). Human resource management practices in small and medium size enterprises: Unanswered questions and future research perspectives. *Entrepreneurship Theory & Practice, 25*(1), 11-26.

Hitt, M. A., Bierman, L., Shimizu, K., & Kochhar, R. (2001). Direct and moderating effects of human capital on strategy and performance in professional service firms: A resource-based perspective. *Academy of Management Journal, 44*(1), 13-28.

Hitt, M. A., Hoskisson, R. E., Johnson, R. A., & Moesel, D. D. (1996). The market for corporate control and firm innovation. *Academy of Management Journal, 39*(5), 1084-1119.

Hitt, M. A., Keats, B. W., & DeMarie, S. M. (1998). Navigating in the new competitive landscape: Building strategic flexibility and competitive advantage in the 21st century. *Academy of Management Executive, 12*(4), 22-42.

Huselid, M. (1995). The impact of human resource management practices on turnover, productivity, and corporate financial performance. *Academy of Management Journal, 38,* 635-672.

Huselid, M. A., Jackson, S. E., & Schuler, R. S. (1997). Technical and strategic human resource management effectiveness as determinants of firm performance. *Academy of Management Journal, 40,*171-188.

Jackson, S. E., Schuler R. S., & Rivero C. J. (1989). Organizational characteristics as predictors of personnel practices. *Personnel Psychology, 42*(4), 727-786.

Kanter, R. M. (1983). *The change masters: Innovations for productivity in the American corporation.* New York: Simon & Schuster.

Kanter, R. M. (1983). The change masters: Innovation and entrepreneurship in the american corporation. New York: Simon & Schuster.

Kaplan, R. S., & Norton, D. P. (1996). *The balanced scorecard: Translating strategy into action.* Boston: Harvard Business School Press.

Kavanaugh, M. J., Gueutal, H. G., & Tannenbaum, S. I. (1990). *Human resource information systems: Development and application.* Boston: PWS-Kent.

Kim, W. C., & Mauborgne, R. (1997, July–August). Fair process: Managing in the knowledge economy. *Harvard Business Review,* 65-75.

Lawson, M. B. (2001). In praise of slack: Time is of the essence. *Academy of Management Executive, 15*(3), 125-135.

March, J. (1991). Exploration and exploitation in organizational learning. *Organization Science, 2*(1), 71-87.

Needy, K. L., Norman, B. A., Bidanda, B., Ariyawongrat, P., Tharmmaphorphilas, W., & Warner, R. C. (2002). Assessing human capital: A lean manufacturing example. *Engineering Management Journal, 14*(3), 35-39.

Penrose, E. (1959). *The theory of the growth of the firm.* New York: Oxford University Press.

Peteraf, M. (1993), The cornerstones of competitive advantage: A resource-based view. *Strategic Management Journal, 14*, 179-192.

Pfeffer, J. (1997). Pitfalls on the road to measurement: The dangerous liaison of human resources with the ideas of accounting and finance. *Human Resource Management, 36*(3), 357-365.

Roslender, R. (1997). Accounting for the worth of employees: Is the discipline finally ready to respond to the challenge? *Journal of Human Resource Costing and Accounting, 2*(1), 9-26.

Rucci, A. J., Kirn, S. P., & Quinn, R. T. (1998). The employee-customer profit chain at Sears. *Harvard Business Review, 76*, 82-97.

Sanchez, R. (1995). Strategic flexibility in product competition. *Strategic Management Journal, 16*, 135-159.

Sanchez, R., & Mahoney, J. T. (1996). Modularity, flexibility, and knowledge management in product and organization design. *Strategic Management Journal, 17* [Winter Special Issue], 63-76.

Scarpello, V., & Theeke, H. A. (1989). Human resource accounting: A measured critique. *Journal of Accounting Literature 8*, 265-80.

Stinchcomb, A. (1965). Social structure and organizations. In J. G. March (Ed.), *Handbook of organizations* (pp. 142-193). Chicago: Rand McNally.

Teece, D. J., Pisano, G., & Shuen, A. (1997). Dynamic capabilities and strategic management. *Strategic Management Journal, 18*(7), 509.

Ulrich, D. (1997). *Human resource champions: The next agenda for adding value and delivering results.* Boston, MA: Harvard Business School.

Welbourne, T. M., & Cyr, L. A. (1999). The human resource executive effect in initial public offering firms. *Academy of Management Journal, 42*(6), 616-629.

Welbourne, T. M., & Katz, J. (2002). Human resource management in entrepreneurial settings: Towards a relational approach. In J. Katz & T. M. Welbourne (Eds.), *Managing people in entrepreneurial organizations: Learning from the merger of entrepreneurship and human resource management.* New York: JAI Press.

Wernerfelt, B. (1984). A resource based view of the firm. *Strategic Management Journal, 5*(2), 171-180.

Williamson, I. O., Cable, D. M., & Aldrich, H. E. (2002). Smaller but not necessarily weaker: How small businesses can overcome barriers to recruitment. In J. Katz & T. M. Welbourne (Eds.), *Managing people in entrepreneurial organizations: Learning from the merger of entrepreneurship and human resource management.* New York: JAI Press.

Wright, P. M., & Snell, S. A. (1998). Toward a unifying framework for exploring fit and flexibility in strategic human resource management. *Academy of Management Review, 23*(4), 756-772.

Wright, P., Gardner, T., Moynihan, L., Park, H., Gerhart, B., & Delery, J. (2001). Measurement error in research on human resources and firm performance:

Additional data and suggestions for future research. *Personnel Psychology, 54,* 875-902.

Zahra, S. A. (1993). Environment, corporate entrepreneurship, and financial performance: A taxonomic approach. *Journal of Business Venturing, 8*(4), 319-340.

Zahra, S. A. (1996). Governance, ownership, and corporate entrepreneurship: The moderating impact of industry technological opportunities. *Academy of Management Journal, 39*(6), 1713-1735.

Zahra, S. A., & Covin, J. G. (1995). Contextual influences on the corporate entrepreneurship-performance relationship: A longitudinal analysis. *Journal of Business Venturing, 10*(1), 43-58.

Zhou, S., & Özsomer, A. (1999). Global product R&D and the firm's strategic position. *Journal of International Marketing, 7*(1), 57-76.

CHAPTER 4

TO HIRE OR NOT TO HIRE? IMPLICATIONS OF ALTERNATIVE STAFFING MODELS FOR EMERGING ORGANIZATIONS

Melissa S. Cardon and Paul Tolchinsky

In discussing staffing issues in entrepreneurship, we often focus on recruiting *permanent* employees, although several scholars have acknowledged that perhaps the staffing needs of small and medium enterprises (SMEs) could also be served by alternative means, such as through professional employer organizations or contingent labor. In this paper, we focus on three specific staffing models in SMEs: hiring workers directly, contracting contingent workers directly or through labor brokers such as temporary agencies, and outsourcing staffing entirely to a professional employer organization (PEO). We argue that the choice of staffing model should be driven by five key organizational considerations, including anticipated speed of growth, mental model of the firm, organizational flexibility, time spent on HR issues, and control over internal firm dynamics, and that each staffing model implies tradeoffs among these factors. While SME managers may incorporate speed of growth and mental models in their staffing decisions, many do not con-

Human Resource Strategies for the High Growth Entrepreneurial Firm, 69–98
Copyright © 2006 by Information Age Publishing
All rights of reproduction in any form reserved.

sider how their staffing approach impacts their time allocation, flexibility, or control over employee issues. Implications for practitioners and managers are discussed.

INTRODUCTION

Human resources are critical for new organizations in ways often unappreciated by researchers who study only established organizations. Founders have trouble establishing a fixed division of labor in young organizations because they are still learning the routines and competencies they need. (Katz, Aldrich, Welbourne, & Williams, 2000)

Founders of small and medium enterprises (SMEs) face many challenges concerning management of their human assets, including recruiting, training, compensating, and retaining those with knowledge and skills critical to the organization's success. One of the most important human issues in business concerns recruitment of essential labor, skills, or prior experience into the firm (Terpstra & Olson, 1993). However, staffing is often problematic for SMEs because small firms lack resources to spend on large scale recruiting efforts, and also often lack legitimacy to attract highly qualified employees (Williamson, Cable, & Aldrich, 2002).

While often the assumption is that new firms focus on recruiting permanent employees, several scholars have acknowledged that perhaps the staffing needs of SMEs could also be served by alternative means, such as utilizing professional employer organizations (e.g., Klaas, McClendon, & Gainey, 2000) or contingent labor (Cardon, 2003). Professional employer organizations (PEOs) are co-employers of those working at SME facilities, providing reduced cost HR programs and services, such as payroll, benefits, and regulatory compliance (Klaas et al., 2000). Contingent labor includes employment of consultants, independent contractors, temporary workers (such as through a temporary agency), or even interns or other seasonal help (Bureau of Labor Statistics, 2004), and implies a more limited fixed labor expense, since contingent worker engagement is variable based upon changing firm needs (Foote & Folta, 2002). While these scholars have argued that SMEs may want to employ a particular staffing model (either PEOs or contingent work), integration of models or consideration of the tradeoffs between these staffing approaches has not yet emerged. Understanding when each model may be an appropriate choice for an SME remains elusive, as does a clear understanding of the related downstream human and organizational implications of the model chosen.

In this paper, we focus on five key factors that should be considered in the choice of SME staffing model, including (1) anticipated speed of growth, (2) mental model for the firm, (3) organizational flexibility, (4) time spent on HR issues, and (5) control over internal firm dynamics. While SME managers do sometimes incorporate speed of growth and mental models in their staffing decisions, many do not consider other HR and employee relations issues that fall within the last three categories of organizational flexibility, time spent on HR issues, and control over internal dynamics of the organization. We suggest that they should, and discuss these issues more specifically below.

We proceed with an overview of key staffing challenges for emerging ventures. We then discuss several alternative models that have been suggested in the literature to help SMEs meet these challenges. Finally we explore factors that may influence the choice of staffing approach, and the tradeoffs that must be made between them. These comparisons have important implications for not only scholarly work concerning HR issues in SMEs, but also for how SME managers approach their HR decisions, specifically the staffing challenges they face.

THE STAFFING CHALLENGE OF EMERGING VENTURES

In many classifications of organizational problems, unavailability of necessary labor, skills, or prior experience resources are left out (Terpstra Olson, 1993). Yet the limitation of managerial capability, especially as it relates to human resources, is more significant than before realized (Thakur, 1999). This is especially critical in small or new organizations, where resources are constrained and formal systems have not yet been developed (Aldrich & Fiol, 1994). Some scholars argue that effective management of human resources is one of the most crucial problems faced by small firms (Deshpande & Golhar, 1994; Hornsby & Kuratko, 1990). In a study of CEOs and founders of SMEs conducted in 1997 and 1998, Heneman, Tansky, and Camp (2000) discovered that staffing, compensation, and reward issues were seen as the most relevant to the future success of their businesses. More specifically, entrepreneurs find the most important factors to their business's success to be (1) developing high-potential employees that can perform multiple roles under various stages of growth, and (2) matching of people to the organization's culture (Heneman et al., 2000).

Despite the criticality of staffing for SMEs, effectiveness in this area is often quite limited. Small firms may have more difficulty in recruiting employees (Williamson et al., 2002), often lack formal HR policies or systems (Markman & Baron, 2002), and face other unique HR challenges stemming largely from their small size (Greening, Barringer, & Macy, 1996). More specifically, Williamson and colleagues (2000, 2002) argue that small firms lack both the resources and the legitimacy to recruit the skills they need. Unlike larger, well-known firms, small business cannot rely on their name, reputation, or market share to attract new applicants or employees (Aldrich & Von Glinow, 1991; Aldrich, 1999). When job-seekers lack knowledge of a firm or its practices or members, SMEs find it harder to establish their legitimacy as a prospective employer (Williamson, 2000).

In addition, founders and managers of SMEs often rely on social networks to attract workers, particularly when the ventures are new (Baker & Aldrich, 1994), which may limit the growth potential or access to requisite skills for the venture (Arthur, 1995). In order for the SME to utilize more legitimate or accepted recruitment or selection practices, such as college campus recruiting or using moster.com or similar web sites, SME managers would have to be able to articulate the job, skills and capabilities needed in a much deeper way than they would when recruiting informally through social networks. This articulation may restrict the SME, as often they need workers who are flexible in their job assignments and capabilities (May, 1997). Moreover, business leaders are often uncomfortable in assessing the qualities, attributes and ultimately the fit of individual applicants into positions. Further, use of these large-scale recruiting strategies requires investment of resources to select the right individuals. Companies like JetBlue, People Express and Southwest Airlines have spent significant amounts of money selecting the right people to ensure the vision and culture of the organization are adhered to. Each has gone out of the mainstream to identify nontraditional candidates, often interviewing 200-300 potential employees to find the 1 or 2 that meet their requirements (Whitesome & Schlesinger, 1995). It is extremely unlikely that firms of fewer than 50 employees would develop the sophisticated personnel systems (Hornsby & Kuratko, 1990) necessary for this given their inadequate financial resources (Aldrich & Auster, 1986; Gatewood & Feild, 1987).

Therefore, many SMEs are likely to adopt what has been phrased a "muddle through" recruitment strategy, entering the labor market without a precise profile of the ideal applicant and simply screening the market for what is available (Williamson, 2000; Windolf, 1986), often using networks of friends and acquaintances of current employees. The successful candidate, in these instances, is often simply the most proximate and accessible candidate. During this muddle through process, it may be important for the SME to consider noninstrumental factors in their hiring, such as the norms, values, and beliefs that exist within an organization and its industry (Heneman et al., 2000; Williamson, 2000). It also may be appropriate for SME leaders to consider alternative approaches to staffing that help alleviate the conflict of finding the critical employee resources for the organization despite their financial and legitimacy constraints.

ALTERNATIVE STAFFING MODELS

A few scholars have suggested that perhaps one effective way for SMEs to meet their staffing challenges is through the use of nontraditional means of employing workers. Two specific sets of recommendations have been made, one suggesting that the use of PEOS will help mitigate HR challenges (Klaas et al., 2000), and the other suggesting that utilization of contingent labor will facilitate entrepreneurial growth (Cardon, 2003). We outline their basic arguments here in order to provide a basis for comparing these models below. We assume that with all three forms of labor contracting (including direct hires as well as these two alternatives), companies will seek the best qualified workers to perform the relevant tasks.

Traditional Hires

Traditionally, workers are hired directly by organizations to fulfill an ongoing need for certain skills, capabilities, or functional task completion (Davis-Blake & Uzzi, 1993). In this model, an organization searches for potential applicants through channels such as friends and family, newspaper ads, college campus recruiting, online candidate clearing sites (e.g., monster.com or jobs.com), or job fairs. Assuming an adequate supply of interested candidates, the company uses a variety of selection tools such as job applications, skill testing, background checks, and personal interviews to select the desired candidate. Once this person is chosen, they are hired directly by the organization and are assumed to continue working for that organization until their skills are no longer needed, they do not perform their job adequately, or they choose to leave the organization. Traditional workers are hired directly by the organization, managed by the organization, and it is assumed they will be ongoing employees of the organization for some time, as long as the quality of their work is good. The firm has legal responsibility for traditional hires as the "employer of record," in terms of compliance with relevant federal and state labor laws.

PEO Hires

In contrast, PEO workers are not hired or employed by an SME at all. Instead, an SME might outsource some of its functions to the PEO, where the PEO handles the SME's workforce by providing compensation programs, regulatory compliance, and other HR-related services (Klaas et al., 2000). PEO workers are legally employed by the professional employer organization (PEO), but are located on site with the SME and do work along side traditional hires within the SME. The PEO company is the legal "employer of record" for these employees, who are then leased to the SME. However, recent court cases suggest that the legal responsibilities for such employees may be shared by the two organizations, since although the PEO technically and legally employs the workers, the SME manages their daily activities and work load, which makes them also at least partially responsibly for compliance with relevant federal and state labor laws.

PEOs were developed in response to the unique HR challenges facing many SMEs. Given the resource and legitimacy constraints of small firms, many don't have dedicated HR personnel, much less departments. Costs associated with hiring highly trained HR professionals on a full time basis are likely to be prohibitive for many smaller organizations (Arthur, 1995). PEOs offer these firms increased access to HR expertise in a cost-effective manner (Cook, 1999). By focusing on human resource management for a number of firms, PEOs can aggregate risk across a larger number of employees, get good rates on benefits, and have a large team of HR experts. The SME gets access to expertise and can outsource HR activities to those with greater ability to perform them efficiently (Greer, Youngblood, & Gray, 1999). SMEs are increasingly relying on PEOs to provide HR services (Cook, 1999), and these services may include benefits, payroll, worker's compensation, safety and health, incentive pay, staffing, performance evaluations, discipline, employment policies, training, employee relations, job design, and even financial planning (Klaas et al., 2000).

In addition to providing greater access to HR expertise and lower costs of benefits, PEOs can greatly facilitate SME success because they allow SME managers to spend less time focusing on employment issues, and more time focused on the main concerns with running their business. The complex and time-consuming nature of many HR activities can pose a significant drain on existing managerial resources (Klaas et al., 2000). When smaller firms do not hire dedicated HR professionals, HR activities often are the responsibility of general managers (Longenecker, Moore, & Petty, 1994), and may interfere with managerial responsibilities that are directly related to revenue production (Cook, 1999). Also, many management decisions involve substantial complexity, and thus the quality of decisions may well be affected by the lack of training and expertise general mangers have in Human Resource issues (Greer et al., 1999; Klaas et al., 2000). Therefore, when firms choose to utilize a PEO, they may be better able to recruit candidates from the greater legitimacy of the larger PEO organization, save money through lowered costs of providing benefits, access greater expertise, and free up managerial time otherwise spent on HR issues to instead focus on advancing the profit-making aspects of the venture. "Clearly, PEOs offer an [effective] approach for addressing some of the major HR concerns faced by SMEs." (Klaas et al., 2000, p. 108).

However, utilization of a PEO is not appropriate or successful for all SMEs. Klaas et al. (2000) suggest that SMEs will be more satisfied with their PEO's role in containing HR costs when the SME is growing rapidly, has experienced HR problems in the past, has values congruent with those of the PEO, and when the SME uses the PEO for multiple services. Furthermore, SMEs will be more satisfied with their PEO in general when the SME is growing and when appropriate attention is paid to the relationship between the representatives of both the SME and the PEO. Their study highlights that even when looking at one PEO, substantial variation exists in how many aspects of HR are outsourced by SMEs, as well as in the satisfaction SMEs found in addressing their HR challenges with this staffing alternative. Klaas et al. (2000) address several factors that may contribute to the relative use and satisfaction with PEOs, and we build on this below in our discussion of the implications of staffing SMEs through PEOs, by traditional means, and through the use of contingent labor.

Contingent Hires

Perhaps a middle option in one sense is the use of contingent labor to address the staffing challenges of SMEs. Cardon (2003) suggests that contingent labor may enable SME growth more so than traditional staffing models can, since it provides a variable cost investment that can be made or discontinued at any point during the growth of the venture. Using contingent workers such as independent contractors and consultants may also bring new ideas and approaches to problems into the organization (March, 1991), which may facilitate creativity and insight in the SME (Cardon, 2003).

Contingent labor includes independent contractors, consultants, temporary workers, on-call or day labor, and even friends who provide help on specific projects, such as installing a local area network for a new business (although this last category is not included in official government calculations). Utilization of contingent work has become much more prevalent and more strategic on the part of organizations. At least 10% of the U.S. workforce, which is more than 12 million individuals, is employed as contingent workers (Cohany, 1996), and 90% of U.S. firms use contingent labor in some capacity (Coolidge, 1996; Matusik & Hill, 1998). Furthermore, these are not just the traditional temporary workers that most people associate with contingent labor. Forty-three percent of U.S. firms use contingent labor in professional and technical functions that have the potential to impact core areas of the firm (Coolidge, 1996; Matusik & Hill, 1998). Organizations may use contingent workers as "technical experts" on important projects (Wysocki, 1996), as well as part of deliberate efforts to drive down fixed costs and enhance the organization's ability to flexibly adapt to rapidly changing market conditions (Coolidge, 1996; Wysocki, 1996) and product or service demands. The traditional perspective is that while permanent employees respond to the stable needs of the organization, contingent workers are used for temporary, unpredictable, or cyclical demand fluctuations (Douglas & Motwani, 1996).

Contingent labor may be particularly important to SMEs, given their limited resources and high needs for flexibility (Stinchcombe, 1965). As Stinchcombe (1965) pointed out long ago, liabilities of smallness and newness generate often conflicting pressures on the firm, where firms must simultaneously keep costs variable in order to maintain flexibility and conserve cash, and rapidly launch growth initiatives, which implies investment in fixed assets to secure a competitive, legitimate, and durable position in the marketplace (Barney, 1991). Cardon (2003) argues that for emerging ventures, using contingent labor may be quite helpful in addressing this challenge, since contingent workers are by definition a variable rather than fixed cost, and utilization of this form of labor negates the high fixed costs associated with hiring and firing permanent workers (Von Hippel, Mangum, Greenberg, Heneman, & Skoglind, 1997). Contingent workers also are typically engaged when they already possess the skills or expertise the organization needs, which minimizes the firm's need to provide costly training programs or large ramp-up times for these workers.

However, contingent labor may also be problematic for SMEs because relying upon them leaves the firm vulnerable to the market availability of the skills they seek (Cardon, 2003). Many firms have difficulty in finding qualified contingent workers when they need them (Hambrick & Crozier, 1985), and this resource access constraint may limit the range of opportunity choices and growth potential for the firm (Cardon, 2003; Thakur, 1999). Further, contingent workers typically have a transactional psychological contract with organizations that engage them (Rousseau & Libuser, 1997), so their goals may not be aligned with those of the organization (Matusik & Hill, 1998). Moreover, just as contingent workers bring new knowledge into the firm (Cardon, 2003), there is a risk that they may also disseminate core firm knowledge out to competitors (Matusik & Hill, 1998), which could be detrimental to maintaining the firm's competitive advantage (Barney, 1991).

Matusik and Hill (1998) suggest a complex matrix of factors that should determine when and how organizations utilize contingent work. For example, they suggest that for firms in dynamic environments, employing limited numbers of contingent workers in core value-creation activities are advantageous, and that in enterprises where it is necessary to continually upgrade the firm's stock of core knowledge, contingent work levels should be higher, since contingent work can stimulate the knowledge-creation process. However, when the risk of dissemination of important knowledge is high, and particularly when these risks outweigh potential knowledge creation gains, contingent labor use should be restricted (Matusik & Hill, 1998).

This discussion suggests that there are several approaches to staffing that may be beneficial for SMEs, including hiring workers directly, hiring contingent workers, or outsourcing staffing decisions to a PEO. While previous authors have mentioned the benefits and risks associated with each approach, we seek to discuss the tradeoffs between these models. We suggest that there are five key considerations that should be taken into account when the staffing model is chosen: anticipated speed of growth, mental model of firm's culture, need for organizational flexibility, extent of control desired, and time available to spend on HR issues.

INITIAL CONSIDERATIONS FOR DETERMINING APPROPRIATE STAFFING OPTIONS

How do managers determine which model to use? It is not necessarily easy for SMEs to determine whether outsourcing will be effective for them or how they should manage the outsourcing relationship (Greer et al., 1999), if they choose to outsource at all. We argue the choice of staffing models should initially be based on two features of the SME: the CEO's internal mental model concerning staffing, and the anticipated speed of growth for the organization.

Internal Mental Model, or the Philosophy of the Founder

Often the approach to hiring in SMEs is focused on selecting someone who fits with the organization culture (Chatman, 1991; Williamson, 2000; Williamson et al., 2002). SME leaders look for those who are able to perform new duties as they are added to the current job, to handle multiple jobs as needed, and who have the ability to take on future jobs as they arise in the organization (Heneman, Heneman, & Judge, 1997). Heneman et al. (2000) discovered that small firm CEOs and founders were very concerned about competencies of their employees and matching these competencies with organizational rather than job requirements. Competencies are the beliefs, values, and interests of workers, rather than the basic knowledge, skills, or abilities, which are more typically used in large organizations as selection tools for job applicants (Chatman, 1991).

This suggests that while many leaders think first and foremost about their product, capital and how to bring the product or service on line, others focus on the kind of company they are trying to raise. Many leaders have in their heads a model or mental image of the type of company they are trying to create, and they think in terms of the critical characteristics or attributes of the organization they wish to influence. Baron and Hannan (2002) found that when asked about their models most leaders expressed them in terms of three dimensions, (1) attachment, (2) coordination/control and (3) selection. Attachment refers to the motives that would bind people to the company, such as the frequent models of love, money or the work itself. Coordination and control refer to the means by which structure was provided within the company. For some, structure was assured by the formal processes and procedures mandated by the organization, while for others it was inherent in the relationships between people and the culture of the company. For still others coordination was achieved through the professional discipline of the employees (i.e., engineering disciplines). Finally, the third dimension of the mental model identified by leaders was the way in which staffing was done in their organizations. Depending on the nature of the business and its markets, the culture of the organization demanded either selecting staff for values and personal fit, for immediate skills or for longer term potential (Baron & Hannan, 2002).

Mental models include images of the culture (habits, behaviors, etc.), espoused values, structures (hierarchy or the lack thereof and levels of decision authority throughout the organization), rules and procedures (or again the lack thereof), interdependencies among the various members of the SME, and compensation (Baron & Hannan, 2002). Founders vary in the clarity of their mental images, some imaging loosely only the antithesis of what they have experienced in other places of employment, while other founders are very explicit about the kind of company (look and feel) that they are trying to create. The mental model chosen by SME leader greatly influences the choices and decisions made concerning staffing and other aspects of Human resource management for the venture. For example, Donald Burr at People Express defined the organization he wished to create, articulated the values it would espouse (what he called "precepts"), envisioned the structures (or lack thereof) required and then went off to hire nontraditional airline staff to make it real. To him it was the second most important job he had, after defining the company mission and business model (Whitesome & Schlesinger, 1995).

The key issue or risk to the founders and leaders is that if they do not have an image of the company they are trying to create then everyone who is hired will create it for them, potentially in ways the leaders do not like. Each individual's approach to their job, their interactions with others once onboard, and their interactions with the customer define and influence the emerging culture of the organization, and in most cases the leader wants to have an important initial influence on this emerging culture, through enactment of their mental model for the venture.

For example, Trilogy leader's mental model of his organization was as fast-paced, highly skilled, innovative and challenging workplace (Austin, 2000; Ramstad, 1998). Joe Liemandt believed that to stay ahead of the competition and attract customers, to be successful, the organization would have to be a place where innovation was continuous and risk-taking was high. Trilogy would require a minimum of hierarchy, and a maximum of coordination. With this in mind, Trilogy determined that the best way to enact the organization was to hire workers directly. They chose "A" players, seeking the most technically skilled people they could find. Rather than network to find best fit, they went to the best colleges and universities in the country and appealed to those seeking cutting edge work assignments in a culture that would highly reward success. They hired first for skills and experience and implemented an extensive training program to acculturate employees into the "Trilogy way" (Austin, 2000). The training that every new employee went through provided the strong socialization necessary to articulate and enact the culture and mental model of the leader. In addition, it transferred the professional processes developed by the leader and the organization to all new employees, through a strong socialization process.

This suggests that the strength of the mental model of the CEO or founder during organizational emergence will have a large impact on the subsequent culture and success of the business (Baron & Hannan, 2002). Within that, the strength of the mental model will significantly impact the recruiting and selection choices, and specifically the relevance of alternative staffing models, for an SME.

Anticipated Speed of Growth

A second major concern for SME CEOs and founders is learning while growing the company; or the need to develop high-potential employees that can perform multiple roles during growth periods of the SME (Heneman et al., 2000; May, 1997). The speed of growth of the organization influences the decisions SME leaders make about staffing in a number of ways. First, the faster the company needs to or intends to grow, the more time is required to staff the organization properly. Fast growth puts a lot of pressure on the organization to "ramp" up hiring. The key in a fast-growing SME seems to be the ability to anticipate the timing and skills needed in order to sustain the growth momentum (Hambrick & Crozier, 1985). As mentioned above, this requires huge investments of time and financial resources. In this situation, either PEO or contingent worker models may be best in the short or medium term, since they provide faster hiring of already skilled workers.

The faster firms grow, the shakier the culture and the less control the SME has on achieving its mental model. Speed does not afford the organization the opportunity to build the cultural foundation necessary to sustain itself. There are a number of examples of SMEs that have not survived simply because the mental model of the leader was either never achieved or "sidetracked" by the numerous staff that came into the organization with their own mental models that swayed the course of the organization. As March (1991) explains, new organizational members bring new ideas, assumptions, cultural norms, and knowledge into a firm. If there are few incumbent workers and many new members, then the potential for the new ideas and norms to overtake the intended mental model is high. Furthermore, where the mental model is strong, hiring new workers is only the beginning, where the real enactment of the mental model occurs through strong socialization or "enculturation" programs (Van Maanen & Schein, 1979). As an organization grows it must manage the entry of new staff into the organization, where faster rates of growth translate into higher needs for post hire processes to ensure proper integration and alignment of new employees.

For example, when Palm Computing spun off from 3COM, leaders anticipated a very rapid growth rate (S. Gill, vice president of human resources, personal communication, March 18, 2003). Their decision was to hire workers directly. From 100 staff members months prior to the spin-off, over the next year Palm added nearly 1000 workers, and all were direct hires. This put a great deal of pressure on the organization to: (1) identify candidates; (2) screen and select; (3) transition these people into new roles, and (4) integrate them with the original and already added employees. The result was often chaos, with new staff not having proper orientation, each bringing their own expectations of the culture of the organization, and few reliable processes for accomplishing the work. Had Palm chosen instead to either contract work to contingent workers or to engage a PEO to manage the staffing and training process, the amount of time, energy, money and resources devoted to this activity could have been invested in a number of other high value added activities during the ramp up of the company (Gill).

When the growth demands or projects of the SME are slower, it may be possible and prudent for the organization to hire workers directly. Slower growth allows the organization time to match the hiring process to the types of individual sought, and to allow for control of work to be based on peers and culture, rather than formal rules or professional norms (Baron & Hannan, 2002). Slower growth also enables the leaders to spend the extra time required in direct hiring, where they can hire people they already know, network with others to identify viable candidates, advertise and interview each candidate personally, and take the time to ensure appropriate socialization of new hires to existing and desired organizational norms. Assuming an SME leader has contacts and a broad base, slow direct hiring is the simplest staffing method and assures the leader they are hiring people they know who will fit into their mental model. One example of this approach is a small startup company in Cleveland, Ohio, ETG, Inc., founded by Don Heestand and two colleagues. Their mental model for the company revolves around dimensions of motivating the staff, having minimum structure in the organization, and building close relationships between the staff and with their customers. Their staffing approach has been to seek the "A" players in the business and to then incentivize them to achieve phenomenal results (Zawacki, 2000). ETG is not on an aggressive growth plan. They seek first to find the best qualified persons they can find. But once found they screen them on (1) need for achievement (self motivated, high need for achievement); (2) motivation (desire to make a lot of money) and (3) a values and cultural fit. Their approach is to go directly to the market for new recruits through an elaborate network of current employees, customers and friends. They look first for current skill and then values and culture fit. They provide minimum training and focus primarily on the natural information process of socialization within the firm.

While this approach offers many advantages, such as the ability to ensure good fit in values and culture between ETG leaders and candidates, it also has disadvantages. For example, because ETG hires friends and acquaintances of current employees and customers, it may be difficult to let workers go if they do not work out. It may also be difficult to truly assess the skills and attributes of the candidates, relying more on the say so of the recommending person. Finally, this method may not ultimately bring to the organization the breadth of knowledge, skill and diversity necessary to provide the dynamic tension needed for creativity and innovation.

Summary and a Model

In summary, as is depicted in Figure 4.1, the anticipated speed of growth of an SME (fast or slow) along with the strength of the leader's

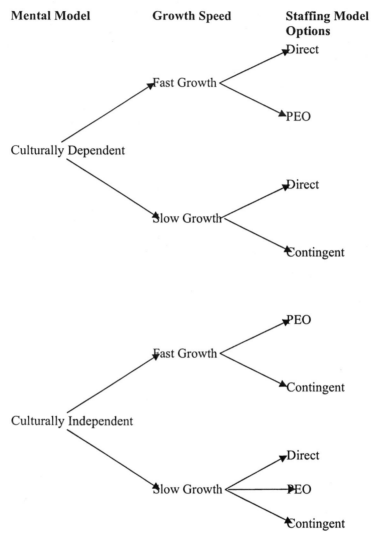

Figure 4.1.   Initial considerations for staffing model choice.

mental model (culturally dependent or independent) will restrict the staffing models most appropriate for that SME. Strong mental models require a lot of time and energy on the part of SME leaders, and these organizations are culturally dependent, since the success of the business model and the leaders' mental model are based on staff acting and behaving in certain ways with customers and each other. Cultural dependence suggests there are specific ways of acting, behaving and performing duties and responsibilities that define the organization in unique ways. In some instances the organization is not even deemed "successful" by the leaders or others if it does not achieve certain internal cultural or philosophical thresholds. These approaches might even be trademarked by the organization.

SMEs with strong, culturally dependent mental models will most likely hire workers directly or outsource their entire staff to a PEO, so that greater assurance of fit between the organization and its new members can be achieved. Further, if the PEO model is utilized, the SME will work diligently to develop a close relationship with the PEO representative, and will make sure the PEO values and culture are aligned with that of the SME and its mental model (Judge & Cable, 1997; Klaas et al., 2000). Contingent labor will likely not be used in an organization with a strong mental model, since acculturation of contingent workers requires large investments in people who have no long-term contracts or relationships with the organization, and resource constrained SMEs would be unlikely to invest significantly in workers with such short or loose attachments (Matusik & Hill, 1998).

Only the speed of growth causes any other consideration. When SMEs are culturally dependent, but growing fast, they may not have time or resources to devote to hiring, training and socializing newcomers, so they may rely upon the PEO staffing model (Klaas et al., 2000). A PEO would have greater access to candidates, existing screening and training programs, and experience and competence at rapidly staffing a fast-growing firm. With either slow or fast anticipated growth, in a strong cultural model, SME leaders would seek a PEO that mirrors the values, culture, and philosophy of the SME, to increase the likelihood of satisfaction and cost savings from the PEO-SME relationship (Klaas et al., 2000).

Culturally independent firms, on the other hand, do not have strong identifiable cultures, and may change cultural factors more easily. SME leaders in these firms are not as concerned about value fit between the organization and candidates, but are more interested in engaging workers' knowledge and skills needed by their organizations. When growth is slow, any one of the three staffing models may be utilized, depending upon which type of worker has the necessary skills, and on additional considerations of time, control, and flexibility, which we discuss below. When growth is fast for culturally independent firms, SMEs will best utilize PEO or contingent work staffing models, since the interest is in rapidly locating workers who already possess the necessary skills, in the most efficient and cost-effective manner. PEOs can again provide greater access, screening, and experience in rapid expansion if SME leaders want to outsource the entire recruiting process, while contingent workers can be engaged and moved around quickly and easily by the SME to perform rapidly changing jobs throughout the growth process. This is particularly helpful in an independent cultural model, when SME leaders are not concerned with matching the values or goals of workers with a preset organizational model.

FURTHER CONSIDERATIONS OF STAFFING MODEL OPTIONS

Once appropriate staffing model options are identified based upon anticipated speed of growth and mental models, or strength of cultural dependence, the choice among them can be made based upon implications of each of the three staffing models for organizational flexibility, control, and time managers spend on HR issues. These three factors are important considerations for SME leaders, and we suggest there are tradeoffs in these factors based upon the three staffing models discussed here. A summary of our arguments is in Table 4.1.

Flexibility Considerations

As previously noted, an important consideration for SME leaders is hiring qualified workers who can rapidly adapt to the changing needs of the emerging and growing organization (Heneman et al., 2000; May,

Table 4.1.   Secondary Considerations of Alternative Staffing Models

	Direct Hire	PEO Hire	Contingent Hire
Flexibility Implications			
Flexibility in staffing	Low	Moderate	High
Flexibility in compensation model	High	Low	Moderate
Time Implications			
Time spent on managing HR issues	High	Low	Moderate
HR expertise required inside firm	High	Low	Moderate
Need to develop HR systems	High	Low	Low
Access to HR expertise	Low	High	Low
Control Implications			
Legal Obligations and Risk	SME	PEO	SME
Management Responsibility	SME	PEO	SME
Control of work based on	Peers/culture	Formal rules	Professional norms
Managerial Risk of bad hires	High	Low	Low
Risk of loss of core knowledge	Low	Low	High
Cost Implications	Wage rate, plus benefits costs	Wage rate, plus markup for overhead	Higher wage rate

1997). This implies that flexibility in staffing is essential. By flexibility in staffing we mean several things. First, it is the ability of the organization to expand and contract the labor force as environmental and organizational conditions warrant (Coolidge, 1996; Wysocki, 1996). It is also the ability to quickly change skill sets needed to respond to market demands. Finally, flexibility in staffing refers to the ability of SME leaders to change compensation and other non staffing related HR systems.

First, SME leaders must be able to adapt organizational size and skill sets to meet changing market conditions. From an SME perspective, a traditional direct hire model is the least flexible approach to staffing. One important factor that limits an organization's flexibility to respond to these changing conditions is the existence of prior legal and psychological contracts with its employees (Matusik & Hill, 1998). Once traditional workers are hired by a firm, there are substantial exit costs associated with firing those workers, including direct severance payments, tarnished reputation as a good employer, and lowered morale among the "survivors," or remaining workers (Brockner, Wiesenfeld, & Martin, 1995; Matusik & Hill, 1998). This makes staffing flexibility with a traditional model quite low.

In contrast, Matusik and Hill (1998) suggest that contingent workers offer the greatest flexibility in staffing levels, because contingent labor is a variable cost (Cardon, 2003) that is incurred only when the services of these workers are needed. "The lower fixed costs of exit associated with the use of contingent work increases the firm's flexibility" (Matusik & Hill, 1998, p. 682). When demand contracts, contingent contracts are not renewed, new contingent labor is not engaged, and therefore labor costs decrease and flexibility is high.

Flexibility in staffing with PEOs is moderate, since these workers have longer-term relationships with the SME organization, and therefore are not quite as "disposable" (Budman, 1994) as contingent workers. However, they are also not direct employees of the SME, and therefore should have a reduced psychological bond with the SME, at least compared to traditional workers. When demand contracts, fewer PEO workers can be used by the SME, but potentially the PEO can place these individuals with other clients, so the negative feelings associated with their job loss should not be great. The risk is that if the SME expands and contracts labor needs frequently, the PEO will have increasing difficulty placing workers in the SME, and the SME may no longer have access to the best and brightest of the PEO's workforce.

If the SME has a culturally dependent approach to HR, such as emphasizing employee empowerment, need for risk-taking, or employee involvement in managerial decision making more than other firms, then other HR systems, such as reward systems, performance evaluation systems, and training programs must be adjusted in idiosyncratic ways to encourage the attitudes and behaviors that differ from what is typically desired in other organizations (Klaas et al., 2000). This idiosyncratic approach is not ideal for PEO-SME relationships (Klaas et al., 2000). PEOs are designed to give cost-effective advantages to firms using traditional HR systems, so that the PEO can design and implement these programs across a number of small firms. If the PEO cannot utilize economies of scale to deliver traditional programs, such as when unique HR practices are desired or necessary, then HR services may not be able to be developed and provided by a PEO in a cost-effective manner for the SME (Klaas et al., 2000).

In sum, flexibility in staffing will be highest with engagement of contingent workers, lowest when directly hiring workers, and moderate when using a PEO. Flexibility in compensation will be highest when directly hiring workers, lowest when using a PEO, and moderate when engaging contingent workers. In terms of flexibility, PEO use may only be best in situations when the culture is independent and only occasionally best when the culture is dependent, but speed is critical in ramping up or down the staffing.

Time Considerations

A second major consideration for SMEs is time. Entrepreneurs are by nature constrained by resources, and one of the most important in addition to cash is time. The classic characterization of entrepreneurs depicts them working extremely long hours, constantly putting out fires, juggling three times as many things as they can possibly handle, and never seeing their families. Therefore, what time they do have, should be focused upon the strategic investment activities of the venture. Performing HR tasks, such as carefully screening applications and assessing the fit and values of candidates, may interfere with managerial responsibilities that are directly related to revenue production (Cook, 1999), which is especially problematic for SME managers who are already resource and time constrained (Klaas et al., 2000).

An important component of time involves the need to develop HR expertise within the firm. As we discussed above, particularly for strong culture organizations, significant resources must be devoted to carefully recruiting, screening, and socializing new organizational entrants with a direct hire model, and the HR expertise required within the firm to do this well is high. Many specialized HR activities are infrequently performed in SMEs (Cook, 1999), and SME managers typically have little experience in filling job vacancies (Heneman & Berkley, 1999) or performing other staffing activities. Therefore internal systems must be developed for finding candidates, taking applications, developing screening systems, conducting interviews, designing competitive compensation systems, and developing and implementing training programs, despite limited experience or skill in these areas. This takes considerable investments of both money and managerial time. However, if invested in, this internal development would be controlled by the SME, and may even become an important competitive advantage for the firm (Barney, 1991).

An important advantage to using a PEO model is that staffing is completely outsourced, so very little HR expertise is required within the firm, there is very limited (if any) need to develop internal HR systems, and yet managers have very high access to competent experienced HR expertise that is housed within the PEO (Klaas et al., 2000). This provides many advantages to SMEs, as their managers can be devoted to important business activities, yet still have sophisticated and competitive systems for managing their workforce. The risk with this model is that the SME is amazingly dependent upon the PEO for these HR systems, and therefore the relationship between the SME and the PEO must be carefully managed and attended to (Klaas et al., 2000).

With a contingent staffing model, the time implications are a bit more complicated. These workers are engaged for only short and fixed durations, and therefore do not require sophisticated socialization, training, or development programs. Therefore, the need to develop internal HR systems is low. However, some HR expertise is required, because these workers must be located, contracted with, monitored, and paid by the SME. Therefore some form of recruiting, performance assessments, and compensation must be administered, although typically at only a basic level. Therefore, a moderate level of HR expertise is required within the firm, and thus a moderate amount of time must be spent on HR issues to ensure that the appropriate contingent workers are being engaged and the work they are doing is satisfactory to the SME. Finally, engaging contingent workers directly implies that any HR expertise needed must be developed internally by the venture, since engaging contingent workers does not come with the advantage of automatic access to these professionals.

Control Considerations of Staffing Model Chosen

The third key area of tradeoffs among staffing models involves control over internal firm dynamics, particularly legal obligations, management responsibility, control of work, risk of bad hires, risk of insider-outsider problems, and risk of core knowledge loss.

One of the advantages of using alternative staffing methods is the transfer of some employment-related risk and legal responsibility to the PEO or contingent worker source (e.g., consulting firm, temporary agency, or independent contractor). These firms, rather than the SME, serve as the employer of record for many HR functions and become at least jointly responsible for managing workers at the SME (Klaas et al., 2000). Responsibility for compliance to work-related legislation, such as Title VII, or the Family and Medical Leave Act, lies with both the SME and the PEO or consulting firm, when one is used. When workers are hired directly by the SME, or when contingent workers are contracted directly by the SME, legal compliance and management responsibility lie squarely on the shoulders of SME management. Legal issues related to co-employment situations, such as when workers are doing work within an SME but are employed by a PEO or temporary firm, have taken on increasing importance in recent years. Prominent cases, such as Microsoft, suggest that both firms are legally culpable for compliance with employment laws.

Along with this legal and management responsibility, however, comes greater control over the job assignments of employees. Role flexibility and adaptation are extremely important in SMEs, as carefully defined highly specialized jobs are quite rare, and changing environmental conditions warrant flexibility and innovation (May, 1997). There is also some risk of opportunism and inappropriate behavior on the part of employees (Williamson, 1996), which may be impacted by the staffing model utilized. It becomes important to understand how work behavior and job responsibilities are controlled in SMEs, in order to mitigate the opportunism problem. Baron and Hannan (2002) point out that the HR blueprint, or set of HR practices utilized, significantly impacts how work is controlled. Consistent with their arguments, we expect that when SMEs hire workers directly, control will primarily be through the culture of the organization, where peer norms strongly influence behavior, particularly for culturally dependent firms. In contrast, when PEOs are used, we expect formal rules to take precedence in guiding worker behavior. As Klaas, McClendon, & Gainey (2000) point out, greater specificity in contracts and services (such as training programs) increases the usefulness and satisfaction the SME will experience with a PEO, indicating that greater reliance on rules is beneficial for SMEs utilizing PEOs. Therefore, appropriate behaviors will be extrinsically guided by the use of rewards and sanctions with a PEO staffing model. We expect contingent workers to be regulated by norms that guide professionals in their chosen job or industry. For example, there is a fairly strong code of conduct or set of professional norms for medical doctors, regardless of what hospital or specialty they are affiliated with, that guides their behavior. We can easily anticipate similar professional norm control in many other professions such as accountants, computer analysts, systems designers, and even college professors. Sales organizations are another good example of firms that rely on the norms and protocols of the disciple to guide and manage behavior (Darr, 2003). Each discipline has a predetermined set of standards and norms that can be seen at play in their particular function.

Although there are always exceptions to these situations, and people who are not guided by strong professional norms of good and appropriate performance, we assume that companies will seek to hire employees who do good work, and to contract with firms that also deliver high quality performance. Unfortunately, we don't have much empirical evidence on this, despite many anecdotal stories of bad employees, poor employment relationships, and improper HR practices.

Given stories of bad hires and bad fit, another potential consideration for SMEs in their staffing decisions is the potential impact of a "bad" hire. New organizational members can have a significant impact on the culture and dynamics of a firm (March, 1991), and given that SMEs can be quite small, the potential for one new worker to impact others is greater than it is for larger organizations. A "bad" hire, either due to a negative attitude, skills deficient from those expected, or differences of opinion with key organizational members may be detrimental to incumbent worker morale, productivity, and even retention of key workers. The level of risk associated with bad hires is greater when that individual is hired directly by the SME, because that person is harder to get rid of. Investment has been made in recruiting, selecting, and potentially even training that person, and firm leaders are likely to be slower in firing a person when such investment has been made. In a PEO or contingent work staffing model, the risk of bad hires is quite low, for two reasons. First, the SME has not made a significant up-front investment in that worker, so the desire to recoup any such investment is missing. Second, the point of using PEO and contingent workers is the greater flexibility they allow, which includes the opportunity to fire or replace people when they are not working out for the SME. If a PEO model is being used, SME leaders would contact the PEO to remove the offending hire, and replace them with a more appropriate individual. If a contingent model is being used, SME leaders would fire the worker and locate a suitable replacement (involving some search and selection costs) or contact the labor provider (e.g., temporary agency) to remove and replace the bad hire.

A final control consideration for SMEs involves the risk of losing core idiosyncratic firm knowledge with the use of contingent or PEO staffing models (Matusik & Hill, 1998). Just as contingent workers can move into firms easily, bringing with them new knowledge that may spark innovative ideas in the SME (Cardon, 2003), they can also leave the firm with private knowledge and share it with other organizations, thus compromising the inimitable elements of the SME's competitive advantage (Matusik & Hill, 1998). Matusik and Hill (1998) argue that when the risk of knowledge dissemination in such a way outweighs the flexibility and cost gains of using contingent labor, firms should either not use contingent workers at all, or at least restrict their use to areas separate from the value-creation activities of the venture. This risk of losing core knowledge is high with contingent workers, but low with direct hires and PEO hires. Direct hires typically remain with firms longer than contingent workers, and may also sign nondisclosure and noncompete contracts, making them less likely to disseminate critical core knowledge outside of the organization. PEO workers also typically remain with an SME for longer tenures than contingent workers do, since they operate essentially the same as direct hires in their daily activities, but are recruited and managed by the PEO rather than the SME. This suggests that the risk of loss of core idiosyncratic knowledge with a PEO staffing model is also low.

In sum, control over internal firm dynamics is highest with a direct hire staffing model, lowest with a contingent hire staffing model, and moderate when utilizing a PEO. A PEO staffing model leaves the SME with lower legal obligations, management responsibility, risk of bad hires, and risk of loss of core knowledge. A contingent worker model also involves less legal obligations and management responsibility, low to moderate risk of bad hires, and a high risk of loss of core knowledge. With direct hiring, the SME has higher legal obligations and management responsibilities, a high risk of bad hires, but a low risk of loss of core firm knowledge.

COST IMPLICATIONS OF STAFFING MODEL

Finally our model suggests that the cost of hiring staff is an important consideration in the final decisions regarding staffing choices. Each of the three approaches we have outlined come with their own unique underlying costs. The "Total Cost" to fill a vacancy is very hard to determine and compare in this situation. It is difficult to suggest that one strategy or another is "more costly"; as each comes with its own set of considerations. Direct hiring may, in fact, end up being the highest cost solution for SME's. The cost of direct hiring includes the cost of advertising, networking time, posting jobs (on the internet or other job sources), and recruiting time on the part of the leader and others. In addition, while the direct hire might lead to an overall lower wage rate, compared to the other two models, benefit costs might be higher.

The PEO situation may be similar in some ways to the direct hire. The leader must "recruit" or find the PEO, interview their leaders and others to determine their comfort level with the PEO and its staff. In addition, the PEO will add-on overhead rates to the wage and benefit rates for the staff member(s) employed. These overhead charges would include the time to provide "oversight" to on-site staff, administer their wage and HR benefits and other costs of doing business as a PEO. In addition, when firms employ skilled and experienced staff from the PEO, their labor rates may be higher per hour.

Finally, with regard to contingent hires, the cost implications are primarily in labor rates. Contingent workers are often more expensive than direct hires, as they markup their labor rates to cover their own overhead costs. While this may not be true for day workers and other less skilled hires, it is typical among consultants, independent contractors and other temporary workers. The cost implications of contingent workers are also dependent on whether or not the worker is directly brokered or not. If directly brokered, the SME may incur advertising and other associated costs as well. If not directly brokered, then the SME may incur a finder's fee, or other agency fee associated with identifying and contracting with the contingent labor.

DISCUSSION AND IMPLICATIONS

In this paper, we have suggested that there are several considerations that may influence the selection and implementation of multiple staffing models in small and medium enterprises, and that there are tradeoffs between these models among these five considerations. Bringing all of these elements together has important implications for both scholarship and practice concerned with staffing these organizations.

Implications for Practice

In terms of practice, we suggest that SME leaders have several important elements to consider when making their early organizational HR decisions. The models presented here offer leaders a simple framework to use in thinking through their staffing options and choices, in order to determine the best approach to staffing given the five key dimensions we have explored.

We suggest that leaders must first determine their mental model of the organization and the anticipated speed of growth for the company. Without clarity on these two points, any approach to staffing will probably not work well. Once these two factors are considered together, additional considerations of control, flexibility, and time can be considered. While direct hires provide greater degrees of control over who works in the organization, this approach also requires significant amounts of time and carries great risk of bad hiring decisions. Leaders who are skilled interviewers, evaluators and assessors, and who have the time and resources to devote to carefully building an effective internal HR system may prefer a direct hiring approach. Where organizational systems are complex (leading to greater HR complexity in compensation, training, and other elements) the SME leader may have no choice but to build internal capability because contingent and PEO hires would be more difficult in these situations.

Where flexibility is essential, a contingent work model may be best, since staffing flexibility is high, compensation flexibility is moderate, and legal obligations and risk of bad hires are minimal. This approach would work best when the organizational culture is independent, time available to spend on HR issues is moderate, and risk of loss of critical organizational knowledge is low.

When time is the scarcest resource, and SME leaders need to focus on critical business functions, a PEO staffing model might be best. A PEO offers a rapidly expanding firm with either a dependent or independent culture great access to HR expertise and knowledge, cost effective HR systems, and moderate flexibility in staffing and compensation, as well as moderate control over internal firm dynamics.

None of the three approaches presented is ideal in every situation. As we have demonstrated, each has its tradeoffs, costs and benefits. However, given a clearly emerging business scenario, leaders must make choices as to their approach to staffing their organizations. What approach a leader takes depends on the amount of flexibility they perceive they will want or need in staffing, the amount of time they can or will devote to the selection process, and finally the amount of control and risk they wish to have and take in the process.

Implications for Research

This model also has important implications for research. The outsourcing of HR in general has received relatively little attention in the literature (Klaas et al., 2000), and within the context of small or emerging ventures, work from only a handful of scholars could be identified. Yet small businesses cannot afford to develop all of their HR systems internally, and many utilize these alternative staffing sources in practice. This suggests that our research in this area is sorely lacking in comparison with what is actually occurring in entrepreneurial firms. Approximately half of the members of the Society for Human Resource Management (SHRM) work in firms with less than 100 employees, yet what we know about how small firms make staffing and other HR decisions is extremely limited (Cardon & Stevens, 2004).

In particular, our suggestions that SME managers consider the tradeoffs and interactions of five key elements in choosing a staffing model indicate the need for scholarship on entrepreneurial decision processes, and on the interaction of these elements of organizational HR design. Scholarship on the interaction of HR components is also quite limited (Heneman & Tansky, 2002), and thus such work could be highly informative for fields of both entrepreneurship and human resource management. Welbourne and Andrews (1996, p. 893) suggest that smaller organizations offer a "unique opportunity for studying human resource management," a call that has been echoed by several (e.g., Heneman et al., 2000) but to date pursued by only a few.

Some specific theoretical questions emerge from this discussion. First, how do concerns for the legitimacy of SMEs as viable employers (Williamson, 2000; Williamson et al., 2002) impact a firm's need to utilize alternative staffing sources, such as PEOs or contingent workers? It would seem that if firms are unable to recruit people with skills necessary for their survival and growth, they would need to outsource or contract workers with those skills, even if those staffing models were not desirable given the considerations we discuss above.

A related issue concerns whether there are conditions under which individuals are more likely to take-on temporary assignments with SMEs than permanent assignments. For example, if individuals are attracted by the more relaxed innovative cultures of SMEs, but concerned about stability and legitimacy of those organizations (Williamson, 2000; Williamson et al., 2002), would they be more likely to take assignments in SMES through labor brokers such as PEOs or consulting firms? This arrangement would provide individuals with benefits such as health care and retirement plans that could be transferred to other SMEs that utilize the same PEO, should the first employer not survive.

A third area of inquiry concerns other potential alternative staffing sources that we do not explicitly consider here, such as extensive use of interns or consulting firms, that may imply different levels of control, time, or flexibility that the broader category of contingent work, under which they are included. For example, the use of interns that are hired directly by the firm is a contingent approach to staffing, but many interns become permanent workers, which may alter how SME leaders consider the recruitment and selection of these workers. Additionally, we have assumed a model in which all workers are full time employees in their home organization. Consideration of how part-time or home workers may be engaged by SMEs might significantly alter the decision processes for the leaders. Many SME's today employ part-time staff or create job-sharing situations that alter the time, control and cost implications of our model. Part-time workers often receive no benefits, limited training and minimal socialization into the company. While part-time workers may add flexibility in staffing, they also add degrees of complexity that might negate the decision to hire them. Theoretical and empirical exploration of this complexity may prove fruitful for both research and in terms of practical application for SME managers.

Finally, we have assumed throughout this chapter that ultimately the individuals employed by organizations through all three means of labor contracting will be high quality performing workers, and that HR practices in all three cases will also be done well. We know anecdotally that this is often not the case, and we need empirical examination of the implications of this. If in an ideal world the three types of labor arrangements we have considered have these seven sets of considerations, what additional concerns might there be for situations in which PEOs or temporary firms are not helpful or productive for SMEs? What is the empirical influence of bad HR practices by the SMEs themselves, the PEOs, or the contingent labor firms on employee productivity, satisfaction, or tenure, as well as on organizational productivity? Such considerations merit empirical investigation before the broad arguments in this chapter can be validated.

In short, there is a broad array of questions that remain concerning how SME leaders make their staffing decisions, and specifically in how they approach nontraditional staffing options. We encourage additional dialogue and empirically study of this phenomenon.

CONCLUSION

Our understanding of staffing in small and emerging ventures has come a long way in the last 20 years, but remains primarily focused on the traditional notion of hiring workers directly into the organization. Given that many SMEs use nontraditional methods of hiring workers, we suggest that more careful consideration of the implications and tradeoffs among these alternative methods should be made. We focused on three specific staffing models in SMEs: hiring workers directly, contracting contingent workers directly or through labor brokers such as temporary agencies, and outsourcing staffing entirely to a professional employer organization (PEO). We argued that the choice of staffing model should be driven by five key organizational considerations, including anticipated speed of growth, mental model of the firm, organizational flexibility, time spent on

HR issues, and control over internal firm dynamics. We provided two graphical depictions of the tradeoffs among staffing models, and encourage application of these to actual staffing decisions made by SME leaders. We also encourage scholarly inquiry into the HR decision-making processes of SME leaders and specifically their use and implementation of nontraditional staffing approaches.

REFERENCES

Aldrich, H., & Auster, E. (1986). Even dwarfs started small: Liabilities of age and size and their strategic implications. In B. M. Staw & L. L. Cummings (Eds.), *Research in organizational behavior* (Vol. 8, pp.165-198). Greenwich, CT: JAI Press.

Aldrich, H., & Von Glinow, M. A. (1991). Business starts-ups: The HRM imperative. In S. Birley, I. C. MacMillan, & S. Subramony (Eds.), *International perspectives on entrepreneurship research* (Vol. 18, pp. 233-253). New York: Elsevier

Aldrich, H.E. (1999). *Organizations evolving*. London: Sage.

Arthur, D. (1995). *Managing human resources in small and mid-sized companies*. New York: American Management Association.

Austin, R. (2000). *Trilogy Software, Inc.* Harvard Business School Press, Case No. 9-699-034.

Baker, T., & Aldrich, H. (1994). *Friends and strangers: Early hiring practices and idiosyncratic jobs*. Paper presented at the Fourteenth Annual Entrepreneurship Research Conference.

Barney, J. (1991). Firm resources and sustained competitive advantage. *Journal of Management, 17*(1), 99-120.

Baron, J. N., & Hannan, M. T. (2002). Organizational blueprints for success in high-tech start-ups: Lessons from the Stanford project on emerging companies. *California Management Review, 44*(3), 8-36.

Brockner, J., Wiesenfeld, B., & Martin, C. L. (1995). Decision frame, procedural justice, and survivors' reactions to job layoffs. *Organizational Behavior and Human Decision Processes, 63*(1), 59-69.

Budman, M. (1994). Throwaway workers? *Across the Board, 31*(4), 38.

Bureau of Labor Statistics. (2004). *Current population survey: Employee tenure summary*. http://stats.bls.gov/news.release/tenure.nr0.htm: United States Department of Labor.

Cardon, M. S. (2003). Contingent labor as an enabler of entrepreneurial growth. *Human Resource Management Journal, 42*(4), 357-373.

Cardon, M. S., & Stevens, C. (2004). Managing human resources in small organizations: What do we know? *Human Resource Management Review, 14*(3), 295-323.

Chatman, J. A. (1991). Matching people and organizations: Selection and socialization in public accounting firms. *Administrative Science Quarterly, 36*(3), 459-484.

Cohany, S. R. (1996). Workers in alternative employment arrangements. *Monthly Labor Review, 119*(10), 31-45.

Cook, M. F. (1999). *Outsourcing human resource functions*. New York: American Management Association.

Coolidge, S. D. (1996). "Temping" is now a career—with an upside for workers. *The Christian Science Monitor, 7*, 1.

Darr, A. (2003). Control and autonomy among knowledge workers in sales: An employee perspective. *Employee Relations, 25*(1), 31-42.

Davis-Blake, A., & Uzzi, B. (1993). Determinants of employment externalization: A study of temporary workers and independent contractors. *Administrative Science Quarterly, 38*, 195-223.

Deshpande, S. P., & Golhar, D. Y. (1994). HRM practices in large and small manufacturing firms: A comparative study. *Journal of Small Business Management, 32*(2), 49-56.

Douglas, C., & Motwani, J. (1996). Temporary workers: Implication on HRM practices and supervisors. *Supervision, 57*, 14-15.

Foote, D. A., & Folta, T. B.(2002). Temporary workers as real options. *Human Resource Management Review, 12*, 579-597.

Gatewood, R. D., & Feild, H. S. (1987). A personnel selection program for small business. *Journal of Small Business Management, 25*(4), 16-24.

Greening, D. W., Barringer, B. R., & Macy, G. A. (1996). Qualitative study of managerial challenges facing small business geographic expansion. *Journal of Business Venturing, 11*, 233-256.

Greer, C. R., Youngblood, S. A., & Gray, D. A. (1999). Human resource management outsourcing: The make or buy decision. *Academy of Management Executive, 13*, 85-96.

Hambrick, D. C., & Crozier, L. M. (1985). Stumblers and stars in the management of rapid growth. *Journal of Business Venturing, 1*, 31-45.

Heneman, H. G., & Berkley, R. A. (1999). Applicant attraction practices and outcomes among small businesses. *Journal of Small Business Management*, 53-74.

Heneman, H. G., Heneman, R. L., & Judge, T. A. (1997). *Staffing organizations*. Middleton, WI: Mendora House/Irwin.

Heneman, R. L., & Tansky, J. W. (2002). Human resource management models for entrepreneurial opportunity: Existing knowledge and new directions. In J. Katz & T. M. Welbourne (Eds.), *Managing people in entrepreneurial organizations* (Vol. 5, pp. 55-82). Amsterdam: JAI Press.

Heneman, R. L., Tansky, J. W., & Camp, S. M. (2000). Human resource management practices in small and medium-sized enterprises: Unanswered questions and future research perspectives. *Entrepreneurship: Theory and Practice*, 11-26.

Hornsby, J. S., & Kuratko, D. F. (1990, July). Human resource management in small business: Critical issues for the 1990s. *Journal of Small Business Management*, 9-18.

Judge, T. A., & Cable, D. M. (1997). Applicant personality, organizational culture, and organization attraction. *Personnel Psychology, 50*, 359-394.

Katz, J., Aldrich, H., Welbourne, T. M., & Williams, P. M. (2000). Guest editor's comments special issue on human resource management and the SME: Toward a new synthesis. *Entrepreneurship: Theory and Practice*, 7-10.

Klaas, B., McClendon, J., & Gainey, T. W. (2000). Managing HR in the small and medium enterprise: The impact of professional employer organizations. *Entrepreneurship: Theory and Practice*, 107-124.

Longenecker, J. G., Moore, C. W., & Petty, J. W. (1994). *Small business management: An entrepreneurial emphasis*. Cincinnati, OH: South Western.

March, J. (1991). Exploration and exploitation in organizational learning. *Organization Science, 2*, 71-87.

Markman, G. D., & Baron, R. A. (2002). Individual differences and the pursuit of new ventures: A model of person-entrepreneurship fit. In J. Katz & T. M. Welbourne (Eds.), *Managing people in entrepreneurial organizations* (Vol. 5, pp. 23-54). Amsterdam: JAI Press.

Matusik, S., & Hill, C. (1998). The utilization of contingent work, knowledge creation, and competitive advantage. *Academy of Management Review, 23*, 680-697.

May, K. (1997). Work in the 21st century: Understanding the needs of small businesses. *The Industrial Organizational Psychologist, 35*(1), 94-97.

Ramstad, E. (1998, September 21). High rollers: How Trilogy Software trains its raw recruits to be risk-takers. *Wall Street Journal*.

Rousseau, D. M., & Libuser, C. (1997). Contingent work in high risk environments. *California Management Review, 39*, 103-123.

Stinchcombe, A. L. (1965). Social structure and organizations. In J. G. March (Ed.), *Handbook of organizations* (pp. 142-193). Chicago: Rand McNally.

Terpstra, D. E., & Olson, P. D. (1993). Entrepreneurial start-up and growth: A classification of problems. *Entrepreneurship: Theory and Practice, 17*(3), 5-21.

Thakur, S. P. (1999). Size of investment, opportunity choice and human resources in new venture growth: Some typologies. *Journal of Business Venturing, 14*(3), 283-309.

Van Maanen, J., & Schein, E. H. (1979). Toward a theory of organizational socialization. In B. M. Staw (Ed.), *Research in organizational behavior* (Vol. 1, pp. 209-264). Greenwich, CT: JAI Press.

Von Hippel, C., Mangum, S. L., Greenberg, D. B., Heneman, R. L., & Skoglind, J. D. (1997). Temporary employment: Can organization and employees both win? *Academy of Management Executive, 11*(1), 93-104.

Welbourne, T. M., & Andrews, A. O. (1996). Predicting the performance of initial public offerings: Should human resource management be in the equation? *Academy of Management Journal, 39*, 891-919.

Whitesome, D., & Schlesinger, L. A. (1995). *People Express*. Harvard Business School, Case No. 9-483-103.

Williamson, I. O. (2000, Fall). Employer legitimacy and recruitment success in small businesses. *Entrepreneurship: Theory and Practice*, 27-42.

Williamson, I. O., Cable, D. M., & Aldrich, H. E. (2002). Smaller but not necessarily weaker: How small businesses can overcome barriers to recruitment. In J. Katz & T. M. Welbourne (Eds.), *Managing people in entrepreneurial organizations:*

Learning from the merger of entrepreneurship and human resource management (pp. 83-106). Amsterdam: JAI Press.

Williamson, O. E. (1996). *The mechanisms of governance*. New York: Oxford University Press.

Windolf, P. (1986). Recruitment, selection, and internal labour markets in Britain and Germany. *Organizational Studies, 7,* 235-254.

Wysocki, B. (1996, August 19). High tech nomads write new program for future work. *Wall Street Journal.*

Zawacki, M. (2000). The Gospel according to Heestand. *Inside Business,* 14-17, 144-145.

CHAPTER 5

THE HIRING CHALLENGE

Recruitment in Small Firms

Alison E. Barber

Although small business owners suggest that hiring qualified workers is one of the greatest difficulties they face, the scholarly management literature has paid little attention to small firms' recruitment. This chapter reviews existing research describing the recruitment practices of small firms and concludes that, rather than mimic the practices of larger, well-established firms, small firms engage in different practices. However, it is unclear whether this distinctiveness leads to more effective recruitment. Studies of the impact of small firm recruitment practices, as well as investigations of the characteristics of job seekers who prefer small firms, are needed before we can make confident prescriptions for this important sector of the economy.

INTRODUCTION

There is no doubt that small firms employ a large portion of the population, both in the United States and abroad. Finding those employees appears to be a challenge. Surveys of small business owners suggest that

Human Resource Strategies for the High Growth Entrepreneurial Firm, 99–113
Copyright © 2006 by Information Age Publishing
All rights of reproduction in any form reserved.

hiring and retaining qualified workers is one of the greatest difficulties they face (Heneman, Tansky & Camp, 2000; Hornsby & Kuratko, 1990). Not only do they struggle in initially attracting employees (Bailey, 2002), they often later lose their employees to larger companies—what Schiller (1983) referred to as "corporate kidnaping"—creating a need for yet more recruiting.

Unfortunately, the scholarly management literature has paid little attention to the recruitment struggles of small firms. Instead, the vast majority of published studies of recruitment focus on large firms. This "large firm bias" has been noted and decried repeatedly (e.g., Barber, Wesson, Roberson, & Taylor, 1999; Carroll, Marchington, Earnshaw, & Taylor, 1999; Heneman & Berkley, 1999; Heneman et al., 2000; Jameson, 2000). It has left us unable to prescribe with any degree of confidence measures that small firms can take to address their recruitment concerns.

Rynes and Barber (1990) proposed that applicant attraction research could advance by the accumulation of solid descriptive findings that would serve as a foundation for prescriptive and theoretical research. Fortunately, we now have a significant number of descriptive studies regarding small firm employment practices, with reasonably consistent findings. The overall conclusion to be drawn from this recent body of work (reviewed briefly below) is that small firms do indeed differ from larger firms in their recruitment practices. As a result, concerns about generalizing from a literature dominated by the study of large firms appear to be well founded.

Although the emphasis on large firms is clearly a limitation from the standpoint of offering useful, practical advice to smaller employers, it may also provide untapped opportunities to advance the state of recruitment research. By focusing almost exclusively on large firms, recruitment researchers have, perhaps unwittingly, restricted variation in ways that limit our ability to identify interesting effects. As Katz, Aldrich, Welbourne, & Williams (2000) noted in the editors' introduction to a special issue of *Entrepreneurship: Theory and Practice* there are "ample opportunity for theory testing in a population (SMEs) that has been largely ignored by many organizational researchers" (p. 8). The goals of this chapter, then, are twofold: to encourage research that will improve our ability to provide useful advice to small firms, and to encourage researchers to use the differences between large and small firms as a means of extending our understanding of a variety of recruitment phenomena.

It is worth noting that the existing literature on small firm hiring practices from which this chapter draws does not differentiate between entrepreneurial start-ups and more traditional small firms. The recent boom in Internet start-up companies, and the desirability of employment in those organizations in their heyday, suggests that certain types of small firms, in specific industries at specific times, can be viewed quite differently from small firms in general. The importance of understanding these phenomena notwithstanding, the focus of this chapter is on the more general case.

RECRUITMENT PRACTICES IN SMALL FIRMS
A SUMMARY OF DESCRIPTIVE DATA

What little research exists on small firm recruitment has focused on describing and documenting small firm recruitment practices and activities. This research, while primarily descriptive in nature, is grounded in theoretical reasoning. For instance, Williamson (2000), citing institutional theory, argued that small firms could gain legitimacy by modeling the recruitment practices of large, well-established firms in their industry. This argument suggests that small firms may profit by mimicking the practices of larger firms; it stops short of suggesting that they actually do engage in such mimicry. Indeed, Williamson noted that small firms may lack the resources required to adopt the formal, bureaucratic recruitment procedures common in large firms. In a similar vein, Barber et al. (1999) argued that large firms are more likely than small firms to find formal recruitment procedures to be economically efficient. They also suggested that institutional pressures to conform are likely to be stronger for large firms because of their greater visibility. Integration of these theoretical arguments suggests a need to identify (a) whether small firms *do* mimic the formal, bureaucratic recruitment practices of large firms, a descriptive issue; and (b) whether small firms *should* mimic the formal, bureaucratic recruitment practices of large firms, a more prescriptive concern.

Research to date has focused on the descriptive question of whether the recruitment practices of large and small firms are similar or different. Methods employed in this research have varied. Studies have been conducted using different categorizations of small firms (e.g., fewer than 100 employees in Heneman & Berkley, 1999; fewer than 500 employees in Deshpande & Golhar, 1994); different locales (primarily, the United States and the United Kingdom); and a variety of industries. Methods have included in-depth case studies (e.g., Carroll et al., 1999) and large-scale surveys (e.g., Hornsby & Kuratko, 1990). Some studies have focused exclusively on small firms (e.g., Bartram, Lindley, Marshall, & Foster, 1995), while others have included large firms in their samples to allow direct comparison (e.g., Barber et al., 1999; Marsden, 1994).

Despite their methodological differences,[1] a number of consistent findings emerge across these studies. In general, they support the argument that recruitment practices differ in large and small firms, and that large firms use more formal and costly procedures than do small firms.

Recruitment Sources. In particular, numerous studies have concluded that small firms use recruitment sources that involve little advance planning and minimal expense. For example, small firms have been found to rely heavily on employee referrals, walk-in applications, and newspaper advertisements (Bartram et al., 1995; Carroll et al., 1999; Heneman & Berkley, 1999; Hornsby & Kuratko, 1990; Jameson, 2000; Marsden, 1994; Wagar & Langrock, 2003) and relatively unlikely to use college placement centers, executive search firms, or other third-party intermediaries (Heneman & Berkley, 1990; Hornsby & Kuratko, 1999).

The few studies that directly compared large and small firm practices reaffirm the degree to which small firms rely heavily on these informal methods and to some extent support the argument that small firms are distinctive in this regard. Although Deshpande and Golhar (1994) found heavy reliance on informal recruitment sources by the small firms in their sample, the sources used by large firms were also primarily informal. However, Barber et al. (1999) found that small firms were significantly more likely to rely on internal referrals and advertisements, and less likely to recruit on college campuses, than were large firms.

Two implications of small firm reliance on informal recruitment sources are noteworthy. First, evidence that small firms tend not to rely on colleges as a major source of new hires reinforces concern about the applicability of existing recruitment research to this employment sector. As many have noted (e.g., Barber, 1998; Rynes, 1991; Wanous & Colella, 1989), campus placement centers quite often are the setting for recruitment research. Perhaps inadvertently, researchers choosing this setting are limiting themselves to the study of large firms.

Second, the heavy reliance of small firms on internal postings and referrals from existing employees may have both positive and negative ramifications. Referrals often have been touted as means to reduce turnover, because employees recruited in this way will have prior knowledge about expectations and also because they will be screened by the employee doing the referral (Carroll et al., 1999). This argument was supported by early recruitment source research showing that employees hired via referrals tend to have longer tenure than employees recruited from other sources (e.g., Decker & Cornelius, 1979; Gannon, 1971). Even though later research failed to replicate these findings (Barber, 1998), small firms may be using this approach because they believe it to be effective, not merely because it is economically efficient and flexible with respect to timing. In addition, it is important to note that studies of recruitment source effectiveness have not differentiated between large and small firms. We do not know whether source effectiveness varies as a function of firm size; therefore it may be true that informal recruitment is more advantageous for small firms than for large.

A potential negative consequence of reliance on informal recruitment sources is the potential for extreme homogeneity within the workforce—a characteristic that can limit organizational effectiveness if taken too far (Kristof, 1996). Firms composed of highly similar individuals may become inflexible, unable to innovate and adapt as the firm's circumstances change (Schneider, Goldstein, & Smith, 1995.) One interesting area of research would explore the optimal degree of homogeneity within small firms.

Although the arguments made by Schneider and colleagues focus on personal qualities such as values and attitudes, it is also true that reliance on internal recruitment sources can have implications for racial/ethnic and gender diversity (Carroll et al., 1999). Heneman, Waldeck, and Chusnie (1996) suggested that segregated social relationships can create barriers to the recruitment of a diverse workforce if hiring is done through these social networks. Indeed, recent evidence suggests that small firms are somewhat less diverse than large firms. According to Headd (2000), small firms tend to employ smaller proportions of women, blacks, and Asians than do large firms. Interestingly, the employment of Hispanics in small firms is relatively large.

Finally, heavy reliance on informal recruitment may introduce additional sources of stress into the work environment. When new employees are recruited from the social networks of existing employees, the opportunity for nonwork conflicts to spill over into the employment setting is high and the risk of favoritism based on personal relationships increases. The "family" atmosphere that is said to characterize many small firms is not necessarily an unmixed blessing (Goss, 1988; Ram & Holliday, 1993).

Other recruitment practices. Studies of small firm recruitment have examined a wide variety of practices in addition to recruiting sources. Several interesting findings appear in individual studies. Although confirmation and replication are needed, these findings warrant discussion.

First, it appears that large firms are engaged in a greater variety of recruitment practices than small firms. Marsden (1994) concluded that large firms used a broader array of recruitment sources overall than small firms did, and Barber et al. (1999) found that large firms employed a wider array of selection techniques than small firms did. Large firms, then, are in a better position to capitalize on the compensatory strengths and weaknesses of different practices. This result is not surprising, given the greater resources that large firms can invest in human resource practices and the greater likelihood that they will have professional human resource staffs (Barber et al., 1999; Heneman & Berkley, 1999). However, it does suggest the importance of comparing sets of recruitment practices when studying the recruitment effectiveness of large versus small firms.

Second, Barber et al. (1999) found that recruitment cycles for small firms were significantly shorter than the cycles common among large firms. They found that large firms began the recruitment practices sooner (relative to the time they needed the employee on board), allowed more time between offer acceptance and start date, and were more flexible with respect to start date. This finding clearly has implications for job searchers, who may want to match the time they have available to search with the search cycles of their desired employers. It may also have implications for recruitment, as a compressed hiring cycle may be attractive to some candidates and unattractive to others.

Finally, Heneman and Berkley (1999) found that a substantial number of the small firms extended job offers verbally, with no written confirmation. Although I know of no data speaking directly to this issue in large firms, most observers would agree that verbal-only offers are rare in the more bureaucratic environment of large firms. Interestingly, the practice of extending offers in verbal form had a stronger impact on recruitment outcomes than any other practice that Heneman and Berkley studied. Overall, the observed impact was negative: it was associated with more rapid filling of positions, but fewer applicants per vacancy and lower probability that applicants would accept offers.

Heneman and Berkley could only speculate as to the reasons for this finding. It stands in interesting contrast to findings regarding generally negative applicant reactions to formal legal statements regarding employment-at-will that are sometimes included in recruitment and hiring materials (Schwoerer & Rosen, 1989; Wayland, Clay, & Payne, 1993). Apparently it is possible to be too formal, as well as too informal, in the final offer stage of recruitment. Research investigating the formality of offers will be more likely to discover interesting phenomena if it includes both large and small firms; by including both, the range of formality is likely to be increased.

QUALIFICATIONS SOUGHT IN RECRUITMENT

One interesting debate in the existing literature on small firm recruitment involves the qualifications sought by large versus small firms (Barber et al., 1999; Bartram et al., 1995; Pritchard & Fidler, 1993). Many have argued that large firms are inclined to begin the recruitment process with a formal job description from which they identify the specific knowledge, skills, and abilities (KSAs) required to perform the job effectively.

Recruitment is then oriented toward identifying individuals who posses those KSAs. Small firms, in contrast, are unlikely to have formally established job descriptions, both because of a general lack of formalized HR procedures but also because of the often fluid nature of jobs in a rapidly growing organization (Katz et al., 2000). Instead, small firms might seek general personal characteristics such as motivation, work ethic, and interpersonal skills that would be of value across a wide range of job responsibilities. As Carroll et al. (1999) argued, small firms might rely heavily on finding employees who would "fit in" to the culture and social environment of their organization.

Heneman et al. (2000) provided evidence in support of this argument. In their survey of CEOs and founders of SMEs, they noted a concern with finding employees whose beliefs, values, and interests were aligned with those of the organization, and significantly less emphasis on finding employees whose knowledge, skills, and abilities matched those of a specific job. In other words, Heneman et al. suggested, leaders of small firms were more concerned with person-organization fit than with person-job fit (Kristof, 1996).

Relatively little research directly addresses the question of whether large and small firms recruit for different types of qualifications. Carroll et al. (1999), on the basis of case studies of 40 small firms in five sectors of the U.K., concluded that the "dominant emphasis" (p. 249) in recruitment was on interpersonal fit. Bartram et al. (1995) found that the qualifications considered most important by small firms were integrity, conscientiousness, and general personality; academic or vocational credentials and work experience were viewed as relatively unimportant. Barber et al. (1999) were unable to document differences in the importance of personal qualities such as motivation and interpersonal ability to small firms versus large. However, they did provide evidence that small firms were less concerned with traditional, objective indicators of ability such as academic credentials than were large firms.

Interestingly, there does appear to be some synergy between the recruitment sources used and the qualifications sought by small firms. Recruits referred to the organization by existing members are likely to share values, beliefs, and other social norms already existing in the organization. Thus referrals can lead to better person-organization fit, which appears to be what the organizations want. Although the merits of extreme levels of fit can be debated, this issue suggests that recruitment practices and their effectiveness should be assessed in light of the organization's goals—in particular, what sort of fit they are trying to achieve through their hiring.

RECRUITMENT AND INDUCEMENTS/JOB ATTRIBUTES

Rynes and Barber (1990) noted that employees are attracted to organizations not only by recruitment practices, but also (and importantly) by the nature of the opportunities offered to the applicant (what they referred to as inducements.) As a result, it is essential to discuss the fundamental attractiveness of jobs in large versus small firms in this chapter. Two points of view will be presented: one treats smallness as a liability, the other as a strength.

Early research into the role of job or organization attributes in job search sought to identify which aspects of work—pay, opportunities for advancement, work climate, etc.—were most influential when applicants chose positions. The variety of attributes available, the complicated tradeoffs that can occur among attributes, and the diversity of individual attribute preferences have made it difficult to provide succinct answers to that question. The question of interest to small firm recruitment, however, is whether the package of attributes offered by small firms is sufficiently appealing. As noted earlier, small firms do struggle in recruitment, and one possible explanation is that they simply are not as attractive as larger firms. This perspective might be referred to as the "liability of smallness" from a recruitment standpoint, in that small firms do not have the resources to provide inducements common in larger firms (Heneman & Berkley, 1999). It is widely known that compensation levels in small firms tend to be lower than in large firms (e.g., Paez, 2003), particularly when traditional forms of compensation (wages and salaries) are assessed. In addition, small firms have been described as offering fewer opportunities for advancement, less training, more stressful interpersonal relationships, and lower job security than can be found in large firms (Carroll et al., 1999; Jameson, 2000).

This perspective is particularly noteworthy in light of previously cited findings regarding recruiting cycles. To the extent that the advance recruitment planning of large firms allows them to present their offers to the marketplace earlier, they may be able to hire their pick of the available candidates, all of whom presumably would prefer to work for the more attractive (large) firms. This would leave the relatively less desirable candidates for the smaller firms—a troubling outcome for this important economic sector.

However, there is an alternative view. Some take the perspective that "small is beautiful," arguing that small firms offer a more personal and supportive working environment, greater responsibility, and a greater likelihood of meaningful work experience, particularly early on in one's career (Carroll et al., 1999; "Graduates Urged," 2000). Individuals who work in small firms may also feel much closer, and more responsible for, the organization's outcomes. This closeness can facilitate performance-based reward systems, and may be particularly attractive to certain types of employees, in particular innovators who anticipate delivering superior performance (Zenger, 1994). Further, there is some evidence that small firms do provide significant opportunities for training and advancement, even if not as great as those provided by large firms (Carroll et al., 1999).

Empirically assessing the attractiveness of large and small firms from an objective standpoint would be extraordinarily difficult, as it would require identifying, measuring, and appropriately weighting a vast set of attributes in a way that would allow for individual differences in preference. An alternative approach would be to assess the preferences of job applicants—that is, to identify whether they view smallness as an asset or a liability. Barber et al. (1999) provide some data to address this issue. In a sample of graduating college students, they found that some applicants did have distinct preferences for large firms, others were indifferent to firm size, and still others had clear preferences for small firms. The group of applicants preferring large firms was significantly larger than the group preferring small firms. Unfortunately, the study did not identify why the job seekers held these preferences. A variety of explanations can be considered. First, applicants might have different attribute preferences, with some desiring attributes present in large firms and others desiring attributes common in small firms. Second, applicants might have different perceptions of what kind of attributes are offered by large versus small firms. Both of these explanations suggest that beauty is in the eye of the beholder . . . in this case the job seeker. Third, applicants may assess their likelihood of gaining employment with large versus small firms, and might self-select into the segment where they believe they will be most successful. Further research into this issue would be useful, as it would allow small firms to target those individuals most likely to be interested in the jobs they offer.

Interestingly, Heneman and Berkley (1999) did demonstrate within a set of small firms that those providing greater inducements were more attractive. In particular, they found that small firms offering superior financial inducements experienced greater recruitment success than similarly sized firms that offered less generous financial packages. Further research in this area might help small firms pinpoint changes in inducements that could have significant impact on recruitment outcomes.

CONVEYING THE RECRUITMENT MESSAGE

Schwab, Rynes, and Aldag (1987) differentiated the recruitment medium from the recruitment message. In addition to identifying what information to provide about their employment opportunities, small firms must also find efficient and effective means of communicating that information. As long as small firms rely on informal recruitment sources, their attributes can be conveyed by word of mouth. But when small firms decide to extend their recruitment networks, the best methods for reaching applicants are unclear.

One medium that merits further investigation is the internet. Internet recruitment can be both inexpensive and fast, qualities important to small firms. Participation in well-known employment sites (e.g., monster.com) could facilitate reaching a much broader pool of applicants. Some evidence suggests that small firms are unlikely to engage in internet-based recruitment, however. Wagar and Langrock (2003), looking at the recruitment practices of Canadian firms with fewer than 100 employees, found that internet recruitment was the least used method for identifying potential employees. Further, it has been suggested that while internet recruitment can be flexible and inexpensive, it is most likely to have positive results only after a sustained period of aggressive use ("Patience Pays Off," 1997); small firms are unlikely to engage in this much recruitment in any medium. Additional work in this rapidly changing area is needed.

Alternatively, researchers could examine the efficacy of radio advertisement, a more traditional tool, as a medium for small firm recruitment. Again, this approach is flexible and relatively inexpensive. It also has an advantage in that it would raise public awareness of the firm within the community; radio advertisements are heard by many individuals who are not seeking work. The importance of such awareness from a recruitment standpoint is addressed below.

Firm familiarity.   One challenge that small firms are particularly likely to encounter is their lack of familiarity to the general public (Williamson, 2000). Recent recruitment research has found that the degree to which a firm is familiar is a particularly important element in applicant attraction (Gatewood, Gowan, & Lautenschlager, 1993; Luce, Barber, & Hillman, 2001; Turban & Greening, 1997). Firms that are larger tend to be more familiar (Turban & Greening, 1997), and even familiarity resulting from negative publicity can have a positive impact on attraction (Luce et al., 2001).

This finding is not surprising, given that the positive relationship between exposure to an object and evaluation of that object was established in the decision-making literature many years ago (e.g., Zajonc, 1968). However, it is disturbing in the context of small firm recruitment. If small firms are rejected (or simply ignored) at the outset because they are unfamiliar, they lack an opportunity to present their merits as an employer. Further, it is unclear how any given small employer might cost-effectively increase its familiarity. In addition to the direct role of size as a factor explaining familiarity, Turban and Greening (1997) found that familiar firms tended to have more media exposure, larger advertising budgets, more formal recruiting materials, and a greater presence in campus placement—all factors that tend to be associated with size. And while some large firms have invested heavily in "image" advertising campaigns to shape the way they are perceived by the public, it is unlikely that small firms could afford to engage in such an intervention.

Further research into the role of familiarity in attraction is warranted. It should be noted that the studies referenced above all use college students as subjects. Although these students were (or were soon to be) searching for jobs, it is possible that job searchers at other stages of their career might view familiarity differently. In addition, the studies focused on the familiarity or unfamiliarity of primarily large firms. By drawing on firms represented in the S&P 500 (Luce et al., 2001) or *Fortune* ratings (Turban & Greening, 1997), the studies are unlikely to have included firms with fewer than 500 employees. As a result we do not know whether familiarity is important in attraction to small firms. It may be that small firms are "forgiven" for being unfamiliar—in other words that being unfamiliar is an expectation and not a concern when the firm is small. On the other hand, it may be that small firms are unattractive simply because they are unfamiliar, and that the impact of familiarity is presently being underestimated due to a restriction in range.

RECRUITMENT EFFECTIVENESS

The existing literature suggests that small firms do not mimic the recruitment practices of large firms. The question of whether or not they should do so remains unanswered. Are the different approaches chosen by small firms truly better for them, or would the adoption of large-firm practices improve their recruiting effectivness?

To address this question thoughtfully, we first must consider what constitutes effective recruitment. Heneman and Berkley (1999), in one of the few studies to explicitly address effectiveness, followed Rynes and Barber's (1990) arguments that attraction is a sequential process, with specific practices likely to have impact at particular phases of the process. They used a set of four outcome measures to capture the effectiveness of recruitment at different phases of the recruitment cycle: the number of applicants per vacancy, average number of days taken to fill a vacancy, job offer acceptance rate, and the six-month retention rate for new hires. The importance of this comprehensive approach was underscored by the fact that they did find certain practices to be effective at one stage and not at others. It is unlikely that a single measure of recruitment effectiveness will capture a sufficient range of important outcomes.

Interestingly, Barber et al. (1999) found recruitment effectiveness to be defined differently by small firms than by large. They used an open-ended item asking survey respondents how they evaluated recruitment effectiveness. Large firms were more likely than small to assess effectiveness on the basis of short-term outcomes such as whether established recruiting goals had been met. Small firms were more likely than large to evaluate effectiveness on the basis on longer-term outcomes (specifically, new hire performance and retention.) Obviously, this difference reinforces the importance of acquiring multiple measures of recruitment success and of capturing both short and long-term outcomes. It also complicates any attempts to compare recruitment effectiveness across large and small firms.

Heneman and Berkley (1999) provide an assessment of the relationship between small firms' recruitment practices and recruitment effectiveness outcomes. The following practices were identified as having a positive impact on recruitment effectiveness: use of walk-ins, employee referrals, past applications, and newspaper ads were related to a lower number of days required to fill positions; the use of worksite tours was associated with lower acceptance rates, while the use of written brochures was associated with lower retention rates; firms who had an HR manager evaluate their applicants experienced higher retention rates; firms who did not put their job offers into writing experienced fewer average days to fill the position but also lower acceptance rates. At this point, then, we can argue that recruitment practices are related to outcomes—in other words, the choices that firms make regarding these practices do matter. However, we are still not in a position to provide empirical evidence as to whether small firms recruit more or less effectively than large. Until this evidence is obtained, questions about the value of mimicking large firm practices will remain unanswered.

CONCLUSION

This chapter has presented an array of issues related to small firms' recruitment practices and outcomes. What can we conclude? First, it does appear that recruitment is a challenge for small firms. Reports "from the field" tell us so, and their credibility is enhanced by certain measurable characteristics (low pay, low familiarity) that suggest small firms may be less visible or less attractive to at least some job searchers. Second, we know that small firms engage in recruitment practices that are somewhat different from those adopted by large firms.

We know far less about whether these differences in practice are beneficial to the small firms, or whether they might be better off mimicking the practices of their larger competitors. This is an important issue, as there is a tendency to believe that large firm practices are "state of the art" and therefore the standard other (smaller) firms should aspire to. But if the costs of these practices are too high relative to the payoff acquired, or if they would lose their effectiveness when transferred into a small firm's culture, then mimicry could be on balance dysfunctional. Contingency models have been proposed for HR strategies in general, and a thorough consideration of how "best practices" in recruitment might vary by firm size could shed needed light.

We also know relatively little about what sorts of individuals might prefer small firm employment, although evidence suggests that those individuals do exist. In addition, it appears that small firms seek applicants with slightly different profiles than those most commonly sought by large firms. Research applying "fit" models to recruitment might yield important insights into the allocation of human capital across large and small firms.

Finally, the differences in recruiting practices of large and small firms provides recruitment scholars with an opportunity to examine variations in many different recruitment practices—variations whose impact might go unnoticed if studied within either the large or the small firm context. Examples include the formality of job offers, use of the internet in recruitment, or the impact of heavy reliance on referrals in hiring.

Given the importance of small firms to the modern economy, and with the expanded research opportunities provided by the study of small firms, it is a bit puzzling that so little attention has been paid to small firm recruitment. It is time for recruitment scholars to move beyond the descriptive work cited above and use what we know to tackle more complex issues, ideally leading to better theoretical understanding and more confident prescriptions for practice.

NOTE

1.   For the purposes of this chapter, research focusing on firms with fewer than 500 employees will be considered small firm research.

REFERENCES

Bailey, J. (2002, February 19). Community colleges can help small firms with staffing. *The Wall Street Journal*, B-2.

Barber, A. E. (1998). *Personnel recruitment research: Individual and organizational perspectives.* Thousand Oaks, CA: Sage.

Barber, A. E., Wesson, M. J., Roberson, Q. M., & Taylor, M. S. (1999). A tale of two job markets: Organizational size and its effects on hiring practices and job search behavior. *Personnel Psychology, 52,* 841-867.

Bartram, D., Lindley, P. A., Marshall, L., & Foster, J. (1995). The recruitment and selection of young people by small business. *Journal of Occupational and Organizational Psychology, 68,* 339-358.

Carroll, M., Marchington, M., Earnshaw, J., & Taylor, S. (1999). Recruitment in small firms: Processes, methods and problems. *Employee Relations, 21*(3), 236-250.

Decker, P. J., & Cornelius, E. T. III. (1979). A note on recruiting sources and job satisfaction. *Journal of Applied Psychology, 64,* 463-464.

Deshpande, S. P., & Golhar, D. Y. (1994). HRM practices in large and small manufacturing firms: A comparative study. *Journal of Small Business Management, 32,* 49-56.

Gannon, M. J. (1971). Sources of referral and employee turnover. *Journal of Applied Psychology, 55,* 226-228.

Gatewood, R. D. Gowan, M. A., & Lautenschlager, G. J. (1993). Corporate image, recruitment image, and initial job choice decisions. *Academy of Management Journal, 36,* 414-427.

Goss, D. M. (1988). Social harmony and the small firm: A reappraisal. *Sociological Review, 36*(1), 114-132.

Graduates urged to join small firms. (2002). *Education and Training, 2*(6), 388.

Headd, B. (2000). The characteristics of small business employees. *Monthly Labor Review, 123*(4), 13-18.

Heneman, H. G. III, & Berkley, R. A. (1999). Applicant attraction practices and outcomes among small businesses. *Journal of Small Business Management, 37,* 53-74.

Heneman, R. L., Tansky, J. W., & Camp, S. M. (2000). Human resource management practices in small and medium-sized enterprises: Unanswered questions and future research perspectives. *Entrepreneurship: Theory and Practice,* 11-26.

Heneman, R. L., Waldeck, N. E., & Chusnie, M. (1996). Diversity considerations in staffing decision-making. In E. E. Kossek & S. A. Lobel (Eds.), *Managing diversity: Human resource strategies for transforming the workplace* (pp. 74-102). Cambridge, MA: Blackwell.

Hornsby, J. S., & Kuratko, D. F. (1990, July). Human resource management in small business: Critical issues for the 1990's. *Journal of Small Business Management,* 9-18.

Jameson, S. M. (2000). Recruitment and training in small firms. *Journal of European Industrial Training, 2*(1), 43-49.

Katz, J. A., Aldrich, H. E., Welbourne, T. M., & Williams, P. M. (2000). Guest editor's comments special issue on human resource management and the SME: Toward a new synthesis. *Entrepreneurship: Theory and Practice,* 7-10.

Kristof, A. L. (1996). Person-organization fit: An integrative review of its conceptualizations, measurement, and implications. *Personnel Psychology,* 49,1-50.

Luce, R. A., Barber, A. E., & Hillman, A. J. (2001). Good deeds and misdeeds: A mediated model of the effect of corporate social performance on organizational attractiveness. *Business & Society, 40*(4), 397-415.

Marsden, P. V. (1994). The hiring process: Recruitment Methods. *American Behavioral Scientist, 37*, 979-991.

Paez, P. (2003). The effects of firm size on wages in Colorado: A case study. *Monthly Labor Review, 126*(7), 11-17.

Patience pays off in internet recruitment. (1997, September). *HRFocus, 74*(9), 12.

Pritchard, C. J., & Fidler, P. P. (1993). What small firms look for in new-graduate candidates. *Journal of Career Planning and Employment, 53*, 45-50.

Ram, M., & Holliday, R. (1993). Relative merits: Family culture and kinship in small firms. *Sociology, 27*(4), 629-49.

Rynes, S. L. (1991). Recruitment, job choice, and post-hire consequences. In M. D. Dunnette & L. M. Hough (Eds.), *Handbook of industrial and organizational psychology* (Vol. 2, pp. 399-444). Palo Alto, CA: Consulting Psychologists Press.

Rynes, S. L., & Barber, A. E. (1990). Applicant attraction strategies: An organizational perspective. *Academy of Management Review, 15*, 286-310.

Schiller, B. R. (1983). "Corporate kidnap" of the small-business employee. *Public Interest, 72*, 72-87.

Schneider, B., Goldstein, H. W., & Smith, D. B. (1995). The ASA framework: An update. *Personnel Psychology, 48*, 747-773.

Schwab, D. P., Rynes, S. L., & Aldag, R. A. (1987). Theories and research on job search and choice. In K. Rowland & G. Ferris (Eds.), *Research in personnel and human resource management* (Vol. 5, pp. 129-166). Greenwich, CT: JAI Press.

Schwoerer, C., & Rosen, B. (1989). Effects of employment at will policies and compensation policies on corporate image and job pursuit intentions. *Journal of Applied Psychology, 74*, 653-656.

Turban, D. B., & Greening, D. W. (1997). Corporate social performance and organizational attractiveness to prospective employees. *Academy of Management Journal, 40*, 658-672.

Wagar, T., & Langrock, L. (2003, July). Small firms offline on internet recruitment. *Canadian HR Reporter, 16*(13), 5.

Wanous, J. P., & Colella, A. (1989). Organizational entry research: Current status and future directions. In K. Rowland & G. Ferris (Eds.), *Research In personnel and human resources management* (Vol. 7, pp. 59-120). Greenwich, CT: JAI Press.

Wayland, R. F., Clay, J. M., & Payne, P. L. (1993). Employment at will statements: Perceptions of job applicants. *International Journal of Manpower, 14*, 22-33.

Williamson, I. O. (2000). Employer legitimacy and recruitment success in small businesses. *Entrepreneurship: Theory and Practice*, 27-42.

Zajonc, R. B. (1968). The attitudinal effects of mere exposure. *Journal of Personality and Social Psychology, 9*, 1-27.

Zenger, T. R. (1994). Explaining organizational diseconomies of scale in R&D: Agency problems and the allocation of engineering talent, ideas, and effort by firm size. *Management Science, 40*(6), 708-729.

CHAPTER 6

PERFORMANCE MANAGEMENT IN SMALL AND HIGH GROWTH COMPANIES

Robert L. Cardy and Janice S. Miller

The chapter presents a model of performance management that identifies critical steps in the process. Key considerations such as purpose of appraisal, type of criteria and their focus are also summarized. Five key assumptions regarding the small and high growth business environment distinguish it from more typical and less entrepreneurial endeavors. Each of these assumptions carries implications for performance management that demand attention so that the performance management system fits and complements characteristics of the organization in which it operates. The chapter advocates a dual purpose appraisal system that includes developmental and administrative functions, emphasis on behavioral as well as outcome assessment, and a move away from task-based performance criteria toward one that also considers values and roles.

Human Resource Strategies for the High Growth Entrepreneurial Firm, 115–133
Copyright © 2006 by Information Age Publishing
All rights of reproduction in any form reserved.

INTRODUCTION

The purpose of this paper is to explore the process of performance management in the setting of small and high growth (S & HG) companies. We will begin with an overall description of performance management, identifying the major components integral to an effective performance management system. We will then consider the setting of S & HG companies. Our thrust here will be on identifying some of the characteristics of these organizational environments that may be important for the conduct of performance management. Following identification of these characteristics, we will turn our attention to effective performance management in S & HG companies. We will identify system characteristics and skills needed for effective performance management in the S & HG setting. The needed system characteristics provide implications for the design of effective performance management systems within these settings, and the needed skills identify management competencies required for performance management within these firms. The system and skill characteristics that we will identify also provide direction for research focusing on performance management in S & HG settings. We next turn to a consideration of the domain of performance management.

PERFORMANCE MANAGEMENT

Performance management is necessary to maintain and improve performance. Without evaluation and feedback, there is no basis for maintaining and improving performance. Maximizing performance requires a careful and committed approach to evaluation and feedback. However, effective performance management is a process that requires much more than simply evaluation and feedback. Performance management includes a number of steps and each must be done adequately for performance to be maintained or to improve.

Figure 6.1 presents a model of the performance management process that identifies each of the steps critical to a complete performance management process. The model is an adaptation of the model presented by Cardy (2004). The model starts with performance. Thus, the first issue for effective performance management is identifying what performance consists of. In other words, just what is performance? Fundamentally, performance consists of either behaviors or outcomes. Performance is commonly viewed as either what people do (behaviors) or what they accomplish (outcomes). We will discuss the behavioral and outcome approaches in more detail when we consider effective performance management in S & HG settings.

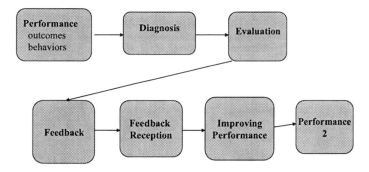

Figure 6.1.   Performance management model.

As depicted in Figure 6.1, performance management includes diagnosis. That is, performance needs to be observed and diagnosed as to the causes for performance and changes that need to be made. Diagnosis is critical if performance is to be improved. Just as with a medical setting in which an accurate diagnosis is needed if the patient is to get well, accurate diagnosis of performance is needed if performance is to be improved. In addition to diagnosing the causes of performance, effective performance management includes evaluation of performance. That is, judgments must be made as to the worth of observed performance. Given the causal factors at play, how should the behaviors or outcomes be assessed? Of course these assessments are of no use to improving performance unless they are conveyed to workers. Thus, feedback is identified in the model as the next critical step. Finally, effective performance management includes taking deliberate and focused actions to improve performance. Depending on the causes identified in the diagnosis stage, performance improvement actions may include training, motivation, or a variety of other possibilities.

In everyday organizational life, the actions identified as separate steps in the model meld into a seamless flow. However, breaking the process into separate steps offers the advantage of clarifying what needs to be done and what skills are needed for effective performance management. Problems in the process can also best be addressed by considering each of the steps and how each is being conducted.

Consideration of the model suggests that there are skills that are key to effective performance management. These key skills are summarized in Table 6.1. As presented in the table, diagnosis, evaluation, and feedback are skills needed for performance management to be carried out effectively. Managers, or whoever is responsible for performance management, need to be able to make fair and accurate diagnostic judgments.

Table 6.1.   Some Key Performance Management Skills

Diagnosis
    Fair & Accurate
Evaluation
    Fair & Accurate
Feedback
    Effective & Limits Emotional Reaction

Diagnosis requires understanding of the performance domain and factors that can influence performance. The manager needs to be familiar with and be able to differentiate between person and system factors. In other words, the manager needs to be able to identify the extent to which performance is due to characteristics of the worker or due to characteristics of the work environment. The manager also needs to be able to observe performance and to make sense of the pattern of the performance.

In addition to diagnostic skills, effective performance management requires skill in evaluation. Performance evaluation must also be done in a fair and accurate manner if the management system is to be an effective tool. Evaluation must be based on appropriate performance characteristics, the characteristics that the organization has identified as defining performance. The manager must be able to keep other characteristics, such as personal characteristics of the worker and affect of the manager, out of the performance evaluation process. Evaluations should not be inordinately easy or tough. Thus, a manager needs to have a sense of the norms in the organization and what is an acceptable evaluation.

Another critical skill area is feedback. Managers need to be able to effectively convey performance evaluations and identify directions for performance improvement. The feedback needs to be conveyed in a way that limits possible emotional reactions from workers. A defensive and emotional response would likely lead to conflict rather than performance improvement. Thus, effective performance management requires that managers have sensitivity to possible emotional reactions and the capability to avoid those reactions.

Extant research and rational consideration suggest key system characteristics regarding performance management. These key system characteristics are summarized in Table 6.2. First, the purpose for the system is an important overarching characteristic. It is common to generally classify the purpose for a performance management system as either administrative or developmental. The purpose for a performance management system has been found to influence performance evaluations and the accuracy of those evaluations (Dobbins, Cardy, & Truxillo, 1988). A per-

**Table 6.2.   Some Key Considerations Regarding
the Performance Management System**

Purpose
Administrative
Developmental
Type of Criteria
Outcomes
Behaviors
Focus of Criteria
Job/Task
Role
Values

formance management system classified as having an administrative purpose would focus on using the performance management system to support personnel decisions, such as layoffs, merit pay distribution, and promotion. With an administrative purpose, the performance management system is being used as an evaluation tool. A performance management system classified as having a developmental purpose would focus on using the performance management system to improve performance, such as through feedback and action planning. With a developmental purpose, the performance management system is being used as a performance improvement tool.

Another key characteristic of a performance management system is the type of criterion used to define and measure performance. Criteria focus the attention and efforts of workers and indicate what is more or less important in terms of performance. Performance criteria are commonly classified as either outcome or behaviorally based. A performance management system employing outcomes as performance criteria offers clear and unambiguous measures. Did the worker achieve the goal? What amount was produced? How many units were sold? These and other related issues are examples of outcome measure of performance. Typically, these types of measures are straightforward and can be easily measured. However, an important disadvantage of outcome criteria is that they don't identify the process by which performance can be improved. It may be clear, for example, that a worker hasn't made the target amount of sales for the quarter. However, what to do about the problem is not clear from the outcome criterion. Clarifying what is needed in order to obtain the desired outcomes is a strength of behavioral criteria. Behavioral criteria identify the types of actions workers should take and should avoid in performing their job duties. The process of performance is the focus of behavioral criteria. However, these behaviors will not necessarily lead to the desired outcomes. In addition, the types of behaviors workers engage in is often a more ambiguous judgment than determining whether outcomes were achieved. In sum, the nature of criteria is an important characteristic of a performance management system, but both outcomes and behavioral criteria have advantages and disadvantages.

Finally, another key characteristic of a performance management system is the focus of the criteria. That is, do the criteria center on task or on some other level of performance? Performance criteria have traditionally been focused on the tasks performed by workers. A job analysis, for example, would define the job as composed of a variety of duty areas and associated tasks. Performance criteria then would be developed for each of these duty areas or tasks. However, some organizations are focusing on roles played by workers, rather than on a fixed set of tasks. The role approach recognizes that the tasks performed by workers can change given differing demands and other circumstances. Another possible approach to capturing and measuring job performance is to focus on values. Organizations often identify their core values as part of their mission statement development and strategic planning. These values can be a basis for developing criteria that measure the extent to which workers are aligned with the core values of the organization.

THE SETTING OF SMALL AND HIGH GROWTH COMPANIES

Organizational environments are not unitary and our purpose here is to focus on the environment of small and high growth companies. Table 6.3 presents our assumptions concerning the S & HG environment. One of our key assumptions is the criticality of performance in S & HG companies. The basis for this assumption is the lack of slack resources in entrepreneurial and small business settings. In large organizations, a poor performer or an episode of poor performance may not make a noticeable difference in performance of the organization. However, in an S & HG environment, a poor performer or an episode of poor performance could mean the loss of a customer and conceivably put the organization out of business.

Our second assumption is that the work processes in small and entrepreneurial enterprises are less fixed than in larger organizations. In part, this assumption is based on the fact that work processes in S & HG settings are less established than in more mature and larger organizations. In addition, the smaller size of entrepreneurial ventures means that work

Table 6.3.   The Small & High Growth Environment: Assumptions

Performance is critical. Poor performance could cost a client or even the business.

The best laid plans can go awry. Work processes are less established and less buffered from environmental forces.

A competitive advantage is closeness to the customer, but customer preferences and needs can change in ways that are difficult to predict. Agility & adaptability are related competitive advantages.

Bureaucracy of rules, procedures, and task descriptions largely does not exist nor is it desired.

Staffing may be inadequate and people may need to take on a variety of duties.

processes are likely less buffered from environmental influences than those in their more mature and larger counterparts. On the positive side, the lack of regimentation in work processes means that small and entrepreneurial ventures have the possibility of being quickly responsive to changing environmental conditions. On the other hand, this lack of establishment and permanence in work processes means that the core of S & HG operations can be characterized as more changeable, even volatile, in comparison to larger firms.

A third assumption is that most small and entrepreneurial ventures are, or at least have the potential to be, close to the customer. If a small or entrepreneurial enterprise is not closely aligned and serves the needs of customers, it probably won't exist for long. Close alignment with customers can be an important competitive advantage for S & HG organizations. However, customer needs and preferences are not static and can be difficult to predict. S & HG organizations need to be agile and adaptive in order to capitalize on their ability to be close to the customer. Being overly structured and fixed in the work process and the consequent services or products can be a serious market disadvantage for a small or entrepreneurial organization.

Fourth, small and entrepreneurial enterprises often eschew bureaucracy. Bureaucracy can, as pointed out in the above assumption, get in the way of remaining close to the customer. However, bureaucracy, rules, set procedures, and careful task descriptions are often simply not preferred in S & HG companies. Many entrepreneurial organizations are started by individuals as alternatives to the way in which their large and former employers did business. Many of S & HG companies are based on a spirit of independence and self-sufficiency, rather than on structure and bureaucracy. It can be the bureaucracy that leads some entrepreneurs to begin their own organizations. Thus, we assume that in many S & HG organizations that highly structured work processes are not desired.

A final key assumption is that staffing in small and entrepreneurial enterprises are at a minimum level. Costs, including labor costs, must be kept low in small organizations. In addition, hiring is a critical decision in S & HG organizations since hiring the wrong person could be devastating to the business. Thus, hiring is not done lightly and S & HG organizations are cautious in making sure that they hire the right people. Cost and personnel concerns have the effect of keeping staffing at minimum levels in S & HG organizations. An important implication of this assumption is that people in S & HG organizations often need to take on a variety of tasks. Since staffing isn't flush, workers may need to wear a variety of hats and perform a wide variety of duties.

IMPLICATIONS FOR PERFORMANCE MANAGEMENT

Performance management is not a one-size-fits-all proposition. In order to be maximally effective, performance management must fit and complement the organizational characteristics in which it operates. We next turn to a consideration of the type of performance management characteristics that might best fit and be most effective in S & HG environments. First, we consider what can be concluded about S & HG environments that may have important implications for performance management.

The above discussion presented our assumptions concerning the typical S & HG organizational environment. What can be derived from these assumptions? What are the characteristics of the S & HG environment that have implications for performance management? Table 6.4 summarizes some potentially important conclusions about the S & HG organizational environment. One conclusion that can be drawn about the typical S & HG environment is that the work process is dynamic. Change is something that can be constant in these organizations. They are not well buffered from environmental volatilities and customers may have various and changing demands. Further, while the tasks and work procedures may not be fixed, performance is absolutely critical in S & HG organizations. Regardless of the dynamic nature of the environment, the very survival of S & HG organizations requires that goods still be produced, services, provided, and sales made. Another important conclusion that can be drawn about the typical S & HG environment is that a breadth of capabilities is needed by workers in order to perform effectively. Finally, the dynamic and unstructured environment coupled with the importance of performance underscores the importance of personal characteristics, such as interpersonal skills and values. That is, people must be able to get along

Table 6.4.

Conclusions
Work process is dynamic.
Tasks & procedures may not be fixed, but performance is still critical.
Breadth of capabilities is needed.
Personal characteristics, such as interpersonal skills, are mandatory.

and communicate and be able to determine what should be done, even if policies and procedures aren't available.

With the above summarization in mind, we next examine the performance management characteristics that might best fit with this organizational environment. We will consider each of the key performance management system characteristics, purpose, type of criteria, and focus of criteria. For each of these aspects, we explore the performance management qualities that might best fit and be most effective in an S & HG environment.

Purpose

As discussed previously, the purpose for a performance management system can basically be classified as either administrative or developmental. In an S & HG setting, performance is critical. Products need to be made, services need to be provided, and/or sales need to be closed. Lack of slack resources amplifies the importance of bottom-line performance in S & HG organizations. Poor performance could just be enough to get an S & HG organization off track or to threaten its very survival. Competitiveness, and maintaining a strategic trajectory, demands that performance management emphasizes performance. For example, using performance measures for a merit pay system or for recognition are ways to achieve needed performance outcomes. Research supports the conclusion that contingent reward and recognition are effective means for improving performance (Cooke, 1994). Further, merit pay and recognition programs can send signals and clarify to workers what is important and how they should allocate their time and effort. In sum, the importance of performance in S & HG organizations leads to the need for a performance management system with an administrative purpose.

The volatility and dynamic environment in S & HG organizations emphasizes the importance of stability in the workforce. Workers who understand the organization and what it is about are important assets and offer some stability in an otherwise changeable environment. The loss of a key employee can be devastating to an entrepreneurial venture. Performance can significantly suffer and customers can be lost due to the departure of an employee. These facts of life can be annoying to large and established enterprises, but can threaten the very survival of S & HG organizations. Retention of employees has been found to be positively influenced by providing feedback and growth opportunities for workers (Cardy & Miller, 2001). It is important that performance management systems in S & HG organizations emphasize feedback and lead to opportunities for improvement. In other words, performance management systems in S & HG organizations should have a developmental purpose.

A dual purpose system would appear to be the most effective in S & HG organizational environments. An administrative purpose that focuses on immediate and bottom line performance is needed, as is a developmental purpose that focuses on feedback and improvement. The administrative and developmental purposes should maximize performance and retention, respectively, two key factors for small and entrepreneurial enterprises.

Type of Criteria

Performance criteria can generally be classified as one of two types: outcomes or behaviors. The criteria of outcomes and behaviors effectively represent end and means, respectively. Thought of in this way, it is clear that an emphasis on both ends and means is important in S & HG organizational environments. Achieving business goals is critical in smaller and entrepreneurial organizations. Thus, the performance management system needs to reflect this reality and emphasize the attainment of important business objectives. However, how these ends are achieved is also particularly critical in S & HG organizations. The process of performance, how customers are treated and the satisfaction of customers regarding interactions with workers can be a pivotal determinant of long-term organizational success. In other words, how things are done can be as important as what is done. This truism implies that performance management in S & HG organizations needs to include both behavioral and outcome criteria.

Focus of Criteria

As discussed previously, performance criteria have typically focused on task performance. The common approach to performance management has been to develop criteria based on an analysis of what is done on the job. A job analysis is done to identify the duties and related tasks that need to be informed in each job. This approach breaks down an overall job into its component parts. Not only can job related performance criteria be identified with this approach, but skills needed to adequately perform the tasks can be identified. These skills can then be used to drive staffing and training efforts. Task-based performance criteria specify what workers need to do in order to perform their jobs at effective levels.

While the task-based approach is rational and provides a clear linkage between job duties and performance criteria, there are some serious disadvantages to the task focus. First, the task level of analysis is, by its very nature, reductionistic. If there are aspects of the job that can't be captured in an analysis of individual tasks, those aspects may be lost in terms of the content of performance criteria. For example, performance criteria based on a task analysis may not reflect some of the customer and interpersonal relations that can separate an excellent performer from an average performer. To the extent that such characteristics are not part of the formal set of tasks that make up the job, the task-based approach will likely overlook them. However, these characteristics may be critical determinants of performance. In addition to being a reductionistic approach, task-based criteria assume that the duties and tasks that make up the jobs in an organization are stable. However, duties and tasks may be anything but stable, particularly in small and entrepreneurial organizations. Criteria based on changing characteristics can be outmoded and useless before they are used. A stable basis is needed for performance criteria. To the extent that duties and tasks associated with jobs are dynamic and evolving, the task-based approach will not provide useful task-level criteria. While the operational details may be in flux, a task-based approach can identify performance outcomes that may remain fairly stable. For example, the work process may vary, but outcomes such as customer satisfaction and amount of sales may remain stable.

Another level which may provide a stable basis for the establishment of criteria, even when work processes are dynamic, is roles. The roles played by workers are collections of related behaviors and responsibilities that can capture what workers actually do in organizations. Tasks may vary and technology may be in continual flux, but the roles played by workers may provide a stable and useful basis for assessing performance. Roles played by workers are beginning to be addressed in research (e.g., Welbourne, Johnson, & Erez, 1998), but much more work is needed to identify the roles that might capture the activities commonly engaged in by workers. Table 6.5 presents descriptions of possible roles that might be engaged in by workers in S & HG organizations. These role titles and their descriptions are meant to be illustrative only and not exhaustively or accurately capture all of the possible roles.

Table 6.5.

Roles
Identify major roles played in organization. Examples:
technical expert
facilitator
team leader
customer service representative

As presented in Table 6.5, some of the roles that might exist in S & HG organizations include technical expert, facilitator, team leader, and customer service representative. The role of technical expert, for example, might include acting as a guide and consultant for teammates regarding technical requirements and proper procedures. A facilitator may overcome conflict and bring people together to accomplish important objectives. The team leader role might include organizing and scheduling and providing a model for others to follow. The role of customer service representative may involve interacting with customers, resolving their problems and complaints, and expediting solutions. An important characteristic of roles is that workers may merge in and out of the roles and play a variety of roles throughout the course of a business day. Thus, the role approach to developing criteria must capture the variety of roles that workers may play. Unlike the typical job analysis approach, the role approach assumes that workers do not consistently perform one set of activities. The role approach is also at a higher level of analysis than the task approach. Thus, details regarding the performance of specific tasks may not be included with performance criteria based on a role approach. However, the role criteria can capture a broad and meaningful set of functions in the organization.

Values offer another possible basis for developing performance criteria. It may not always be clear in S & HG settings just what should be done and how. However, the values that should be brought to bear on any work situation may be clear and stable. As discussed previously, policies and procedures may not be available or desired in many S & HG settings. Thus, what should be done, may not always be clearly specified. The appropriate values can guide workers when there is ambiguity or question as to how to proceed. Values-based criteria can signal to workers what is important and what actions should take priority, even when specific procedural guidelines are not available. Identifying core values can begin with a consideration of an organization's mission statement and strategic materials, which often include statements concerning core organizational values. Core values might include, for example, the characteristics of integrity, innovation, and customer orientation. What these characteristics mean and what form they might take in the context of the organization must be determined in order for usable performance criteria to be generated.

Values and roles offer options to the typical task level and may provide a more stable basis for developing criteria in dynamic organizational environments. The task-based approach, if used at a general level, can specify job-related objectives. As discussed previously, obtaining business goals is important in S & HG organizational environments. Thus, the task-based approach can be useful for identifying outcome criteria that are critical to the survival of the business. Roles and values, on the other hand, specify the process that workers need to engage in while striving to obtain those goals. Figure 6.2 presents a conceptualization that summarizes the relationships between the types and foci of criteria. As presented in the figure, outcome criteria are derived from an examination of business goals and behavioral criteria are derived from an analysis of roles and values in the organization. We contend that both outcome and behavioral criteria are needed for effective performance management in S & HG organizations.

The development of behavioral criteria reflecting roles and values can be accomplished using the critical incident technique (Flanagan, 1954). For example, behavioral performance criteria have been developed based on roles (Welbourne et al., 1998) and values (Henry, Keys, & Schaumann Reese, 2002). The critical incident technique has been widely used to develop behavioral criteria based on an analysis of tasks involved in per-

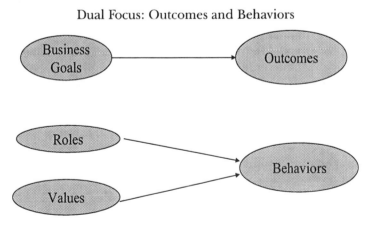

Figure 6.2.   Performance management system recommendations.

Table 6.6.

Some Features of Recommended System

Focusing on both outcomes & behaviors can create a balanced environment.

Identifying outcomes & behaviors can clarify & make real to everyone what is expected and how to perform at a high level.

Behaviors can be basis for job aids to help assure high performance.

Customers can be an important source for assessment.

forming a job. The critical incident technique can be easily applied to role and value-based approaches by replacing the job-based performance dimensions with core values or with role dimensions. These values or role dimensions could then generate behaviorally anchored rating scales (BARS) (Bernardin & Beatty, 1984) which might become a behavioral basis for appraisal.

In sum, our overall recommendation regarding effective performance management in S & HG organizations is that the system includes both outcomes and behaviors. Further, the outcome criteria should be based on an analysis of business goals and the behavioral criteria should be based on and analysis of roles and/or values. Table 6.6 specifies additional features of our recommended performance management system.

As summarized in Table 6.6, the performance management system should support a balanced working environment. What we mean by balance, is a system that orients workers to achieving business objectives, but not at the expense of the process by which these goals are obtained. Likewise, it is important to the viability of S & HG organizations that the process does not overshadow the importance of obtaining needed business outcomes.

Another feature summarized in the table is the importance of clearly defining performance in terms of behaviors and outcomes. A performance management system that clearly identifies and encourages both means and ends is needed for entrepreneurial enterprises to obtain long-term success. Criteria can serve as more than simply measuring sticks. If clearly and unambiguously defined, criteria can signal to everyone what is important and what needs to be done. These signals can certainly direct workers, but can also inform customers as to what the organization is really about.

Another feature of the recommended performance management system is the use of criteria for performance improvement, not just measurement. For example, job aids have been found to be an effective means for improving performance levels (Tyler, 2000). Behavioral descriptions of role characteristics and values can serve as aids to remind and guide workers in the conduct of their jobs. The behavioral descriptions could be used to generate employee guides that could be easily accessed by workers.

Satisfied and loyal customers are key to the success of S & HG organizations and it is critical that the customer perspective is included in the performance management system. External customers may have a different view of performance than coworkers or managers. In addition, long-term success requires an understanding of customer expectations and preferences. In the recommended performance management system, the customer voice is integrated into the performance management system. However, more than simply satisfaction judgments, customers can evaluate and provide useful feedback on behavioral specifics. Customers are less likely to be useful when evaluating the attainment of business outcomes unless they are service outcomes, since that is not likely their concern or part of their knowledge base. However, customers could be a valuable source for input regarding the means employed by workers. Indeed, making the effort to align well-defined customer outcomes with performance management dimensions is a good way to develop a high performing and customer-focused organization (Bernardin, Hagan, Kane, & Villanova, 1998). It is logical that attention to customer feedback could be one important factor contributing to the high growth characteristic of the S & HG firm.

Implications for Performance Management Skills

Given the importance of performance management to S & HG firms, it is paradoxical that entrepreneurs and small business owners often fail to have the needed human resources (HR) or management training and background to implement successful performance management. Furthermore, small firms are less likely than their larger competitors to have abundant HR resources or dedicated expertise in the performance management realm. This means that it falls to the general manager, who might be trained as an engineer or technical expert, to develop an appropriate performance management system. For this to happen, this manager may also need to be convinced of the importance of good management of the human resource.

One way to make the case for high quality performance management systems is by demonstrating the cost of lost productivity from poorly executed appraisal processes, as well as the intangible cost to morale that ensues from employees feeling wrongly or poorly evaluated. Performance management failures and their detrimental effects can significantly damage the workplace environment in small firms where individuals interact closely and there are few secrets. Executives in smaller organizations should be receptive to these concerns. The implication for performance management within S & HG firms is that skills must be developed in areas of diagnosis, evaluation, and feedback.

Diagnosis is a critical step in the performance management process because it drives subsequent evaluations and remedies. Because of its importance, raters engaged in diagnosis must attend to an array of factors that can influence performance. For example, they should consider situational or system factors as well as person factors. This involves determining what portion of job performance is due to motivation or ability and within one's control, versus the portion that is a function of factors extraneous to an individual. An accurate diagnosis means determining whether, for example, weak sales performance reflects a failure to pursue leads or, alternatively, the appearance of new competition in the market. Holding someone accountable for system factors makes little business sense, since making judgments on criteria unrelated to job performance does not suggest a path to improvement that is within individual control. Accurate diagnosis is essential in that it underlies the steps a person undertakes to address a performance problem.

Consequently, the diagnosis portion of the performance management process in S & HG firms relies upon careful consideration of an array of actors that influence performance. Quick and informal observation is inadequate, and may be subject to actor/observer bias or errors of attribution (Weiner, 1980) that occur automatically and subjectively. What is required is examination of repeated observations of a pattern of performance, as repeated observations reduce the potential for diagnostic bias.

From an interpersonal standpoint, it is worth noting that erroneous diagnosis can also underlie conflict and lost productivity, which are negative outcomes in any organization, but particularly harmful to small firms and those in high growth environments. Conflict is potentially particularly disruptive in small organizations.

Accurate diagnosis implies that a rater is able to justify evaluations, providing objective data wherever possible as supporting evidence. This is not to de-emphasize the role of subjective evaluation. Even in cases where objective outcomes are available, subjective judgment nonetheless occurs and cannot be ignored. Cognitive research suggests that raters automatically use subjective judgment, and these automatic judgments may be accurate as well. However, the automatic judgment process may also be errorful, and lead to significant cost. For example, an incorrect subjective judgment can result in a lower evaluation than an individual deserves, subsequent pay consequences, perhaps even a grievance or expensive legal procedures. At a minimum, faulty subjective judgments may impede the working relationship between rater and rate.

Similarly, interpersonal affect is known to influence ratings (Cardy & Dobbins, 1986, 1994; Tsui, & Barry, 1986). For example, positive affect has been found to produce the highest ratings, followed by ratings awarded in neutral affect situations, and finally by ratings associated with negative affect. This finding is relevant in the small firm setting in particular because of the closer working conditions and potential for more frequent one-on-one interaction than would be expected in a large organization. Within S & HG firms, abundant opportunities exist for developing nonperformance judgments (i.e., affect, subjective evaluations). Although personal acquaintance and affect may enter into ratings, a rater must be able to justify evaluations for the system to be perceived as fair and to maintain trust.

FEEDBACK

People need and want to know how they are doing. Feedback from others not only provides motivation, but it also supplies direction, making it possible to amend performance strategies. Supervisors in S & HG firms face the challenge of providing feedback that accomplishes this goal. Because negative feedback from superiors is more informative than positive feedback (Ashford & Tsui, 1991), supervisors also must be able to deliver negative feedback that is simultaneously sensitive and forward-looking. Considering that most raters in S & HG environments are not trained in feedback delivery, it is not surprising that many are uncomfortable in this role.

Feedback acceptance depends not only on its credibility but also on its delivery. The rapidly changing milieu in which the typical S & HG firm operates, underscores the critical importance of adopting a future-focused approach to feedback delivery. Dwelling on past performance events is less helpful than using the feedback session to accomplish goal setting for subsequent performance. Since the way feedback interacts with goal setting is a function of feedback clarity, managers in S & HG firms need to take steps to limit possible emotional reactions to feedback. One way to accomplish this is by adopting a performance focus as opposed to a trait focus during a review session. For example, to minimize emotional responses, a manager would discuss task performance and progress toward objectives rather than a ratee's personality or personal characteristics.

Creating an unthreatening environment for feedback delivery means clearing the calendar to provide ample time for thorough discussion, and eliminating phone calls and interruptions that imply feedback is a bothersome task of little importance. Details such as a room arrangement that does not underscore power differences and body language that welcomes conversation are important ways to minimize emotional trappings of feedback sessions. With emotional reactions minimized or eliminated, feedback stands a better chance of being heeded and used to improve performance.

SUMMARY

This review has addressed some unique aspects of the entrepreneurial environment that have performance management implications for S & HG firms. First, the system's purpose must be examined and consensus reached within the organization as to what that purpose is. This paper has recommended a dual approach, valuing the developmental aspects of performance management, while carefully balancing the administrative functions of supporting personnel decisions and conducting evaluation. Since performance management works best when customized to its environment, it is important to create a fit between this process and the S & HG firm.

Most S & HG organizations little resemble more familiar bureaucracies where tasks, roles, and processes are highly codified. These firms face dynamic environments, and their members prefer them for their fluidity and ability to adapt and change. Successful performance management in the S & HG firm should complement their less structured or rigid work processes. Thus, emphasis on roles and values as performance criteria makes sense. In that a role approach assumes varying worker activities and a values approach guides workers through ambiguity, these more dynamic criteria are positioned to serve the S & HG organization well.

We further recommend a balance between emphasis on outcomes and behaviors in these firms. While outcome criteria evolve from business goals and are critical to organizational survival, customers are in a position to evaluate behavioral criteria and should be encouraged to do so. The closeness to customers that is characteristic of S & HG firms strongly supports making them part of evaluation processes.

Finally, we caution that a more personal S & HG work environment composed of individuals who interact closely makes it imperative that managers learn to diagnose and evaluate accurately, and provide feedback in a future-oriented and sensitive way. Lost productivity and impaired morale are potentially more harmful in S & HG firms than in ones that are more bureaucratic or possess greater slack. Manager ability and motivation to implement high quality performance management processes are certainly not innate, and often requires a conscious commitment to develop. However, the benefits to the S & HG organization should make this investment more than worth the effort.

REFERENCES

Ashford, S. J., & Tsui, A. S. (1991). Self-regulation for managerial effectiveness. *Academy of Management Journal, 34*, 251-280.

Bernardin, H. J., & Beatty, R. W. (1984). *Performance appraisal: Assessing human behavior at work.* Boston: Kent.

Bernardin, H. J, Hagan, C. M., Kane, J. S., & Villanova, P. (1998). Effective performance management. In J. W. Smither (Ed.), *Performance appraisal: State of the art in practice* (pp. 3-48). San Francisco: Jossey-Bass.

Cardy, R. L. (2004). *Performance management.* Armonk, NY: M. E. Sharpe

Cardy, R. L., & Dobbins, G. H. (1986). Affect and appraisal accuracy: Liking as an integral dimension in evaluating performance. *Journal of Applied Psychology, 71*, 672-678.

Cardy, R. L., & Dobbins, G. H. (1994). *Performance appraisal: Alternative perspectives.* Cincinnati, OH: South Western.

Cardy, R. L., & Miller, J .S. (2001). *Customer equity and HRM: The potential for a new framework.* San Diego, CA: Society for Industrial and Organizational Psychology.

Cooke, W. N. (1994). Employee participation programs, group based incentives, and company performance. *Industrial and Labor Relations Review, 47*, 594-610.

Dobbins, G. H., Cardy, R. L., & Truxillo, D. M. (1988). The effects of individual differences in stereotypes of women and purpose of appraisal on sex differences in performance ratings: A laboratory and field study. *Journal of Applied Psychology, 73*, 551-558.

Flanagan, J. C. (1954). The critical incident technique. *Psychological Bulletin, 51*, 327-358.

Henry, D., Keys, C., & Schaumann Reese, L. (2002). Value-based job analysis: An approach to human resource management in rehabilitation agencies service people with developmental disabilities. *Journal of Rehabilitation Administration, 25*, 1-17.

Tsui, A. S., & Barry, B. (1986). Interpersonal affect and rating errors. *Academy of Management Journal, 29*, 586-599.

Tyler, K. (2000). Hold on to what you've learned. *HRMagazine, 45*, 94-102.

Weiner, B. (1980). *Human motivation.* New York: Holt, Rinehart, & Winston.

Welbourne, T. M., Johnson, D. E., & Erez, A. (1998). The role-based performance scale: Validity analysis of a theory-based measure. *Academy of Management Journal, 41*, 540-555.

CHAPTER 7

COMPENSATION STRATEGY IN NEW VENTURES

David Balkin and Michele Swift

Taking a life cycle approach, we examine the dominant compensation issues that occur at the early stages of growth in new ventures and apply organizational justice and agency theory to derive propositions relating to those key issues. Of particular interest are new ventures anticipating rapid growth such as those in technology-intensive markets. The dominant compensation issues analyzed in this chapter include (1) the distribution of equity among members of the team of founders, (2) the design of the pay package for key employees who are nonfounders, and (3) the compensation strategy for broad employee groups who are hired as the organization grows in size. A total of eight research propositions are developed predicting relationships between selected pay strategies and stage of growth for new ventures that foresee or experience rapid growth.

INTRODUCTION

The majority of research in entrepreneurship and new ventures has focused on topics considered strategic to the firm's growth. As a result, relatively little research in the entrepreneurship domain has addressed

Human Resource Strategies for the High Growth Entrepreneurial Firm, 135–160
Copyright © 2006 by Information Age Publishing
All rights of reproduction in any form reserved.
135

human resource issues (Balkin & Logan, 1988). Both life cycle literature and feedback from CEOs of small firms though have highlighted the importance of needing appropriate human resource practices (Aldrich & Langton, 1997; Heneman, Tansky, & Camp, 2000) to support the firm as it grows, especially compensation and reward systems. However, most compensation research has focused on larger firms with the resources to establish comprehensive compensation systems (Gerhart & Milkovich, 1990; Gerhart & Trevor, 1996). Compensation systems in small firms are informal, undocumented and therefore less visible, so at this point little research has been published in this domain. As a result, the compensation models that have been developed are not necessarily applicable to firms in the early stages of growth given that these firms usually have limited resources, are at a higher risk of failure, are experiencing continual change, and have fewer choices in terms of compensation options. Additionally, they do not address the question of how to reward the founders for their risk and contribution to the startup of the new venture. This paper attempts to fill that gap by addressing a key aspect of growing a new venture, the issue of compensating and rewarding the founders, key and nonkey employees in the absence of a formal compensation system and uncertain access to financial resources.

Compensation and rewards have been shown to affect an individual's decision to join a firm and their desire to remain with a firm. However, since new ventures are typically struggling to grow and achieve profitability, the ability to attract, motivate and retain employees can be especially challenging given the new venture's limited financial resources and the uncertainty regarding the future of the firm. Having a compensation and reward system that enables the new venture to attract and motivate employees while operating within the financial constraints of the firm is particularly important to the performance and survival of the small firm and organization life cycle literature indicates survival is a key objective of firms at the early stages of their life cycle (Kazanjian, 1988).

Extensive research has been done linking compensation to employee performance (Kraizberg, Tziner, & Weisberg, 2002) and demonstrating what types of compensation are appropriate in order to achieve desired employee behaviors and organizational outcomes (Gomez-Mejia & Balkin, 1992). Reward systems are key to eliciting and reinforcing behaviors that support firm strategy (Balkin & Gomez-Mejia, 1990) which means they can have a substantial positive or negative effect on the small firm's performance, especially during the firm's early stages. The risk of failure is higher during the early stages, often because the firm is operating in an uncertain environment and its customer segment has not been fully determined and developed. This suggests that the early stages represent the greatest uncertainty for the firm. As the firm grows during these stages, it also experiences the greatest amount of structural change (Greiner, 1998; Kazanjian, 1988) which makes eliciting and rewarding appropriate performance on an ongoing basis critical to the continued growth and success of the firm. Given this, the crucial questions facing a new venture during its early stages of growth then becomes when the firm has limited financial sources, is uncertain of its continued existence, and is in a state of continual change, how do you design a reward system that recognizes founders for their risk and contribution, compensate employees and managers so their interests are aligned with the founders, and is a fair and equitable system that recognizes differences in individual contributions?

In an uncertain state where continual change is occurring, such as in a new venture, achieving this alignment requires flexibility both in determining the appropriate components of the monetary reward system and being able to continually adjust the reward system to reflect the changing needs of the business. As the size of the firm's workforce increases, job roles also change resulting in differentiation in the degree of task importance and complexity among the workforce (Lawrence & Lorsch, 1967). The reward system has to take into account the changing roles of employees whose activities will reflect relative degrees of importance and uncertainty. Considering that firms tend to be smaller during the early stages of development and it is during these stages that job responsibilities are continually evolving, a reward system model is required that reflects the nature of these organizations and is flexible enough that it can change as the organization grows and evolves.

In addition, as the firm continues to grow, it may have access to financial resources that were not previously available or were inaccessible during the initial growth stages. For example, banks are more likely to lend money to a firm with an established base of customers and financial assets which provide collateral that can reduce the lender's financial risk. However, at the startup stage a firm has few assets that can be used for collateral by banks. This requires viewing compensation in the context of a total reward system that can be adjusted to reflect the changes in the firm's internal and external environment. In a total rewards perspective (Parus, 1999) compensation includes psychological rewards, learning opportunities, and recognition, in addition to monetary rewards in the form of base pay and incentives (Graham, Murray, & Amuso, 2002). A total rewards perspective also requires flexibility to ensure that as the firm grows and changes the interests of its employees remain aligned with those of the firm and its founders while also recognizing the varying contributions of the firm's early and key employees relative to the firm's later employees. While the total rewards perspective also encompasses nonfinancial rewards, we limit our discussion of rewards here to the critical issues that are concerned with financial rewards.

In this chapter, we take a life cycle approach to examining reward systems applicable to new ventures as they grow, focusing on the founding employee(s), and next, key employees and other employees added as the firm grows. Using organizational justice and agency theory, we identify the compensation issues applicable to the early life cycle stages and the implications of those issues to the types and structure of monetary rewards offered in order to reward the founders as well as attract, motivate and retain both key and other employees during these stages. In the next section, we present the growth model to be used as the basis for identifying critical reward decisions during early stages of new venture growth after which we develop research propositions regarding the form and basis of the reward system appropriate at early growth stages of firms.

GROWTH MODELS

A number of life cycle and growth models have been developed to explain the process a firm goes through as it grows (Bhave, 1994; Churchill & Lewis, 1983; Hanks, Watson, Jansen, & Chandler, 1993; Kazanjian, 1988;). All of these models outline the key activities that occur within each of the stages of growth, why these specific activities are critical to the firm, and the systems required to help move the firm into the next stage. Given the similarities between the various models, rather than utilize all of them as the basis for developing a new venture compensation and rewards model, we have chosen to follow the stages identified by Kazanjian (1988) in his growth model. An advantage of this model is that it was developed as result of studying high-technology firms which tend to be fast growing and which is the context where our propositions are focused, and it recognizes the dominant issues associated with each growth stage and the activities and systems required in order to resolve those issues. Additionally, Kazanjian found that issues related to attracting, developing and retaining employees were prevalent at all the stages of growth. Rewarding employees is a key component of being able to address these issues.

As with other life cycles models, the Kazanjian (1988) model explains the growth of the firm through the maturity stage when its products are well established in the market. However, we will be focusing on the early stages of a firm's existence. During the initial stages of a firm's existence, a firm tends to be experiencing the most uncertainty in terms of continued existence, has a smaller workforce, and is likely to be experiencing a higher level of growth. As a result, these stages represent the period during which a firm is the most dynamic and is undergoing the most changes. These factors also affect a firm's ability to provide compensation and the level of importance associated with various tasks and functions. This influences the types of compensation appropriate for rewarding the various tasks being performed in a firm.

The compensation and reward system models that currently exist tend to assume a more stable environment with more options for the types of compensation offered and therefore have limitations when applied to a new venture going through these early stages. For example, the use of job evaluation requires a relatively stable set of jobs in order to provide accurate assessments of job worth (Milkovich & Newman, 2002). In a dynamic environment often associated with early growth stage firms, job evaluation may not be a useful means to compare the worth of different jobs. A new venture also has resource constraints and considerations with regards to rewarding employees not typically present in the larger or more mature organization, which affects the types of compensation and rewards it can offer to employees.

In this chapter we are attempting to reduce the gap in the compensation literature that overlooks how pay is managed in the subset of new ventures that are small, growing firms experiencing high rates of growth as well as financial resource limitations, such as high-technology firms. As such, we will be focusing on the first three stages of the Kazanjian model (1) conception and development, (2) commercialization and (3) growth—which we refer to as (a) startup, (b) launch and (c) growth.

PAY STRATEGIES IN NEW VENTURES

The literature on compensation examining pay policies in small firms (e.g., Balkin & Logan, 1988) provides some insights into how compensation is managed in new ventures, which are also likely to be small in size during early growth stages. However, the total population of small firms is more diverse and also includes older, mature companies as well as family firms. New ventures differ and can be viewed as a subset of small firms. In many cases new ventures are founded by a team of individuals and are small only when they are young. Additionally, most new ventures are started with the expectation of rapid growth and larger size as they achieve their planned growth objectives.

Pay levels in small firms (defined as less than one hundred employees according to theU.S. Bureau of Labor Statistics) have been reported to be below the median rate of pay in the market (Deshpande & Golhar, 1994; Milkovich & Newman, 2002). Similar market patterns for benefits levels are also observed for small firms. The rationale for these rates of pay is that small firms compare their pay and benefits with peers that are similar in size in the market, and they are also likely to economize on pay and benefits due to the lack of slack resources available for higher rates of compensation.

There are also fewer benefits choices available to employees in small firms due to the fact that larger firms can negotiate a broader array of benefits programs at lower costs by spreading benefits costs over a larger pool of employees, an option not open to firms small in size (Martocchio, 2003). For example, a larger firm is able to enroll a large group of employees for a vision care benefit program, so that it can obtain a lower cost for vision care per employee from the provider of the benefit. Small-sized firms do not have this option.

The proportion of total pay that consists of performance contingent pay incentives is on average less than 10% for employees in small firms. This proportion is no different from the proportion of performance contingent pay incentives for large firms (Deshpande & Golhar, 1994). This finding suggests that in general a modest proportion of employees' pay is placed at risk independent of firm size. Interestingly though, small firms are more likely to have a policy of broad employee participation of stock options, while large firms (defined as having more than 1000 employees) are likely to provide stock options on a more limited basis to a select group of key employees (Justis, Chan, & Werbel, 1991; Rosen, 2002). The rationale favoring broad employee participation in small firms is that there is less potential for dilution of stock ownership to shareholders when a firm is small, since the number of employees receiving options will be a small number.

The use of simple, whole job methods of job evaluation is likely to be applied in a small firm (Milkovich & Newman, 2002). This type of job evaluation produces only a simple ranking of jobs according to their value. Larger firms, with a more complex array of jobs, are most likely to use a more sophisticated quantitative method of job evaluation. The quantitative job evaluation methods produce more precise measures of differences in job worth and require a greater investment in effort and resources to implement. However, small firms often do not have the staff resources or expertise necessary to implement and maintain these types of systems.

The role within a small organization that is responsible for implementing pay policies is most likely to be a human resource management generalist or an outside consultant (Greer, Youngblood, & Gray, 1999). If the firm maintains an internal HR generalist, this position will have a broad set of other HR responsibilities such as staffing and employee relations in addition to dealing with pay concerns. The development of an internal compensation specialist role is usually associated with larger organizations where they have the resources to develop and maintain a more sophisti-

Table 7.1.   Pay Policies in Large and Small Firms

Pay Policy	Large Firm Policy*	Small Firm Policy**	Rationale
Pay level	Meet or above market level	Below market level	Peer comparisons; scale economies
Benefits level	Meet or above market level	Below market level	Peer comparisons; scale economies
Benefits choices	Diverse	Basic	Peer comparisons
Stock options	Limited participation	Broad participation	Dilution concerns
Pay incentives (% of total pay)	Small portion < 10%	Small portion < 10%	Peer comparisons
Job Evaluation	Quantitative method	Whole job method	Administrative ease
Compensation role holder	Specialist in compensation	HR Generalist or Consultant	Technical complexity of pay system
Union influence in pay policy	Yes	Not important	Union threat effect related to size

Note: *Large firms are > 1,000 employees. **Small firms are < 100 employees.

cated compensation system. Finally, union pay patterns are not likely to influence small firms, due to the fact that they are difficult and costly to organize. Thus, the union threat effect is not very potent for the small organization (Rees, 1979). A summary of these pay policy differences between large and small firms are summarized in Table 7.1.

The next section of this chapter examines early growth stages of new ventures with respect to compensation strategies. We will start with a description of the business strategy context at each stage of growth and explain the linkages between business and pay strategy.

Startup Stage

During the startup stage of a new venture the focus of the founders is on defining its market and developing the product to meet a need in the market (Churchill & Lewis, 1983; Hanks et al., 1993; Kazanjian, 1988). The founders are involved with activities such as building a product prototype, creating a formal business plan to present to financial investors, and testing and evaluating the prototype to verify its performance and ensure the functionality of its features. The level of uncertainty and degree of business risk is highest at the startup stage. Moreover, resources are scarce at this stage since sales to the customer has yet to take place and the new venture is consuming cash without being able to replace it with incoming resources.

The organization structure at the startup stage is simple (Greiner, 1998; Hanks et al., 1993) and is likely to consist of a team of founders who collaborate with each other in flexible roles to achieve goals that move the business closer to achieving important performance milestones. Due to a lack of financial resources at the startup stage, some of the founders may work on a part-time basis while they keep their jobs with employers in order to provide themselves with enough income to maintain their standard of living. The resources used to sustain a new venture are likely to consist of the founders' personal savings and the founders' unpaid labor (also referred to as sweat equity). These resources are limited and likely to be exhausted within a six to twelve-month period of time unless the venture is able to achieve planned growth milestones and provide a positive flow of cash to cover its expenses.

Monetary compensation for the founders at the startup stage is either unavailable or provided as a token amount to cover basic living expenses due to the scarcity of cash. The critical compensation issue at the startup stage concerns the relative distribution of equity to the founders (i.e., founders' stock). Equity represents potential future wealth for each founder contingent on the success of the startup enterprise. Importantly, equity also represents control of the enterprise when a coalition of founders own more than 50% of the stock. When a coalition of founders (or a single founder for that matter) controls a majority of stock they can determine the direction the business takes when there is disagreement over the strategic goals of the organization. Therefore, the distribution of equity concerns more than just wealth, for it represents the value of the contribution that each founder brings to the startup team, and the relative influence that each founder may have on the direction of the enterprise. Consequently, the decision to distribute equity to founders is likely to be emotionally charged. A distribution of equity that is perceived as unfair by one or more founders can be expected to undermine the degree of teamwork produced by the founding team of entrepreneurs (Ensley, Allison, & Amason 2002). Due to the potential for conflict between founders over the perception of a fair distribution of equity, the principals often turn to trusted advisors or consultants to provide a recommendation for a decision rule to fairly distribute equity between the new venture founders (Shepherd & Zacharakis, 2001). These characteristics associated with the startup stage of a new venture are summarized in Table 7.2.

The organizational justice literature suggests there are two distribution rules that can be used to distribute equity to founders: (1) the rule of equality, and (2) the rule of equity (Greenberg, 1987). The application of the equality rule would result in an equal distribution of founders' shares to each member of the founding team, while the equity rule would distribute shares in proportion to the value of each founder's inputs. The under-

Table 7.2. Relationship Between Early Life Cycle Stages, Organization Characteristics, and Compensation Decisions

Characteristic	Start-Up	Launch	Growth
Strategic business focus	Product development	Acquire financial resources	Sales and market share growth
Sales revenues	None	Small	Substantial
Earnings	None	Low to none	Moderate
Risk profile	Very high	Moderate to high	Moderate
Organization structure	Team of founders	Group of founders and key nonfounders	Differentiation by function into units
The role of HR	Shared founder responsibility	Embedded in role of managers or consultants	HR Generalist position created
Dominant compensation issue	basis of allocation of equity to founders -Equal or unequal distribution of equity	Design of pay for non-founder key employees -Eligibility for equity -Mix between variable and fixed pay	Compensation strategy for broad employee groups -Pay for person or job -Internal vs. external equity -Variable vs. Fixed pay -L/T vs. S/T pay

lying assumption of the equality rule is that each founder's contribution to the new venture is approximately of similar value. In addition, allocating equal shares of equity to each founder on the team preserves social harmony and is less likely to cause conflict and disruption to team motivation (Deutsch, 1949; Ensley et al., 2002; Henderson & Fredrickson, 2001).

Based on the above discussion, the equality distribution rule is likely to be selected by founders as the basis to distribute equity in a startup for several reasons. First, the roles of founders within a startup team are usually quite flexible. Each founder will wear several hats and often the enacted roles of each founder will overlap. Moreover, it will be difficult to separate and determine the value of the marginal contribution of each founder. The expectation that each founder is adding equal value to a startup may indeed be realistic. Therefore, we will consider the equality distribution rule to be the general case governing the allocation of founder equity.

Additionally, new ventures with a founding team are not dissimilar to partnerships where the equality distribution rule has long been incorporated as an established practice. Partnerships are a legal form of organization that are often used by professionals in accounting, law, consulting and medicine. Each founding partner in a partnership receives an equal share of the organization's profits, and consequently assumes an equal burden to assume the partnership's financial liabilities (Mann & Roberts,

1994). The equality distribution rule provides an impetus for the partners to collaborate with each other over the governance of their firm so that a norm of collegiality is nurtured within the partnership which reduces the potential for conflict among the partners. Conflict between partners has long been recognized as a major threat to the success of a partnership. Thus, the founding team of a new enterprise can be viewed analogous to a partnership, consisting of individuals who are dedicated to building a successful organization.

Finally, the need to preserve social harmony and avoid shirking on the founding team is particularly critical at the startup stage since this stage is characterized by high levels of uncertainty and heavy work demands placed on each founder (Greiner, 1998). By reinforcing teamwork and reducing the potential for conflict by establishing rules with provisions for owning equal amounts of equity and having an equal voice over the operation of the enterprise, the founders are more likely to make personal sacrifices of time and energy that are necessary to propel the new venture toward achieving its growth goals. This leads us to the first research proposition.

Proposition 1:   In general, the startup stage of a new venture will be characterized by the founders receiving equal amounts of equity.

There may be special circumstances however where the equality distribution rule would not be appropriate for the allocation of equity among the members of the founding team of a new venture. In these circumstances, the equity distribution rule may be perceived by founders as a fair way to distribute stock. The equity rule distributes the amount of founders' shares in proportion to the value of the inputs that each founder provides to the new venture. The equity distribution rule should be applied only when there is a significant and noticeable difference between the amount or quality of inputs provided by one or more founders with respect to the others. The presence of an asymmetrical distribution of founder inputs may involve one or more of the following situations: (1) noticeable differences in level of commitment displayed by the founders to work on a startup as measured by amount of time devoted to startup activities or intensity of effort; (2) noticeable differences in monetary resources contributed by founders as startup capital; and (3) noticeable differences in the value of the founder's skills or knowledge that is applied to a startup.

An example of a significant and noticeable skill discrepancy between founders would be one where a founding team consists of several recent MBA graduates and a Nobel Prize winning scientist. The celebrated scientist may have rare and special talents that give the startup strong credibility in the scientific and financial communities and this would represent an asymmetrical contribution to the new venture provided by the scientist. The rationale for the application of the equity distribution rule in this example would be that the star scientist deserves a larger amount of founder stock than that of the other founders whose skills as recent MBA graduates are relatively unproven. This leads us to the next proposition.

Proposition 2:   When there are significant and noticeable differences in levels of commitment, contributed capital or skill between founders, the amount of equity allocated will be in proportion to the perceived value of each founder's inputs to the new venture at the startup stage.

Launch Stage

The launch stage of a new venture is focused on the acquisition of necessary resources (Kazanjian, 1988) and activities that bring the product into the market and into the hands of the customer (Churchill & Lewis, 1983). Sales revenues begin to flow to the enterprise at the launch stage, providing cash beyond what was available from the founders' personal savings which had financed the earlier startup stage and this additional cash is used to pay for expenses. Value chain activities such as supply chain logistics, manufacturing, marketing, sales, information systems, distribution logistics and post-sale customer service are also beginning to be established (Hanks et al., 1993; Kazanjian, 1988). The degree of business risk and uncertainty has subsided at the launch stage compared to the startup stage, although risk and uncertainty are still higher than at later stages.

One of the key business risks at the launch stage happens when the product needs to move beyond the early adopter customer of a product and find the market for the mainstream adopter who is looking for a product that is easy to use and free of problems. Early adopters buy a product because they want the latest technology or most innovative service and are willing to tolerate early versions of the product that are not user friendly. What distinguishes early adopters is that they have the technical skills to fix the product flaws themselves or with minimal assistance (Moore, 1991). The difficulty in finding the mainstream market has unhinged many technology firms that pioneered innovative, new technologies only to be surpassed by firms applying fast follower strategies that offered similar products that were more reliable and easier to use. For example, America Online, a fast follower, became the most popular residential internet service provider due to the ease of use of its service with colorful graphics and icons, grabbing the market for residential Internet service from earlier, pioneering firms that assumed greater technical sophistication on the part of the residential internet customer.

Financial issues become the "dominant problem" focus at the launch stage because substantially more financial resources are needed (Churchill & Lewis, 1983; Kazanjian, 1988) to develop competencies to manufacture, market, and sell the product. At this stage, the enterprise management must decide whether to invest in establishing its own production capabilities or outsource those activities to another party. Similarly, the new venture must decide whether to hire a professional sales force or develop a partnership with a firm with established market distribution channels to sell the new venture's product as an extension of its own product lines. Outsourcing some of the critical value chain activities may be the lowest cost option yet also the riskiest for the new venture, because outsourcing often leads to the loss of control (Leiblein, Reuer, & Dalsace, 2002) of the knowledge of making and selling the product to others so there is greater vulnerability to rivals who would appropriate the product and the customers for their own purposes (Greer et al., 1999).

At the launch stage, debt or equity financing are now more likely to be available due to the availability of assets that can be secured as collateral for a business loan. While the founders are able to assume some of the important roles involved with managing value chain activities of the growing business, other value chain activities will need to be managed by hiring some key and nonfounder employees who have the knowledge and experience to take the venture past the launch stage to the point where rapid growth is anticipated (Greiner, 1998; Kazanjian, 1988).

Based on this discussion of activities occurring during the launch stage, one can expect some basic differentiation to occur within the organization into functions such as manufacturing and marketing to take place (Hanks et al., 1993; Lawrence & Lorsch, 1967). Other supporting activities such as human resources are embryonic and may be subsumed within the roles of key employees (either founders or nonfounders) inside the organization, or alternatively the human resource activities may be provided by external consultants (Greer et al., 1999). The availability of resources to cover compensation expenses should have improved during the launch stage. Reserves of cash may be available from debt or equity financing to pay the salaries of nonfounder and key employees hired into the new venture. Some cash from the sales of the product to early adopters may also trickle in, adding to the availability of financial resources to pay for employment expenses. Despite the latent availability of financial resources to cover compensation expenses though, there is a competing need to reinvest these resources into the business to fuel future growth in order to realize the long-term potential of the business model (Churchill & Lewis, 1983).

The critical compensation issue at the launch stage of a new venture concerns how to attract and motivate key employees who are nonfounders and who must be added to the firm to take it to the next level of anticipated growth (Greiner, 1998). Examples of key employees at the launch stage would include a chief financial officer, a vice president of marketing or director of engineering. The sources of supply for the key nonfounder employees are likely to be large corporations, which provide fertile environments for these valuable contributors to perfect their professional skills with the latest technologies and the most abundant investments in formal training. A challenge facing the founders of a new venture is how to design an appropriate compensation package for key nonfounder employees who are already employed and receive competitive salaries and benefits from their current employers (Balkin & Bannister, 1993; Gomez-Mejia & Balkin, 1992).

A primary concern in the design of the compensation package for key and nonfounder employees will be whether the founders are willing to share a significant amount of equity with the nonfounder key employees (Timmons, 1994). If a significant amount of equity is distributed to newcomers, it may result in a dilution of the equity holdings of the founders and this situation could be resented. Founders may feel that since they assumed the greatest burden of risk at the startup stage it follows that they deserve the lion's share of equity in the new business, and may have serious reservations about sharing any of it with newcomers. Due to our earlier discussion explaining why the distribution of equity is both controversial and emotional to founders, we expect that in most cases founders will be willing to share a limited amount of equity with incoming key nonfounder employees. On the other hand, giving key nonfounder employees only a token amount of equity may not provide enough upside potential in pay to entice a talented professional manager to give up a secure corporate career and income to become part of the management team of a riskier new venture. The ambivalence of the founders over redistributing equity to other nonfounder employees suggests that the form of compensation for nonfounders is a crucial decision that must be sorted out. A summary of these characteristics and issues associated with the launch stage of a new venture are presented in Table 7.2.

It is suggested that while the pay package will likely include an equity component, the focus will be on the appropriate mix of fixed and variable pay components. The pay mix will have to be such that it allows key nonfounder employees added to the management team the opportunity to share in the success of the firm if it reaches its anticipated growth goals. The fixed pay component will consist of salary and benefits with the salary and benefits levels calibrated to market comparisons of similar size firms at similar stages of growth (Milkovich & Newman, 2002). Consequently, due to resource constraints typical of smaller, early stage firms, the fixed pay component will not be the most prominent part of the pay package and is likely to be modest compared to what larger corporations pay their employees (Balkin & Logan, 1988).

Variable pay is the other component in the design of the remuneration package for key and nonfounder employees at the launch stage. Variable pay consists of a menu of pay incentives linked to achieving the growth and performance goals of the new venture (Bloom & Milkovich, 1998; Gerhart & Milkovich, 1990; Stroh, Brett, Baumann, & Reilly, 1996). The pay incentives should include an individual performance cash bonus, a pay incentive tied to short-term organization performance such as profit sharing, and long-term incentives such as stock options or phantom shares. Phantom shares are long-term financial incentives that are similar to stock bonuses but result in a cash distribution that does not dilute the equity holdings of the founders (Taulli, 2001). Taken together as a total compensation package, the combination of equity and nonequity fixed and variable components of pay may equal or exceed the compensation offered at larger corporations where nonfounder key employees are being recruited. Due to the greater degree of risk and uncertainty that is concomitant with joining a new venture, its variable pay component is expected to be emphasized compared to the fixed salary (Miceli & Heneman, 2000; Stroh et al., 1996) and benefit component. The resulting pay configuration offers higher upside pay potential for key nonfounder employees but also greater pay variability than the pay design provided by larger corporations. In other words, the bulk of the compensation package design for key nonfounder employees is expected to be highly leveraged and contingent on meeting future growth and performance milestones for the new venture. Thus, risk is shared between the founders (principals) and nonfounders (agents) by utilizing a pay system design that facilitates incentive alignment between these two different classes of managers, founders and nonfounders (Fama, 1980; Jensen & Meckling, 1976). Based on the proceeding discussion, we offer the following propositions.

> **Proposition 3:**   The amount of equity allocated to key nonfounder employees will be smaller than the amount of equity allocated to founders at the launch stage.

Proposition 4:   The variable pay component of the pay design for key nonfounder employees will be emphasized in the pay design adopted during the launch stage.

Growth Stage

Once a new venture's product crosses over from the early adopters to the mainstream adopters and achieves market acceptance by a broad group of customers, a period of rapid growth is likely to follow. The focus of the new venture at this stage is to distribute its product in volume while attaining profitability (Churchill & Lewis, 1983; Kazanjian, 1988). The growth stage for an organization is likely to be accompanied by major expansion in the scope of its physical facilities and size of the workforce. Achieving rapid growth may be beneficial because the firm is at a point where it considers itself to be in a race with rivals to achieve scale economies based on market share enabling it to be able to outspend competitors in developing the most innovative new products that strengthen its foothold in the market.

The benefits of rapid growth have been observed in successful high technology firms aiming to provide the *de facto* technology standard by virtue of having more users than competitors offering a competing technology standard (Farrell & Saloner, 1985; Schilling, 1998). By taking advantage of the *network effect* that makes a technology more valuable as the user base increases in size, the growth stage may determine whether a firm becomes a profitable market leader, or finds itself serving a narrow, specialized market niche and just trying to survive. The ability to sustain rapid growth is usually an important factor that determines whether a large user group can be formed and then becomes locked into and committed to using a technology due to switching cost barriers so that it gains broad acceptance as the standard (Katz & Shapiro, 2001; Schilling, 1998).

While an acceleration of the rate of growth is expected and desired in the growth stage, too much growth can put an unbearable strain on the operations of a business. For example, a company spending too much of its available cash on expansion may have difficulty meeting its financial obligations to creditors resulting in a cash flow crisis. Therefore, management in some cases may want to control its rate of growth, which sometimes means turning down a growth opportunity when the firm is already operating at full capacity (Covin, Slevin, & Covin, 1990). An important decision that needs to be made during the growth stage is how much growth is expected and desired. Growth may take the form of either a steady evolutionary increase in sales volume or an exponential growth in sales. Firms that are growing at exponential rates, such as those on the *Inc*

500 list of fast-growing companies, must develop highly flexible human resource management systems that can respond to the changes in its organization structure caused by the inflow of massive numbers of employees. While we recognize that some new ventures desire more modest growth rates than others, we focus our attention on firms experiencing rapid growth during the growth stage. For a new venture that expects to become a market leader, the period of rapid growth leading to market leadership occurs during the growth stage.

During the growth stage the increase in number of employees will give rise to hierarchy and functional specialization in which employees' roles are more differentiated from each other (Hanks et al., 1993; Kazanjian, 1988). At this point the role of human resource management is likely to be turned over to a professional in human resource management due to the increased technical knowledge required by the incumbent to advise managers about human resource policies and procedures. One major impetus for having an experienced human resource management person on staff is that complying with government regulations covering employment law, employee benefits, and diversity issues necessitate developing systems which can become time-consuming and complex as a firm increases in size.

At the growth stage nonkey employees will be hired and deployed to work as subordinates and perform work delegated from the group of key employees who are either founders or nonfounders. As the complexity and sophistication of the work at the new venture increases with the volume of serving many new customers, some of the founders may no longer be competent to perform their jobs effectively and may need to be replaced (Churchill & Lewis, 1983). For example, as a firm expands in size from ten employees at the launch stage to several hundred employees at the growth stage, the job of chief financial officer (CFO) becomes increasing complex and technical. At the growth stage the CFO may need the skills to manage cross technology licensing deals, raise cash with venture capitalists, deal with investment bankers to facilitate an initial public offering (IPO), and implement a sophisticated accounting information system to control for internal expenditures. These job changes are likely to cause the skills of the existing CFO to become obsolete and create the need for either the current CFO to develop new skills or the firm to identify a suitable replacement. Potential replacement employees with the necessary professional skills may be recruited from the outside or promoted from within as nonkey employees are developed and promoted to take on important tasks.

In either situation, as the organization becomes increasingly differentiated in its structure, these changes affect how employees feel about the organization (Ambrose & Schminke, 2003) and a compensation system needs to be developed that is fair and consistent (Milkovich & Newman, 2002) and yet recognizes the contributions of these diverse employees. The critical compensation decision during the growth stage concerns the overarching design or architecture of the compensation system so that it provides remuneration that can attract, retain and motivate a diversified workforce (Gomez-Mejia & Balkin, 1992). In other words, during the new venture's growth stage a formal compensation strategy needs to be defined and a compensation system implemented.

To recap, during the growth stage the firm is experiencing rapid expansion with the addition of many new employees, resulting in continuous change in the structure and reporting relationships as people are moved both horizontally and vertically as new opportunities are presented. The compensation strategy at the time of the growth stage should provide policies for the basis, design and administration of pay that are flexible and adaptive in order to deal with changing circumstances and sudden environmental shifts. Several dimensions of the pay strategy are sensitive to change and environmental turbulence and are expected to be aligned with a flexible, "organic" compensation strategy (Gomez-Mejia, 1992; Lawler, 1990). These strategic pay dimensions include the following choices: (1) to emphasize external pay equity or internal pay equity; (2) to pay on the basis of the person or the job; (3) to give pay incentives high prominence in the pay design or low prominence; and (4) to adopt a long-term time orientation for pay or a short-term time orientation. Each of these pay dimension choices are now examined at the growth stage and a summary of the characteristics of the growth stage is presented in Table 7.2.

Emphasis on external or internal pay equity. Firms at the growth stage are likely to decide to put a high emphasis on external pay equity, which translates into making frequent and comprehensive external market pay comparisons in order to facilitate the extensive recruiting of new employees to support the goal of rapid growth. When a firm puts a high priority on external pay equity it needs to provide flexible pay ranges that offer market competitive salaries to incoming employees. Milkovich and Newman (2002) refer to this practice as "market pricing," where external pay equity drives the compensation decision making. Thus, job vacancies with incumbents even in scarce supply can still be filled because a pay strategy with an emphasis on external pay equity lets pay rates be adjusted to reach a competitive market equilibrium without using control points that try to preserve internal consistency between an employee's pay level with those of other significant pay referents.

Firms at the growth stage are less likely to emphasize internal pay equity which is often at odds with external pay equity. Internal pay equity aims to provide internally consistent salaries to employees based on the relative worth of their job inputs as measured by job evaluation (Collins & Muchinsky, 1993; Milkovich & Newman, 2002), a tool used to determine the value of a job across several factors common to all jobs. The logic of job evaluation depends on having stable job content so that each job can be measured consistently based on its quantifiable worth to the organization. Unstable job content caused by rapid growth and dynamic change makes the process of job evaluation problematic for the same reasons that job based pay is deemed lacking in merits when applied at the growth stage. We can thus expect that internal pay equity will be given a lower priority than external pay equity. Therefore, we expect that new ventures at the growth stage will adopt pay policies emphasizing external pay equity which is consistent with having a flexible, organic compensation strategy (Gomez-Mejia, 1992).

> **Proposition 5:**   External pay equity will be emphasized as the basis for determining base salary ranges for employees at the growth stage of a new venture.

Person versus job as basis of pay.   When the *person* is the basis of pay, a firm pays according to the amount of knowledge and skills an employee brings to the organization. As an employee develops new skills that can be utilized by the firm, additional pay is allocated to the base salary. The greater the variety of tasks an individual has mastered under a knowledge or skill-based pay policy, the higher the base salary. Thus, a skill-based pay policy rewards employees for their versatility to the firm by being able to enact a broad variety of roles (Murray & Gerhart, 2000). By encouraging a multi-skilled workforce, a knowledge or skill-based pay system gives managers flexibility to deploy employees rapidly in response to growth induced shocks to the organization. A *job-based* approach, on the other hand, pays an employee based on a fixed set of tasks that are documented within a job description. When a job-based pay approach is selected, base pay rates can only be changed when the individual changes jobs. In dynamic environments associated with rapid growth, job content is changing constantly making task domains unstable and difficult to document for purposes of pay. Moreover, it is costly and impractical to frequently rewrite job descriptions in reaction to growth induced changes in the job content. Because job based pay is less flexible in dynamic environments, casting uncertainty on the accuracy of the job content, it is problematic to use this approach during periods of rapid growth (Lawler, 1994). Therefore, we expect that firms at the growth stage will adopt pay and merit policies that pay for the person, not the job. This leads to the next proposition.

Proposition 6:   The person as the basis of pay will be selected as the approach for determining increases to base salaries for employees at the growth stage of a new venture.

Proportion of pay incentives.   At the growth stage the proportion of pay incentives to total compensation is expected to be a prominent feature of the compensation system design. In other words, management is expected to provide compensation containing a relatively large portion of variable pay which consists of pay incentives, and a relatively modest portion of fixed pay which consists of salary and benefits. Having a flexible pay package design, with a substantial degree of pay variability, offers several benefits at the growth stage. First, the prominent use of pay incentives such as cash bonuses, profit sharing, and stock options provides opportunities for broad classes of employees to share in the success related to anticipated growth of the company during its high growth trajectory period (Kruse, 1993). The pay incentives can be used to recognize employees who contribute to achieving planned growth goals. Second, the level of business risk and uncertainty due to rapid growth is still significant and building in variability in the pay system allows management to economize on meeting its labor cost obligations if there is a decline in organization or subunit performance (Weitzman, 1984, 1985). The use of variable pay also provides an environment of shared risk with the founders so that nonfounder employees' have similar incentives to prospect for opportunities for growth (Bloom & Milkovich, 1998; Miller, Wiseman, & Gomez-Mejia, 2002; Stroh et al., 1996). If the incentives are properly aligned, both founders and nonfounder employees will share success when the firm is prosperous, and experience some loss of economic benefits when the firm misses its expected performance or growth goals.

Finally, a prominent level of variability in the design of the pay system reduces the employment risk to employees if the firm experiences a cash flow crisis which is not unusual during the growth stage. If the firm has an urgent need to conserve cash due to economic shocks, the flexibility provided by variable pay allows management to automatically reduce compensation expenses by eliminating employee bonuses or profit-sharing benefits until the firm improves its financial performance (Weitzman, 1984, 1985). Without the flexibility provided by variable pay, the firm is more likely to use layoffs to reduce labor costs, since it would have fewer alternatives to reduce its employment costs short of eliminating jobs. Therefore, we argue that firms at the growth stage are expected to use variable pay prominently in the design of the pay system.

Proposition 7:   Variable pay will represent a substantial portion of total pay for employees at the growth stage of a new venture.

Time orientation for pay incentives.   Closely related to a policy that emphasizes pay incentives in the compensation design is a policy that articulates the time orientation, short-term or long-term, used to measure performance and distribute pay. A firm at the growth stage of its life cycle anticipates that most of its financial success will occur in future periods, indicating a long-term focus, when it achieves its growth goals and operates at a higher level of profitability. At the growth stage it is important to provide employees with performance goals having a long-term focus and

Table 7.3.   Relationship Between Compensation Decisions and Propositions

Stage	Dominant Compensation Issue	Propositions
Start-up	Basis of allocation of equity to founders • Equal or unequal distribution of equity	P1: In general, the start-up stage of a new venture will be characterized by the founders receiving equal amounts of equity. P2: When there are noticeable differences in levels of commitment, contributed capital or skill between founders, the amount of equity allocated will be in proportion to the perceived value of each founder's inputs to the new venture.
Launch	Design of pay for non-founder key employees • Eligibility for equity • Mix between variable and fixed pay	P3: The amount of equity allocated to key nonfounder employees will be smaller than the amount of equity allocated to founders at the launch stage. P4: The variable pay component of the pay design for key nonfounder employees will be emphasized in the pay design adpoted during the launch stage.
Growth	Compensation strategy for broad employee groups • Pay for person or job • Internal vs. external equity • Variable vs. fixed pay • L/T vs. S/T pay	P5: The person as the basis of pay will be selected as the approach for determining base salaries for employees at the growth stage of a new venture. P6: External pay equity will be emphasized as the basis for determining base salary ranges for employees at the growth stage of a new venture. P7: Variable pay will represent a substantial portion of total pay for employees at the growth stage of a new venture. P8: A long-term time orientation of pay incentives for employees is expected to be adopted at the growth stage by new ventures.

bolster them with the long-term rewards because short-term and long-term goals are often at cross purposes (Galbraith & Merrill, 1991; Hill & Snell, 1989). For example, in the short-run it may be prudent to downsize the workforce to be able to reduce costs and improve quarterly profits, but in the long-run downsizing can undermine the innovation process due to both voluntary and involuntary turnover of employees. A focus on short-term goals such as quarterly profits at the growth stage could disrupt the innovation process (by cutting R&D budgets to be able to claim higher profits) leading to more serious problems from the long-term perspective. For example, by economizing on R&D spending in a current period, a firm in the long-term may have a paucity of new products to respond to a competitor's moves leading to loss of market share (Hoskisson, Hitt, & Hill, 1993). Therefore, due to the importance of sustaining an employee focus on long-term performance during the growth stage, a long-term time orientation of the pay incentives is expected.

Proposition 8:   A long-term time orientation of pay incentives for employees is expected to be adopted at the growth stage by new ventures.

A summary of the eight research propositions and their relationship to the dominant compensation issues identified for each of the stages of a new venture's growth are summarized in Table 7.3.

CONCLUSION

As new ventures move through the startup, launch, and growth stages, they face different dominant compensation decisions. The decisions they face are affected by the firm's structure, financial position, and the size of the firm's workforce in each stage. Given that the high growth venture is constantly adding new employees during the early stages, the venture requires a compensation system that is flexible and can address changing compensation issues.

During the startup stage the new venture consists of a team of founders which may receive little or no compensation for the effort they are exerting to start the new venture. Their contribution is in anticipation of future success which makes the question of ownership a key issue. The equality distribution rule is likely to be used as the basis for distributing ownership in order to encourage and maintain teamwork and collaboration among the founders. It assumes equal contributions from the founding team and encourages continued equal contributions. However, when there are significant and noticeable differences in the founders' skills or their contribution to the new venture then distributing equity based on varying levels of contribution requires using the equity distribution rule rather than the equality rule for distributing ownership.

When the venture reaches a point where additional employees beyond the team of founders are needed to grow the firm beyond the startup stage (Greiner, 1998), the dominant compensation issue shifts to how to attract and motivate those individuals (Greiner, 1998; Kazanjian, 1988) considering that the people with the critical skills needed are often employed by larger firms with more financial resources. Attracting these key people requires a different type of compensation package given that even though the salary portion of the compensation package would be competitive with that offered by other small growing firms it is also likely to be less than that offered by larger firms (Balkin & Logan, 1988). As a result, providing these key employees with an incentive to join the new venture may require that the founders share some of the ownership as well as make variable pay a prominent component of the total compensation package. This provides key nonfounder employees with the opportunity to achieve a total potential compensation level greater than what is offered by larger firms where variable pay is not a significant portion of the pay package. Linking incentives to firm performance also allows the founders to share their risk with employees and align the interests of the key nonfounder employees with their interests, which is to grow the firm (Fama, 1980; Jensen & Meckling, 1976).

The growth stage is characterized by a rapid increase in the workforce resulting in increased functional specialization, the creation of a more complex hierarchy, and roles that are continuously changing and becoming more differentiated (Kazanjian, 1988). With this growth a more defined compensation system is required but a concern is what the design and structure of it should be. The objective is to pay a diverse group of employees fairly but also allow for constantly changing roles and an increasing complex hierarchy. Additionally, while the firm has more financial resources than were available in earlier stages there are still financial constraints in that the financial resources are needed to fund continued growth. All of these factors require that the venture's pay policies be adaptable and flexible (Gomez-Mejia & Balkin, 1992).

To achieve this flexibility, compensation is likely to be based on the knowledge and skills that the person brings to the organization and what the external labor market has established as a competitive salary for those skills. Similar to the launch stage, incentive pay is also expected to be a prominent portion of the compensation package. Additionally, linking incentives to growth and performance objectives helps to ensure the focus remains on the long-term growth and performance of the firm and it provides employees with an opportunity to share in the success of the venture

(Kruse, 1993). It also allows the firm the flexibility to decrease compensation rather than reduce its workforce should the venture not meet its performance objectives (Wietzman, 1984, 1985). This approach to pay allows the firm to remain flexible and maintain a long-term orientation.

While many new ventures have the objective of growing rapidly and becoming a market leader in their specific product market, many firms do not fit that description. In addition, some new ventures are not founded by a team of individuals. The propositions developed in this chapter are oriented toward ventures that have a team of founders and adopt a high growth strategy, which is typical of firms in high technology industries. In contrast to what was presented here, a new venture may not adopt a high growth strategy or it could be started by a single individual. Both of these differences would result in different compensation decisions in some or all of the stages of growth. Additionally, while high-technology ventures may involve either high-tech manufacturing or professional services such as technology consulting, these propositions assume that the high-growth firm is more similar to high-tech manufacturing or software development firms. In contrast, if the new venture offered professional consulting services this could affect the dominant compensation decisions made by the venture. In all of these instances, the new venture would address their compensation issues differently resulting in a compensation system with a different configuration.

REFERENCES

Aldrich, H., & Langton, N. (1997). Human resource management practices and organizational life cycles. In P. Reynolds & W. Bygrave (Eds.), *Frontiers of entrepreneurship research* (pp. 349-357). Babson Park, MA: Center for Entrepreneurial Studies Babson College.

Ambrose, M. L., & Schminke, M. (2003). Organization structure as a moderator of the relationship between procedural justice, interactional justice, perceived organizational support, and supervisory trust. *Journal of Applied Psychology, 88*(2), 295.

Balkin, D. B., & Bannister, B. (1993). Explaining pay forms for strategic employee groups in organizations: A resource dependence perspective. *Journal of Occupational and Organizational Psychology, 66*, 139-151.

Balkin, D. B., & Gomez-Mejia, L. R. (1990). Matching compensation and organizational strategies. *Strategic Management Journal, 11*, 153-169.

Balkin, D. B., & Logan, J. W. (1988). Reward policies that support entrepreneurship. *Compensation and Benefits Review, 20*(1), 18-25.

Bhave, M. P. (1994). A process model of entrepreneurial venture creation. *Journal of Business Venturing, 9*, 223-242.

Bloom, M., & Milkovich, G. T. (1998). Relationships among risk, incentive pay, and organizational performance. *Academy of Management Journal, 41*, 283-297.

Churchill, N. C., & Lewis, V. L. (1983). The five stages of small business growth. *Harvard Business Review, 61*(3), 30-50.

Collins, J., & Muchinsky, P. (1993). An assessment of the construct validity of three job evaluation methods: A field experiment. *Academy of Management Journal, 36*, 895-904.

Covin, J. G., Slevin, D. P., & Covin, T. (1990). Content and performance of growth-seeking strategies: A comparison of small firms in high- and low-technology industries. *Journal of Business Venturing, 5*, 391-403.

Deshpande, S. P., & Golhar, D. Y. (1994, April). HRM practices in large and small manufacturing firms: A comparative study. *Journal of Small Business Management*, 49-57.

Deutsch, M. (1949). A theory of cooperation and competition. *Human Relations, 2*, 129-152.

Ensley, M. D., Allison, A. W., & Amason, A. C. (2002). Understanding the dynamics of new venture top management teams cohesion, conflict, and new venture performance. *Journal of Business Venturing, 17*, 365.

Fama, E. F. (1980). Agency problems and the theory of the firm. *Journal of Political Economy, 88*, 288-308.

Farrell, J., & Saloner, G. (1985). Standardization, compatibility, and innovation. *RAND Journal of Economics, 16*(1), 70-84.

Galbraith, C. S., & Merrill, M. C. (1991). The effect of compensation program and structure of SBU competitive strategy: A study of technology-intensive firms. *Strategic Management Journal, 12*, 353-370.

Gerhart, B., & Milkovich, G. (1990). Organizational differences in managerial compensation and financial performance. *Academy of Management Journal, 33*, 663-691.

Gerhart, B., & Trevor, C. O. (1996). Employment variability under different managerial compensation systems. *Academy of Management Journal, 39*, 1692-1712.

Gomez-Mejia, L. R. (1992). Structure and process of diversification, compensation strategy, and firm performance. *Strategic Management Journal, 13*, 381-397.

Gomez-Mejia, L. R., & Balkin, D. B. (1992). *Compensation, organizational strategy and firm performance.* Cincinnati, OH: Southwestern.

Graham, M. E., Murray, B., & Amuso, L. (2002). Stock-related rewards, social identity, and the attraction and retention of employees in entrepreneurial SMEs. In J. A. Katz & T. M. Welbourne (Eds.), *Managing people in entrepreneurial organizations* (Vol. 5, pp. 107-145). Amsterdam: Elsevier Science Ltd.

Greenberg, J. (1987). A taxonomy of organizational justice theories. *Academy of Management Review, 12*, 9-22.

Greer, C., Youngblood, S., & Gray, D. (1999). Human resource management outsourcing: The make or buy decision. *Academy of Management Executive, 13*(3), 85-96.

Greiner, L. E. (1998, May-June). Evolution and revolution as organizations grow. *Harvard Business Review*, 55-67.

Hanks, S. H., Watson, C. J., Jansen, E., & Chandler, G. N. (1993, Winter). Tightening the life-cycle construct: A taxonomic study of growth stage configuration in high-technology organizations. *Entrepreneurship Theory and Practice*, 5-30.

Henderson, A. D., & Fredrickson, J. W. (2001). Top management team coordination needs and the CEO pay gap: A competitive test of economic and behavioral views. *Academy of Management Journal, 44*, 96-118.

Heneman, R. L., Tansky, J. W., & Camp, S. M. (2000, Fall). Human resource management practices in small and medium-sized enterprises: Unanswered questions and future research perspectives. *Entrepreneurship Theory and Practice*, 11-26.

Hill, C. W. L., & Snell, S. A. (1989). Effects of ownership structure and control on corporate productivity. *Academy of Management Journal, 32*, 25-46.

Hoskisson, R. E., Hitt, M. A., & Hill, C. W. L. (1993). Managerial incentives and investment in R&D in large multi-product firms. *Organization Science, 4*, 325-341.

Jensen, M. C., & Meckling, W. H. (1976). Theory of the firm: Managerial behavior, agency costs, and ownership structure. *Journal of Financial Economics, 3*, 305-360.

Justis, R. T., Chan, P. S., & Werbel, J. D. (1991). Reward strategies for franchising organizations. *Journal of Small Business Strategy, 2*, 16-23.

Katz, M. L., & Shapiro, C. (2001). Network externalities, competition, and compatibility. *American Economic Review, 75*, 424-440.

Kazanjian, R. K. (1988). Relation of dominant problems to stages of growth in technology-based new ventures. *Academy of Management Journal, 31*, 257-279.

Kraizberg, E., Tziner, A., & Weisberg, J. (2002). Employee stock options: Are they indeed superior to other incentive compensation schemes? *Journal of Business and Psychology, 16*, 383-390.

Kruse, D. L. (1993). *Profit sharing: Does it make a difference?* Kalamazoo, MI: W.E. Upjohn Institute for Employment Research.

Lawler, E. E. III. (1990). *Strategic pay.* San Francisco: Jossey-Bass.

Lawler, E. E. III. (1994). From job-based to competency-based organizations. *Journal of Organizational Behavior, 15*, 3-15.

Lawrence, P., & Lorsch, J. (1967). Organization and Environment. Homewood, IL: Irwin.

Leiblein, M. J., Reuer, J. J., & Dalsace, F. (2002). Do make or buy decisions matter? The influence of organizational governance on technological performance. *Strategic Management Journal, 23*(9), 817.

Mann, R. A., & Roberts, B. S. (1994). *Business law* (9th ed.). St. Paul, MN: West.

Martocchio, J. J. (2003). *Employee benefits.* Burr Ridge, IL: McGraw-Hill Irwin.

Miceli, M. P., & Heneman, R. L. (2000). Contextual determinants of variable pay plan design: A proposed research framework. *Human Resource Management Review, 10*, 289-305.

Milkovich, G. T., & Newman, J. M. (2002). *Compensation* (7th ed.). Burr Ridge, IL: McGraw-Hill Irwin.

Miller, J. S., Wiseman, R. M., & Gomez-Mejia, L. R. (2002). The fit between CEO compensation design and firm risk. *Academy of Management Journal, 45*(4), 745.

Moore, G. A. (1991). *Crossing the chasm.* New York: Harper Business.

Murray, B., & Gerhart, B. (2000). Skill-based pay and skill seeking. *Human Resource Management Review, 10*, 271-287.

Parus, B. (1999, February). Designing a total rewards program to retain critical talent in the millennium. *ACA News*, 20-23.

Rees, A. (1979). *The economics of work and pay*. New York: Harper & Row.

Rosen, C. (2002). *Employee stock options are here to stay*. http://www.nceo.org

Schilling, M. A. (1998). Technological lockout: An integrative model of the economic and strategic factors driving technology success and failure. *Academy of Management Review, 23*(2), 267-284.

Shepherd, D. A., & Zacharakis, A. (2001). The venture capitalist-entrepreneur relationship: Control, trust, and confidence in co-operative behavior. *Venture Capital, 3*(2), 129-150.

Stroh, L. K., Brett, J. M., Baumann, J. P., & Reilly, A. H. (1996). Agency theory and variable pay compensation strategies. *Academy of Management Journal, 39*, 751-767.

Taulli, T. (2001). *Stock options: Getting your share of the action*. Princeton, NJ: Bloomberg Press.

Timmons, J. A. (1994). *New venture creation* (4th ed.). Burr Ridge, IL: McGraw-Hill Irwin.

Weitzman, M. L. (1984). *The share economy*. Cambridge, MA: Harvard University Press.

Weitzman, M. L. (1985). The simple macroeconomics of profit sharing. *American Economic Review, 75*, 937-954.

CHAPTER 8

HR AND THE HIGH-GROWTH SME

The Role of Professional Employer Organizations

Brian Klaas, John McClendon, Tom Gainey,
and Hyeuksueng Yang

Small and Medium Enterprises (SMEs) face significant challenges in their efforts to effectively manage human resources. Because of these challenges, many SMEs have explored using Professional Employer Organizations to obtain a wide array of HR services. While PEOs have the potential to offer many benefits for SMEs, a number of factors have emerged that might threaten the feasibility of this form of governance and the PEO's ability to achieve positive outcomes for client organizations. For SMEs considering use of a PEO, numerous questions are raised by this combination of potential benefits from PEO utilization and threats to the feasibility of the PEO model. In this paper, we have attempted to identify some of the more significant questions, our current knowledge base with regard to these questions, and areas where future research might be beneficial.

Human Resource Strategies for the High Growth Entrepreneurial Firm, 161–188
Copyright © 2006 by Information Age Publishing
All rights of reproduction in any form reserved.

INTRODUCTION

It is well established that the management of human resources can play a critical role in affecting the performance and growth of the small and medium enterprise (Baron, Burton, & Hannon, 1996; Welbourne & Cyr, 1999). In many ways, high-growth small and medium enterprises (SMEs) are more vulnerable to deficiencies in how human resources are managed (Sexton, Upton, Wacholtz, & McDougall, 1997). When firms are at critical junctures with regard to their growth, the failure to retain a key employee or to make valid judgments when hiring can derail the firm's strategy. Similarly, when HR practices sour interpersonal relationships within the SME, the effect on strategy execution is likely to be particularly significant given social structures common within smaller firms (Hannon, Burton, & Baron, 1996; Holoviak & DeCenzo, 1982).

It is less clear, however, what SME leaders should do to ensure the effective delivery of HR services and programs. Lacking sufficient economies of scale, responsibility for HR issues often resides with the general manager and his/her administrative staff—individuals who typically have little background or training in HR. Even among larger SMEs, the capacity to build and develop an effective HR staff is sometimes limited (Cook, 1999). From a governance standpoint, then, questions exist regarding the effectiveness of using internal staff members to provide HR services. As a result of these questions, many SMEs have explored using market-based governance to obtain HR services. To date, the Professional Employer Organization (PEO) is the most common mechanism used by SMEs to obtain integrated HR services via market governance (Klaas, McClendon, & Gainey, 2000).

While many argue that Professional Employer Organizations have the potential to improve organizational performance and growth, it should be noted that there are significant challenges associated with making effective use of a PEO. Indeed, these challenges may limit a PEO's ability to achieve positive outcomes for client organizations. Significant questions exist regarding the conditions under which firms will benefit from using a PEO and what SMEs should do to ensure they actually benefit from PEO utilization. Given these questions, there is a need for research to examine PEOs and their impact on high-growth SMEs.

In this chapter, we begin by examining how HR tasks typically are performed in SMEs in the absence of a PEO and when in-house task performance might actually yield advantages for the SME. Following this, we examine the structure of PEOs in order to assess how they can generate value for the SME. We will then examine factors that might limit the degree to which an SME actually realizes these potential benefits. As we will show, this combination of potential benefits from PEO utilization and threats to the PEO model has created significant questions regarding the role of PEOs in small and medium enterprises. This paper identifies these significant questions and discusses what evidence exists that addresses these questions as well as where additional research is needed.

THE IN-HOUSE MODEL OF HR FOR SMES

It is important to acknowledge that most SMEs do not make use of a PEO. These SMEs provide HR services using internal resources (Cook, 1999). For many SMEs, however, this means that some HR programs and services are more informal or ad-hoc in nature. It may also mean that other HR programs and services are simply not provided (Holoviak & DeCenzo, 1982). Consider the following hypothetical structure for HR in an SME that does not use a PEO. The SME leader may contract with an accounting firm for payroll related activities and they may obtain insurance programs directly from an insurance vendor. With regard to issues such as hiring and firing, performance management, pay and rewards, and employee development, the SME leader is likely to play a key role. Very often under this arrangement, these activities will be performed more informally and in a more ad-hoc fashion.

The outcomes that result from such an arrangement are likely to vary greatly across firms. For example, such a model might impose more modest demands on an SME leader in what might be viewed as a steady-state environment. For example, where there is modest growth and low turnover among employees, the HR environment might be less demanding. Such an environment might impose even more modest HR demands if the current employees have mastered their jobs and feel some personal connection with the SME leader. In such an environment, the need for professionally-designed HR systems and support may be less critical. Within such environment, strong personal relationships may be sufficient to ensure the continued, effective performance of the existing stock of employees.

It is in more demanding HR environments where such an approach might create more difficulties for the SME leader. For example, where growth needs require that the firm make large numbers of critical hires, the consequences of even modest improvements in selection practices are likely to be substantial (Heneman & Judge, 2003). Similarly, where business processes place greater demands on performance management and employee development systems, well designed HR programs are likely to have a greater impact on HR outcomes.

One might also argue that retaining a more informal and ad-hoc approach to managing HR is also likely to yield benefits for the firm (relative to moving toward PEO utilization), when the firm's business processes or culture are so idiosyncratic that outside vendors are likely to have difficulty understanding how to use HR practices within that organization. HR expertise should be used in a way that reflects the particular needs of the firm. Where those needs are highly idiosyncratic, it may be difficult for the vendor to adjust its services to reflect those idiosyncratic needs (Klaas, McClendon, & Gainey, 1999). Under such conditions, retaining a more informal and ad-hoc approach to HR may be preferable to relying on HR systems that are more formalized but less reflective of the needs of the firm.

It is important to acknowledge that not all SMEs rely on more informal and ad-hoc HR systems in the absence of using a PEO. An SME is defined to include firms that have up to 500 employees. While in-house HR professionals are clearly not an option for smaller SMEs, for larger ones it is clearly a viable alternative. Maintaining an internal staff would allow for the SME to obtain professional HR expertise and also to rationalize the process of making HR decisions. For smaller SMEs, the choice is between a more informal and ad-hoc approach to HR and reliance on a third-party vendor. For the largest SMEs, the choice is between in-house HR and reliance on a third-party vendor. For larger SMEs, the choice about whether to use a PEO is similar to the choice facing larger firms about whether to move toward BPO outsourcing within the HR arena (LePak & Snell, 1999). Outsourcing offers economies of scale and efficient access to expertise. These benefits are likely to be particularly significant in this setting because many HR tasks would be performed relatively infrequently within even the largest SME. As such, HR staff members are likely to have less opportunity to accumulate expertise in different functional activities. On the opposite side of the ledger, internal HR staff members are likely to accumulate higher levels of firm-specific knowledge. Such knowledge, other things equal, is likely to enable service providers to tailor HR services and programs to business conditions and organizational culture.

THE PEO MODEL AND THE POTENTIAL
BENEFITS FROM PEO UTILIZATION

The co-employment relationship is central to the structure and operation of the PEO. When an SME signs a contractual agreement with a PEO, the PEO and the SME become co-employers of those working at SME facilities. In essence, the SME and the PEO agree to share responsibilities as an employer (Klaas et al., 2000; NAPEO, 1993). While the SME retains the right to hire, reward, and dismiss employees, the PEO becomes the employer of record for other human resource functions (Baron & Kreps,

1999). PEO responsibilities would typically include such transactional activities as payroll, benefits, and regulatory compliance. PEOs may also assume responsibility for HR programs designed to improve the quality and motivation of the SME workforce as well as managerial skills and behavior. For example, a PEO might offer programs designed to help managers conduct effective interviews, provide constructive feedback to subordinates, and devise effective reward programs. They may advise management on employee relations issues, provide training programs to build human capital, and audit HR practices within the firm to ensure that the SME is making effective use of the programs and services available to them through the PEO (Hirschman, 1997).

Potentially, PEOs have a number of means by which to affect SME performance and growth. Because of economies of scale, PEOs are able to efficiently perform a number of routine, administrative tasks that otherwise would consume the energy and time of the SME leader. By saving time in a cost-effective manner, a PEO may enable SME leaders to focus on activities more directly related to core business processes (Klaas et al., 2000). The potential also exists for PEOs to affect valuable HR outcomes within the SME. While SME leaders retain responsibility for such issues as hiring, evaluation, and firing, the PEO can affect how such issues are handled through the programs and services offered (Klaas, in press). To the extent that the PEO can positively affect how SME leaders make decisions about staffing, training, evaluation and rewards, and employee relations, they may be able to affect employee behavior in a number of different ways. Absenteeism, performance and productivity, safety practices, and turnover all may be affected. And as the strategic HR literature suggests, improved performance, turnover, and absenteeism often generates financial benefits for the firm (Huselid, 1995; Becker & Gerhart, 1996).

A final way that PEOs may be able to affect financial outcomes for SMEs relates to the potential for cost-savings. Cost savings may result if the PEO is able to significantly reduce the cost of insurance and benefit programs. Many of the major PEOs serve as a co-employer for tens of thousands of employees. Using the co-employment concept, the PEO may be able to treat all worksite employees as their own from the standpoint of insurance and other benefit programs (Cook, 1999). As a result, the ability to aggregate risk across a large number of employees allows them to obtain a competitive rate for benefit programs. Increased size also provides PEOs with greater leverage in negotiating favorable rates with benefit providers (Klaas et al., 2000). More favorable rates may also result from PEO initiatives designed to improve safety practices within client organizations. Since workers' compensation rates are experience rated, reducing the accident rate among client organizations may lead to lower rates and greater cost savings (Hirschman, 2000). By obtaining lower rates on insurance programs, SMEs may be able to reduce their overall labor costs. Alternatively, the cost savings could be used to offset the cost of more strategic HR programs, thus allowing firms to obtain improved HR outcomes without incurring additional costs.

While the PEO model has the potential to offer a number of benefits for client SMEs, there is substantial variation across SMEs in the objectives they pursue through PEO utilization. For example, while perhaps most SMEs use a PEO primarily to save money or time, there is a significant number that also want services that are likely to affect HR outcomes (Klaas et al., 2000). Similarly, variation also exists among PEOs in what objectives they attempt to pursue for client organizations (Cook, 1999).

THE PEO MODEL: POTENTIAL THREATS TO THE EFFECTIVENESS OF PEO UTILIZATION

While the PEO outsourcing model offers mechanisms which might allow client organizations to experience cost savings, time savings, and improved HR outcomes (Cook, 1999), a number of factors exist that may limit whether an SME will actually receive these benefits (Klaas, in press). First, increasingly, legal questions exist surrounding the co-employment concept. Many of the advantages that results from using the co-employment concept depend on the degree to which PEOs can treat worksite employees as common law employees for the purpose of benefit programs (Hirschman, 1997). And recent IRS rulings have raised questions about the ability of PEOs to do this—which is a direct threat to the PEO business model (Harris & Linsenmayer, 2003). For example, a recent IRS ruling indicated that retirement programs sponsored by PEOs would be subject to taxation because worksite employees are not common law employees of the PEO. A subsequent ruling indicated that PEOs will be permitted to retain tax benefits if they create multi-employer retirement programs. However, with multi-employer programs, if any client organization fails the nondiscrimination test relating to highly paid versus lesser paid employees, all client organizations would be deemed as in noncompliance (Harris & Linsenmayer, 2003). While this does permit PEOs to rely on the co-employment concept, it also creates additional burdens for PEOs and may necessitate a very different type of PEO-SME relationship.

Second, increased costs associated with workers' compensation programs have led to the failure of some of significant PEOs (e.g., HR Logic). Further, issues relating to how workers' compensation programs have been managed have led CNA to stop providing workers' compensation insurance to PEOs in the state of Florida (Cole, 2002; Braga, 2002). These recent developments are significant because a key element in a typical PEO business model is the ability of the PEO to obtain savings in insurance programs for client organizations. With regard to workers' compensation, it is usually argued that cost savings are possible because the PEO is able to introduce safety practices within client organizations, aggregate risk, and obtain better rates through negotiating leverage afforded by their size (Cook, 1999). It has been suggested, however, that some PEOs aggressively pursued growth even if it meant adding clients with a significant risk-profile, clients who perhaps were unwilling to make the changes necessary to reduce the accident rate. While in the short-run, PEOs were able to offer reduced insurance rates, over time accident rates climbed and, with that, insurance costs. This rise in insurance rates was exacerbated by business conditions facing the insurance industry itself—conditions which made providers more conservative when assessing risk (Braga, 2002). It has also been suggested that the PEO structure has sometimes been used to, in essence, hide workplaces with an unacceptable risk profile from insurance providers. The potential for such behavior is part of what led some workers' compensation providers to limit the coverage provided to PEOs or to change the pricing structure (Cole, 2002).

It is clear that some PEOs achieved cost savings and revenue growth by utilizing practices that could not be sustained over time. While this raises questions about practices of particular PEOs, it does not necessarily challenge the previously described logic underlying the PEO business model. However, it does highlight the difficulties facing PEOs. PEOs likely to survive in the current climate may well be those that are effective in managing workplace safety issues and in selecting clients that both have an acceptable risk profile and a willingness to cooperation with efforts to improve safety.

A third potential challenge relates to the type of service provided by the PEO and the way those services are delivered. Many PEOs focus more on the transactional side of HR (Klaas, McClendon, Gainey, & Yang, 2003). They focus on offering cost and time savings and attempt to achieve these goals by outsourcing tasks that are well suited to market-based governance (Baron & Kreps, 1999). Cost and time savings are achieved largely through the outsourcing of routine HR activities (e.g., payroll, benefits administration, and regulatory compliance) and such tasks can be more easily specified in contractual terms (LePak & Snell, 1999). Further, because such tasks can be standardized across organizations, market competition has the potential to be a viable tool for ensuring effective task performance. The standardized nature of the tasks also allows for economies of scale within the PEO to generate substantial efficiencies and, thus, savings for the SME (Greer, Youngblood, & Gray, 1999).

Where a PEO maintains such a focus, it is unclear whether HR outcomes would be affected. As such, a key benefit associated with using a PEO is likely to depend on the type of PEO utilized (Klaas, in press). Even where a PEO incorporates services designed to affect employee behavior and motivation, questions exist over whether the PEO model will be effective. Much of this concern is driven by the fact that PEOs must provide services to large numbers of small clients, meaning that service providers may have limited opportunity to interact with SME leaders and employees. Without frequent interaction, questions exist about whether the PEO will have a sufficient understanding of conditions at the firm to offer effective advice and guidance regarding human resource issues. The literature on strategic HR suggests that HR practices should be tailored to reflect a firm's culture and business strategy (Arthur, 1992; Becker & Huselid, 1999; Wright, Smart, & McMahan, 1995). Questions exist about whether PEO service providers will have sufficient knowledge about client organizations to ensure that HR practices and programs are tailored to meet the unique needs of the firm. And if the HR services are "generic" in nature, will they impact employee behavior and motivation in a way that is consistent with the needs of the firm?

A fourth potential challenge for the PEO model relates to whether efforts to improve the management of HR through PEO utilization actually allows for firms to develop resources that would create sustainable competitive advantage (SCA). How organizations manage people is typically seen as a possible source of SCA (Becker & Huselid, 1999; Barney, 1991). Effective HR practices and programs can create valuable outcomes in terms of employee performance and productivity—outcomes that are difficult for other firms to achieve. Further, because the effective management of people is dependent on tacit knowledge, as well as routines and norms that are not easily understood, the source of improved performance and productivity is less susceptible to imitation by competing firms. However, when a firm achieves improved HR outcomes by using a PEO, questions exist about whether the SME retains sufficient control over the source of SCA. Further questions exist about whether other firms might be able to achieve the same outcomes simply by also making use of the same PEO. This question is particularly significant if the SME invests in helping the PEO develop the competencies to affect behavior within the SME. Quite clearly, the value of this investment declines if the PEO can readily transfer the relevant routines, norms, and tacit knowledge to other SMEs.

A fifth challenge relates to the potential for opportunism often associated with the use of market governance. As Transaction Cost Economics and the make or buy literature suggests (Walker & Weber, 1984; Williamson, 1996), the potential for opportunism by the vendor depends on the nature of the transaction and also the nature of the relationship between the parties. The potential for opportunism is thought to be greatest when an asset-specific investment is required in order for the vendor to provide services and when there is incomplete contracting (Hart, 1988). Within the context of a PEO-SME relationship, asset-specificity and incomplete contracting are likely to be greatest when the PEO provides more strategic HR services as well as the more transactional. More strategic services are likely to require some investment in understanding an SME's business and culture. Further, it is difficult to know in advance the exact nature of the services required in more strategic areas, making incomplete contracting more likely. As such, SMEs using PEOs to obtain the widest range of outcomes are likely to experience the greatest risk of opportunism.

Having said this, it is important to note that some of the most severe cases of PEO fraud and abuse were committed by PEOs providing largely transactional HR services (Cole, 2002). This suggests that controlling for opportunism can prove to be challenging even for SMEs using a PEO primarily for transactional purposes. While market governance has the potential to be effective when transactional services are provided, that effectiveness depends on effective contracting and monitoring as well as the effective flow of information about PEO services and costs among SMEs within a given market (Helper & Levine, 1992; Williamson, 1996). As such, while market governance clearly can be effective with regard to transactional services, it is important to recognize that SMEs are not immune from opportunism simply because their PEO utilization is limited to transactional services.

POTENTIAL BENEFITS AND POTENTIAL THREATS: QUESTIONS RAISED ABOUT PEOS AND THEIR IMPACT ON SMES

While PEOs may well have the potential to generate substantial benefits for SMEs and contribute to their growth and performance, it is also true that SMEs face some significant challenges when attempting to make effective use of a PEO. As a result, numerous questions exist about the effects of PEO utilization on SME outcomes, about the conditions under which SMEs are most likely to benefit from PEO utilization, and about SME and PEO practices that might enhance the prospects of an SME benefiting from PEO utilization. In the remainder of the paper, we will identify these questions and then discuss both the evidence available from existing research and areas where future research is needed.

Why PEOs? Why Not Business Process Outsourcing?

In reviewing the potential benefits associated with outsourcing as well as the potential challenges for SMEs and PEOs, it is clear that the co-employment relationship has traditionally played a critical role within the PEO-SME relationship. But should it? Do alternatives exist for SMEs wanting to obtain HR services and programs without co-employment? Vendors such as Exault and Fidelity Employer Services provide integrated HR outsourcing to large clients such as IBM and Bank of America and do so without the co-employment relationship (Cook, 1999). Is it possible that business process outsourcing models would be relevant for smaller organizations as well? By moving to the BPO model, concerns about the legal status of the co-employment relationship would be negated as would concerns about whether the co-employment model was being used to, in essence, disguise the presence of high-risk employers in the PEO's workers' compensation pool. However, questions remain about whether BPO providers would be able to obtain competitive rates for insurance programs for client organizations. Cost savings might be achieved by virtue of the BPO agreeing to serve as a marketplace for alternative providers and by using expertise in risk management to find lower-cost ways of providing coverage (Cole, 2002). Whether these cost-savings would match the savings available through the PEO model remains to be seen and, clearly deserves attention. Another open question is whether—under ideal circumstances—the co-employment model helps create a strong link between the PEO and the SME. For example, if the PEO needs to improve safety practices within each client to ensure that their rates overall remain low, it is likely that the PEO will establish a stronger presence within the SME and develop stronger ties. In doing so, they might well be better positioned to then offer advice and counsel about how best to manage employee relations issues and ultimately affect HR outcomes within the firm (Klaas, in press). It may well be that the co-employment relationship forces at least some PEOs to strengthen their relationship with SME leaders and this relationship may be critical to the PEO's ability to change other HR practices within the organization. At its best, then, co-employment may serve as a tool to help move the SME-PEO relationship from an arms-length relationship to one where stronger personal ties exist.

Questions about the impact of the co-employment relationship on the link between PEO service providers and SME leaders clearly calls for research and is related to the more general issue of how PEO leaders affect change within client SMEs. For PEOs that focus on more strategic HR services, changing managerial behavior and practices is critical to their ability to deliver results. It is possible that the co-employment relationship encourages a stronger link between PEO service providers and SME leaders—which ultimately enables the PEO to affect change within the SME.

What is the Proper Role for PEOs?
Strategic or Transactional?

Clear distinctions exist across PEOs in their focus with regard to HR services. Whereas some focus primarily on transactional services (e.g., payroll and benefits administration), others try to provide a broad array of HR services—the strategic as well as the transactional. As noted above, while transactional service would traditionally be seen as well suited to outsourcing, questions remain about the likely effect of outsourcing more strategic HR services. When PEOs move toward providing a broad array of HR services, they become involved with services that may require some understanding of conditions at the client organization. Absent that understanding, HR service provided by a PEO may not be adequate to affect employee behavior and motivation. This might seem to suggest the need for PEOs to invest in understanding conditions at each individual client in order to offer firm-specific advice. However, to the extent that the SME pays for this asset-specific investment, it becomes, consistent with transaction cost economics, vulnerable to opportunistic behavior. These concerns raise questions about whether firms that use a PEO to obtain a full-range of services will experience any benefits relative to a firm that uses a PEO simply for transactional services.

This issue was partially addressed in study sponsored by the Society of Human Resource Management (Klaas et al., 2003). In this study, 49 PEOs and 516 clients working with these PEOs were surveyed. The mean number of SMEs served by these 49 PEOs was 229.92 and the mean number of employees served was 4599.34. The largest PEO served more than 4000 SMEs and more than 68,000 employees. The smallest PEO represented five SMEs and 100 employees.

PEO leaders were asked to provide information on PEO characteristics, including the type of services offered by the PEO. As part of this, PEO leaders indicated what percent (on a five-point scale) of their clients received services in seven areas within HR that have the potential to be more strategic (e.g., training and development). SME leaders were asked to provide information on, among other things, HR outcomes within the SME. SME leaders indicated how satisfied they were with such things as employee performance, motivation, turnover, and absenteeism. Hierarchical linear modeling was then used to examine whether HR outcomes were higher in firms that were affiliated with PEOs that offered a broader array of strategic HR services (controlling for other characteristics of the PEO and the SME). HR outcomes in firms affiliated with PEOs that offered a broad array of services were found to be more favorable than in SMEs affiliated with firms that used PEOs that focused more on transactional HR activities.

It is important to stress that these results do not suggest that it is necessarily preferable to use a PEO that provides a broad array of HR services. Rather, the results indicate that the limitations associated with an outsourcing model do not prevent more strategic HR services from affecting employee behavior and outcomes and that it may be possible, therefore, for firms to benefit from utilizing a full-service PEO. In other words, while there may be significant challenges associated with using a PEO to obtain a broad range of HR services, these results of the above described survey suggest that it may be possible to overcome these challenges.

Full Service Versus Transactional PEOs? Should Different SMEs Choose a Different Kind of PEO?

The research referenced above (Klaas et al., 2003) suggests that SMEs may be able to obtain more favorable HR outcomes if they use a full-service PEO rather than one focused on providing transactional services. But would all firms be able to obtain these benefits and might some firms actually be more likely to experience these improved HR outcomes than others. In a survey of more than 700 clients of a single PEO, it was found that satisfaction with PEO services was influenced by the quality of the SME-PEO relationship as well as the degree of value congruence between the vendor and the PEO (Klaas et al., 2000). This finding highlights the possibility that SME characteristics may play a role in determining the benefits generated from using a given PEO.

Theory also suggests that a PEO's ability to affect HR outcomes is likely to depend on characteristics of the client (Klaas, in press). For example, client receptivity is likely to be critical in determining how strategic HR services offered by a PEO affects HR outcomes. More strategic HR services are often designed to guide SME leaders on employee relations issues that are typically viewed as core areas of responsibility for the general manager of an organization (Becker & Huselid, 1999). Because of the nature of the co-employment relationship, PEOs are limited in their ability to ensure compliance with their advice on these employee relations matters (Cook, 1999). Further, contractual mechanisms within market governance are of limited value in resolving disputes over the process by which to accomplish required tasks (Connor & Prahalad, 1996; Dow, 1987). Thus, where there is a lack of receptivity to the advice provided by the PEO, the PEO is less likely to be able to affect HR outcomes within the organization.

Client receptivity is also critical because one way that PEO utilization affects HR outcomes is through the learning that occurs when SME leaders observe the consequences when they follow guidance offered by the PEO. Much knowledge about employee relations issues is tacit in nature, and best understood through experience (Ulrich, 1996). For example, within an organizational hierarchy, tacit knowledge is thought to be transmitted when subordinates follow the directives of a superior and observe the consequences of the approach taken. With the PEO-SME relationship, however, a similar mechanism does not exist for ensuring the transmission of tacit knowledge (Connor & Prahalad, 1996). Thus, where there is a lack of client receptivity, SME leaders are less likely to follow PEO recommendations, making it less likely that tacit knowledge will be transmitted to SME leaders. And transmission of this tacit knowledge, over time, is likely to affect HR outcomes within an SME.

Attitudes within the SME regarding the importance of human capital and the need to effectively manage that human capital may also be relevant in determining the likely affect of using a PEO that offers a full-range of HR services. While transactional HR services can easily be compartmentalized and then outsourced to the PEO, many more strategic HR services require the active involvement of SME leaders. Cooperation by SME leaders is critical in determining the impact of more strategic HR services and that cooperation may depend on whether SME leaders perceive human capital as critical to the success of their firm. As such, attitudes and beliefs among SME leaders may play a critical role in determining whether an SME should use a full-service PEO as opposed to one focusing largely on transactional HR activities.

Similarly, communication behavior within the SME-PEO relationship is likely to be more critical when working with a PEO providing a full-range of HR services. With transactional HR activities, tasks are largely routine and, for the most part, are highly standardized across client organizations. Communication between vendor and client revolves around routine information exchange. By contrast, HR programs that are designed to affect employee behavior and attitudes are likely to require full and open communication between the PEO and the SME. In order to help SME leaders effectively use the more strategic HR services that the PEO makes available, PEO service providers may need to understand the personalities and culture within the SME. Further, communicating the need for change in how people are managed may require highly-developed communication patterns (Klaas, in press). As such, unless SME leaders are willing to communicate extensively and openly about a wide range of managerial and organizational issues, it may well be that the SME would have difficulty fully benefitting from utilizing a PEO that offers more strategic as well as transactional HR services.

Consistent with theory, evidence suggests that the effect of utilizing a PEO that offers a broad array of HR services (rather than just transactional services) depends on communications behavior, client receptivity, and the perceived importance of human capital (Klaas et al., 2003). In the SMRM sponsored survey described above, SME leaders responded to three item scales (each with coefficient alphas above .80) for (a) communications behavior; (b) client receptivity, and (c) the perceived importance of human capital. Using HLM procedures, each variable was found to moderate the impact of using a PEO that offers more strategic HR services. This finding is consistent with the argument that some clients may be better positioned to benefit from a PEO offering a full array of services. As such, this finding highlights the importance of PEOs assessing client characteristics and screening clients based on the issue of fit. Having said this, it is important to stress that little is known about how client receptivity, beliefs in the importance of human capital, or the willingness to communicate emerge within an SME (or within the context of an SME-PEO relationship). For example, does client receptivity emerge over time as the result of positive interactions with the PEO? Can PEO service providers affect change in how SME leaders perceive human capital and, if they can, how is such change affected? While it may be that questions of this sort cannot be addressed via conventional methods, longitudinal case studies may permit insights in this regard.

Can Offering Strategic HR Services Yield Benefits?

Using a PEO for more strategic as well as transactional HR services appears to offer benefits to client organizations in terms of improved HR outcomes (Klaas et al., 2003). It is less clear why those benefits actually occur. It might simply be that PEOs that offer more strategic HR services are making available standardized and generic programs relating to hiring procedures, employee communication and feedback, employee training, and employee relations. While the HR programs and services might well be standardized and generic, they may still represent a significant improvement over what would have been done in their absence. For example, simply offering standardized decision-aids and tools for the selection process may be sufficient to improve the quality of hires relative to what would be done otherwise. Making available standardized paper and pencil tests as well as decision-aids for developing a structured interview may be sufficient to make a significant improvement in workforce quality.

Alternatively, the effect generated by more strategic HR services may result from more complex processes. While the full-service PEO may offer a variety of standardized tools to help SME leaders address strategic HR issues, the positive effect observed in the study referenced above (Klaas et al., 2003) may depend on efforts by the PEO to utilize firm-specific knowledge to advise SMEs on what tools should be used and how they should be used. It may also depend on advice and counsel provided by the PEO regarding how to use the available tools and resources to address HR problems that the SME is currently facing. Similarly, it may depend on the capacity of SME leaders to link the services available from the PEO to the unique needs of the firm

In sum, ambiguity exists regarding the degree to which generic HR tools offered by a PEO will lead to improved HR outcomes and also about the degree to which the PEO must develop firm-specific knowledge about SME clients. This issue has significant applied implications both for SMEs considering use of a PEO and PEOs designing service delivery models. If the impact of more strategic HR services depends on the development of firm-specific knowledge and offering firm-specific advice and solutions, it may be necessary to utilize service delivery models that encourage repeated interaction between clients and the same set of service providers within the PEO. Such a need might call into question more efficient models of service delivery—models that revolve around call centers and, increasingly, self-service software applications.

This issue also has implications for governance within the SME-PEO relationship. If, in fact, improved HR outcomes arise through standardized applications, standard market governance mechanisms may, in fact, be well suited for PEO-SME relationships that offer both transactional and strategic HR services. However, if firm-specific knowledge and services are required, asset-specific investments are likely to be required (Greer et al., 1999; Klaas et al., 1999). And in light of incomplete contracting, vulnerability to opportunism may arise. And consistent with make or buy literature, under such conditions the relationship between the client and vendor may play a critical role in constraining opportunism (Ghoshal & Moran, 1996; Gulati, 1995). Where trust develops over time between parties, opportunism may be less likely to emerge (Coleman, 1990). Where trust exists, the psychic costs of behaving opportunistically may deter such behavior (Nooteboom, Berger, & Noorderhaven, 1997). If the above referenced positive effect on HR outcomes is a result of PEOs developing firm-specific solutions, the appropriate governance model for ensuring effective service may well differ from standard market governance models. Contractual mechanisms may not be sufficient and may need to be supplemented by greater emphasis on the development of trust and a strong PEO-SME relationship. This issue of why strategic HR services yield benefits have clear implications for both SMEs and PEOs, and as such, there is a need for research to examine the process underlying the positive effect associated with strategic HR services.

Can Using a PEO Lead to Sustainable Competitive Advantage?

Obtaining sustainable competitive advantage (SCA) is thought to require resources that are valuable, rare, and difficult to imitate (Barney, 1991). Increasingly, the HR system is seen as having the potential to create such resources (Becker & Gerhart, 1996; Becker & Huselid, 1999). Questions might be asked about whether SMEs can create these resources by using an outside provider such as a PEO. In many ways, this issue is relevant only for SMEs considering use of a PEO that provides both transactional and more strategic HR services. When using a PEO that provides only transactional HR services, the focus is on outsourcing routine, administrative activities in order to save time or reduce costs (Cook, 1999). While that may lead to valuable outcomes, given that mechanisms used to achieve these outcomes are highly standardized, other firms are likely to be able to achieve the same outcomes by affiliating with the same or a similar PEO and using contractual mechanisms effectively. This would seem to preclude sustainable competitive advantage (Barney, 1991).

By contrast, it may well be that using a full-service PEO could create resources that lead to SCA. As noted above, previous research found that improved HR outcomes were observed in association with using a PEO that offered strategic as well as transactional HR activities. Further, characteristics of the SME and the SME-PEO relationship interacted with the availability of strategic services. This suggests that it may be difficult for some SMEs to obtain improved HR outcomes simply by affiliating with a PEO that offered strategic HR services. Clients who are skeptical regarding the value of investing in human capital and those who display little interest in learning from or communicating with the PEO in regard to people management issues may be less likely to obtain the same benefits as other SMEs. The potential for SCA is also introduced by the difficulty of evaluating the HR services and programs that are targeted at employee behavior and outcomes (Greer et al., 1999). Because of the role tacit knowledge plays in managing people effectively (Barney, 1991), it is not always easy to communicate and justify a given approach to managing people—even when that approach is likely to be effective. As such, it may be difficult for SMEs to compare the services offered by PEOs and make a selection based on the quality of their more strategic HR services. While it is perhaps easier to compare benefit plans, it is likely to be more challenging for SME leaders to assess in advance the quality of the tools and advice that will be made available to help the SME manage people more effectively.

Barriers to imitation can also be found in the fact that it may often be necessary for PEO service providers to educate SME leaders regarding the need for change in how they approach managing people. Again, because HR practices are based on tacit knowledge, such education may occur slowly and may require the development of trust between SME leaders and PEO service providers. There is likely to be an additional barrier to imitation if a PEO's ability to affect HR outcomes depends on the development of firm-specific knowledge. Such knowledge is unlikely to develop quickly—which suggests that a PEO's ability to affect HR outcomes may emerge over time and only if both parties remain committed to achieving that long-term objective.

It is important to note that these arguments about PEOs and SCA are based on a number of assumptions and research has not directly examined if PEOs allow for SCA. In part, this may be because longitudinal data on financial performance is often difficult to obtain from SMEs—at least compared to publicly traded firms. While this barrier to data collection is likely to remain, it may be possible to examine issues that are suggestive as to whether PEO utilization could lead to SCA. Specifically, by examining potential barriers to imitation within the SME-PEO relationship, it might be possible to at least draw inferences regarding the potential for SCA. For example, by studying multiple clients of the same full-service PEO, it might be possible to assess the degree to which different clients are benefitting from PEO utilization and what factors are allowing some to benefit more than others. It might also be noted that case study or ethnographic approaches to studying these issues might ultimately prove more feasible than conventional empirical methods.

What Should an SME Consider When Selecting a PEO?

SMEs differ in what they want from a PEO and, for some, cost and time savings are the primary objectives (Klaas et al., 2000). The services desired by these SMEs are largely routine and administrative and, as such, traditional mechanisms within market governance might well be appropriate when selecting such a transactionally-oriented PEO. Requiring careful specification regarding the services to be provided and the costs of those services allows for effective comparison across alternative vendors. Careful examination of contractual provisions necessary to protect SME interests also play a critical role (Cook, 1999).

However, the challenges currently facing the PEO industry may also suggest additional considerations. First, while rapid growth has characterized the PEO industry for much of the last decade (Hirschman, 2000), it is increasingly important to examine how that growth was achieved. For example, for some PEOs growth was achieved by offering cost savings on insurance programs almost regardless of SME characteristics. Little attention was paid to an SME's history with regard to workplace accidents or the SME's willingness to cooperate with PEO efforts to alter safety practices, ensure regulatory compliance, or otherwise affect change within the PEO. Recent developments with regard to workers' compensation insurance have made this a dangerous practice for PEOs and is seen as having led to the demise of several significant firms (Cole, 2002). Growth achieved without being selective as to clients increasingly may be an indication that the PEO is facing undue risks and, thus, may have difficulty sustaining operations over time. Further, it appears that some of the greatest abuses by PEOs occurred when the PEO was facing significant pressures as a result of accepting undue risks (Braga, 2002).

The importance of being selective with regard to clients is also suggested by the IRS's recent ruling regarding the co-employment relationship and the need for PEOs to use multi-employer retirement plans (Harris & Linsenmayer, 2003). Under such multi-employer systems, if any client fails the nondiscrimination test, the entire system fails. As such, it is increasingly important for SMEs to select PEOs that have selected other clients that are willing to cooperate with such regulatory requirements.

Together, these developments raise questions about the degree to which the PEO-SME relationship can be treated as an arms-length relationship—even for SMEs wanting transactional services. If reductions in insurance costs depend increasingly on reducing accident rates, PEO-SME cooperation may be more critical. Similarly, given the increasing importance of ensuring compliance across all clients with regard to the nondiscrimination issue, characteristics of the SME-PEO relationship may take on increasing importance. As such, when selecting a PEO, it becomes increasingly important for SMEs to consider a PEOs client base and its capacity for fostering a cooperative relationship with that client base. Unfortunately, little is known about how clients assess a vendor's capacity for forming cooperative relationships nor about how they should make such assessments. Research examining the decision-making process of SME leaders when selecting a vendor may be justified.

For SMEs wanting a PEO that affects a broader range of outcomes, the selection task is even more difficult. Consideration must also be given to the quality of HR programs and expertise offered by the PEO. Evaluating such programs and expertise may be difficult to do in advance—even by individuals with expertise in human resources. Moreover, in addition to evaluating the content of HR programs, decision-makers must also evaluate how these programs will be delivered. If HR programs and expertise must be tailored to meet the needs of individual firms, some level of firm-specific knowledge must develop. As such, if firm-specific knowledge is needed, it may be necessary that the service delivery model permit repeated interaction between a given set of PEO service providers and a PEO. Even if firm-specific knowledge is not needed by PEO service providers, the service delivery model is likely to be critical. Strategic HR services often depend on changing managerial behavior and practices. Whether such change occurs, depends on the way in which services are delivered. As such, SME leaders considering a full-service PEO may need to consider whether the service-delivery model utilized makes it likely that they and other SME managers would respond constructively to PEO initiatives.

Once again little is known about the validity of SME leader judgements regarding the quality of HR services and programs or the quality of the service delivery model. Moreover, little is known about how SME leaders should evaluate more strategic HR services and programs and the delivery of those services and programs. Ample research has examined how selection decisions are made and how to improve the selection process when hiring employees within the context of organizational governance systems (Heneman & Judge, 2003). And this research has proved to have great value from an applied standpoint. Given the growing importance of market governance mechanisms, research examining the selection process with regard to vendors is called for in order to offer insights regarding common problems with the selection process as well as how SMEs might best avoid such problems.

As noted above, it is necessary that both the content and the delivery of strategic HR programs and services be assessed. One emerging trend relating to the delivery of strategic HR services and programs is the reliance on information technology to communicate with mangers about the appropriate approach for managing people and to guide managers through HR decisions. The administrative efficiency associated with such tools suggests that they may be well suited to the SME-PEO relationship. However, it is important to stress that questions might well be raised in light of work in the communications literature relating to information richness (Daft & Lengel, 1986). In general, personal communication is thought to be superior to other forms of communication when efforts are made to establish norms, deal with sensitive issues, or persuade. However, with advances in technology, the information richness of web-based communication is perhaps superior to other forms of written communication. Moreover, given the ease of access associated with such technology-based communication, it may well be that it is utilized more readily than personal communication with PEO service providers. Such ease of access may, to some extent, offset the loss of information richness. Unfortunately, little is known about the role of technology in facilitating communication between PEOs and SMEs. As such, research in this context may well help SME leaders assess alternative service delivery models. From the standpoint of different types of HR communication tasks, when does technology function as effectively as personal communication with regard to the actual exchange of information, attitudinal change, and satisfaction with the communication process? Given that PEOs—drawn by the promise of administrative efficiency—are increasingly incorporating such technology (Cook, 1999), it is important for researchers to explore what HR communication tasks are best suited to technology-driven delivery and how technology can be integrated with personal communication.

How Should an SME Manage a PEO-SME Relationship?

The distinction between SMEs that use a PEO primarily for transactional services and those that use a PEO for both transactional and more strategic HR services is once again relevant here. With regard to SMEs that use a PEO primarily for transactional services, they are using services that are performed, for the most part, in a standardized way across multiple clients (Cook, 1999). Little asset-specific investment is needed in order for payroll and benefit services to be offered, which means that there are few switching costs associated with leaving a vendor should they be dissatisfaction with the services provided. Moreover, the routine nature of the services provided can be more easily specified contractually (LePak & Snell, 1999). As a result, conventional market governance mechanisms have the potential to provide for effective delivery of services. While questions might be raised about the ability to standardize services relating to workplace safety, the PEO's incentive (under current conditions) to reduce accidents is perhaps stronger than the SME's. As such, while the PEO may have to invest time and resources to understand how best to reduce accidents within each individual SME, the incentive-structure with regard to workers' compensation insurance is likely to place the burden for that investment upon the PEO—thus minimizing concerns about asset-specificity and opportunism.

The conclusion offered above is based largely on what theory would suggest based upon the transaction cost literature (Shelanski & Klein,

1995; Williamson, 1996). Specific evidence within this context is limited to the previously referenced study (Klaas et al., 2000) which examined customer satisfaction with PEO services within a single PEO. It was found what while overall satisfaction was affected by social exchange type variables (e.g., strength of the relationship with service providers), satisfaction with cost reduction was unrelated to this variable and much more strongly affected by contract characteristics. It should be stressed, however, that while there is some support for this argument, the available empirical evidence is limited.

Very different issues are raised for SMEs pursuing both transactional and strategic HR services. In large part, this is because the factors that determine HR outcomes are very different from the factors that determine cost and time savings (Klaas, in press). The factors that determine whether a PEO will improve an SME's HR outcomes make it unlikely that the traditional tools associated with market governance will be sufficient. In order for HR outcomes to be affected, greater levels of asset-specific investment are likely to be required, thus making the SME more vulnerable to opportunistic behavior. This vulnerability is heightened by the fact that the services required to affect HR outcomes are less routine and, therefore, less easily specified within the PEO contract (Klaas et al., 1999). This then raises questions about whether opportunism can be constrained via social exchange processes. Within the alliance literature, for example, it has been suggested that the development of strong ties between parties can constrain opportunism (Nooteboom et al., 1997; Ring & Van de Ven, 1992). This literature argues for SME leaders investing in the relationship with their PEO, developing frequent and open communication, and engaging in a pattern of reciprocal accommodation with the PEO. It is important to note that while surveys of PEO clients suggests that relationship variables are related to such outcomes as client satisfaction and HR outcomes (Klaas et al., 2000, 2003), this research does not necessarily demonstrate that opportunistic behavior is actually constrained by the strength of the relationship.

It is also important to stress that there is no evidence to suggest that traditional market governance mechanism decline in importance when firms use a PEO for both transactional and more strategic HR services. For example, surveys of PEO clients suggest that HR outcomes are positively affected by the degree of contractual specificity (Klaas et al., 2003). While it is often suggested that careful negotiations designed to protect one's interest can interfere with the development of trust within a relationship (Ghoshal & Moran, 1996), no evidence of this was found in the assessments provided by PEO clients.

Having said this, ambiguity remains regarding how SMEs should approach the issue of contractual specification. Specifying outcomes and processes in advance remains challenging in light of ambiguity regarding the nature of the task. Within the context of other outsourcing relationships where task ambiguity is significant, the interests of vendors and clients are sometimes linked by incentive programs (Cook, 1999). For example, within the context of the SME-PEO relationship incentives might be established for improvements in turnover rates, employee satisfaction with HR services, and other HR metrics. By focusing on HR metrics within the contract, process issues (about which there is substantial ambiguity) need not be specified with the same level of detail. While such contractual mechanisms offer potential, little is known about their effect within this context, the willingness of the parties to adopt them, or what metrics should be used. It should be noted that some PEOs market themselves as employers of choice and attempt to highlight their ability to affect behavior through processes that inevitably are somewhat ambiguous. Links between PEO incentives and HR outcomes may lend credibility to claims made by the PEO and enhance the development of a partnership between the PEO and the SME.

PEOS AND SMES: FUTURE RESEARCH DIRECTIONS

We have attempted to address what is known about key issues relating to whether and how SMEs should use a PEO and what PEOs may need to consider when determining how to structure their services. While our discussion was informed by both relevant theory and research, many critical questions remain. This section attempts to highlight areas where research might help SMEs understand whether and how to use a PEO.

One key area that merits additional research relates to differences across SMEs in terms of characteristics that might affect whether and how a PEO should be used. SMEs differ in terms of their size, growth rate, prospects for survival, and stability of business processes. These differences are likely to affect the need for human resource services and programs, the ability to provide such services using internal staff members, and the willingness to invest in the implementation of human resource programs and services. Consider, for example, a firm that is at the low end of the size continuum for SMEs and that has been operating for several years with only modest growth and high levels of stability in terms of business processes and employment. With such a firm, there will be fewer opportunities for the PEO to affect workforce quality through more strategic HR services. The payoff from having access to more strategic HR services is likely to be higher when the firm has a higher hiring rate and when it needs to respond to more rapid change in business processes.

Consider also a firm that is in the initial start-up phase with significant questions about the viability of the business model and its ability to obtain sufficient capital. Is such a firm likely to benefit most from: (a) developing a relationship with a full-service PEO; (b) obtaining transactional services from a PEO; or (c) delaying use of a PEO? In part, the answer to this question may depend on what is required to execute the business plan. In service-intensive environments, acquisition and development of human capital may be critical to the executive of the business plan—making it more attractive for the firm to invest in developing a relationship with a full-service PEO. By contrast, where execution of the business plan revolves around development of a technology or product by founders of the organization, it may well be that investing in a relationship with a PEO at the initial start-up phase may yield fewer benefits.

The benefits from affiliating with a full-service PEO are likely to be strongest where there is rapid growth, where there is more rapid change in business processes, and where there are fewer questions about the viability of the business plan.

One might expect that similar benefits might result for a similarly situated firm that is on the high end of the size continuum for SMEs. However, it should be noted that larger SMEs are in a position where it is likely to be more feasible to employ internal HR staff members. As such, these larger SMEs are faced with questions regarding whether it would be preferable to obtain a full range of HR services from a PEO or from an internal staff member.

Quite clearly, SMEs are not homogenous and the benefits from using a PEO are likely to vary with SME characteristics. While research has examined the impact of PEO use on firm-level outcomes, little attention has been given to how the effects might vary with some of the SME characteristics identified above. Given the substantial diversity across SMEs, it is important for future research to explore how different kinds of SMEs are likely to be affected by PEO use.

Another area where future research might be called for relates to factors that make clients receptive to receiving services in more strategic areas of HR. From a strategy standpoint, some leading PEOs have decided to shift from transactional-only services to providing a broader range of services. What is less clear is how many SMEs are willing to pay for this broader range of services. Further, even when clients select service packages that include strategic HR services, it is unclear how SME leaders are likely to be receptive to the advice and counsel that are provided when such services are delivered. Strategic HR services require that the PEO affect how SME leaders behave within the organization, meaning that the effectiveness of these PEO services depends on the client's willingness to change their behavior. But little is known about how receptive SME leaders are to such advice and counsel or what factors determine levels of client receptivity.

Is client receptivity malleable within the sales process or within the context of the service relationship? Or is it necessary that high levels of receptivity exist at the outset of a PEO-SME relationship? And if so, what determines this receptivity? Are there individual differences among SME leaders that explain why there are differences in receptivity? Do individual differences relating to openness, propensity to trust, resistance to change, or social awareness affect client receptivity? Or is client receptivity more a function of beliefs regarding the utility of investing in human resource interventions and beliefs regarding the capacity of employees to generate significant process improvements for the firm? Related to this, client receptivity may also be determined by past experiences of the SME leader relating to HR programs and services. Past work experience where HR programs clearly enhanced the firm's competitive situation might create receptivity to PEO programs and initiatives.

Another area for future research relates to understanding the process by which PEOs affect outcomes through more strategic HR services. Does this impact occur because SMEs gain access to highly standardized HR programs in such areas as selection, training, and performance management? Or does this impact occur because SMEs are able to offer advice and counsel that reflects the particular conditions facing the firm? In many ways, this is a critical issue. PEOs offer services to large numbers of small organizations. If standardized HR services are primarily responsible for changes in HR outcomes, the need for gaining firm-specific information regarding each client diminishes. Clearly, this would have significant implications for the appropriate service delivery model.

Another important issue regarding how PEOs affect HR outcomes relates to the issue of cultural fit between the PEO and the SME. Does the impact of a PEO depend on the degree of compatibility between the PEO and the SME? Organizations develop cultures as a result of the leadership team and as a result of business processes and environmental pressures. Arguably, advice given about reward programs, employee relations, and staffing should be consistent with a given organization's culture. But it is likely that advice given by the PEO will be driven by their own culture and business environment. In other words, it is unlikely that the advice and programs provided by the PEO will be untainted by the culture within the PEO and their experiences in providing services to other SMEs. It is important, therefore, for future research to examine the degree to which cultural fit between the PEO and the SME moderates the impact associated with the use of PEO services.

In addition to these more substantive concerns, future research might also benefit from addressing several methodological issues. First, in assessing the impact of PEO services, it would be desirable to ultimately capture the impact of PEO services on financial performance. To date, research has focused on intermediate outcomes and has not examined whether the benefits that result from PEO use offset the costs. In part, this is a result of the fact that financial performance measures for SMEs typically are not published. Moreover, SMEs often are resistant to share such financial data when surveyed. However, overcoming these challenges would allow research to document the overall financial impact of PEO use. Such documentation would be valuable to SMEs considering whether to use a PEO and it would address concerns about whether improved HR outcomes justify the costs associated with PEO use. Moreover, measures of intermediate outcomes might be more effectively measured. To date, measures of intermediate outcomes relating to employee behavior and performance rely on subjective assessments by the SME leader. Objective measures of employee behavior and/or measures of employee attitudes may help validate the findings that have been obtained to date.

A final methodological suggestion for future research relates to the fact that, in past research, measures relating to the SME-PEO relationship were obtained from the SME leader as were measures relating to client receptivity and other attitudes that might moderate the impact of PEO services. Given the potential for social response bias, it may well be desirable to obtain measures regarding key characteristics of the client from service providers that work closely with the client as well as from SME leaders.

CONCLUSION

SMEs face significant challenges in efforts to effectively manage their human resources. While PEOs offer a model for delivering human resource programs and services in a way provides significant opportunities for firms to benefit from PEO utilization, the PEO model faces significant threats as well. For SMEs considering use of a PEO, numerous questions are raised by this combination of threats and opportunities.

We have attempted to identify some of the more significant questions, our current knowledge base with regard to these questions, and areas where future research might be needed.

REFERENCES

Arthur, J. B. (1992). The link between business strategy and industrial relations systems in American steel mini-mills. *Industrial and Labor Relations Review, 45*, 488-506.

Barney J. (1991). Firm resources and sustained competitive advantage. *Journal of Management, 17*, 99-120.

Baron, J. N., Burton, D. M., & Hannon, M. T. (1996). The road taken: Origins and evolution of employment systems in emerging companies. *Industrial and Corporate Change, 5*, 239-275.

Baron, J. N., & Kreps, D. M. (1999). *Strategic human resources*. New York: John Wiley & Sons.

Becker B. E., & Gerhart, B. (1996). The impact of human resource management on organizational performance: Progress and prospects. *Academy of Management Journal, 39*, 779-801.

Becker, B. E., & Huselid, M. A. (1999). Overview: Strategic human resource management in five leading firms. *Human Resource Management, 38*, 287-302.

Braga, M. (2002, August 19). No comp, no company. *Sarasota Herald-Tribune*.

Cole, C. (2002, November 22). Workers' comp crisis leaves many out in cold. *Bradenton Herald*.

Coleman, J. S. (1990). *Foundations of social theory*. Cambridge, MA: Belknap Press.

Connor K. R,, & Prahalad, C. K. (1996). A resource-based theory of the firm: Knowledge versus opportunism. *Organizational Science, 7*, 477-501.

Cook, M. F. (1999). *Outsourcing human resource functions*. New York: American Management Association.

Daft, R. L. & Lengel, R. H. (1986). Organizational information requirements: Media richness and structural design. *Management Science, 32*, 554-557.

Dow, G. (1987). The function of authority in transaction cost economics. *Journal of Economic Behavior and Organization, 8*, 13-38.

Ghoshal, S., & Moran, P. (1996). Bad for practice: A critique of the transaction cost theory. *Academy of Management Review, 21*, 7-12.

Greer, C. R., Youngblood, S. A., & Gray, D. A. (1999). Human resource outsourcing: The make or buy decision. *Academy of Management Executive, 13*, 85-96.

Gulati, R. (1995). Does familiarity breed trust? The implications of repeated ties for contractual choice in alliances. *Academy of Management Journal, 38*, 85-112.

Hannon, M. T., Burton, M. D., & Baron, J. N. (1996). Inertia and change in the early years: Employment relations in young, high technology firms. *Industrial and Corporate Change, 5*, 503-536.

Harris, S. C., & Linsenmayer, K. E. (2003). *401(k) plans*. Seattle: Employee Benefits Institute of American.

Hart, O. (1988). Incomplete contracts and the theory of the firm. *Journal of Law, Economics and Organization, 4*, 119-139.

Helper, S., & Levine, D. (1992). Long-term supplier relations and product-market structure. *Journal of Law, Economics, and Organization, 8*, 561-581.

Heneman, H. G., III, & Judge, T. (2003). *Staffing organizations*. Madison, WI: Mendota House Press.

Hirschman, C. (1997). All aboard: The boom in employee leasing may bring good career opportunities for HR professionals. *HR Magazine, 42,* 80-86.

Hirschman, C. (2000). For PEOs, business is still booming. *HR Magazine,* 45, 42-48.

Holoviak, J. J., & DeCenzo, D. A. (1982). Effective employee relations: An aid in small business's struggle for survival. *American Journal of Small Business, 6,* 49-54.

Huselid, M. A. (1995). The impact of human resource management practices on turnover, productivity, and corporate financial performance. *Academy of Management Journal, 38,* 635-672.

Klaas, B. S. (In press). Professional employer organizations and their role in small and medium enterprises: The impact of HR outsourcing. *Entrepreneurship Theory and Practice.*

Klaas, B. S., McClendon, J., & Gainey, T. (1999). HR outsourcing and its impact: The role of transaction costs. *Personnel Psychology, 52,* 113-136.

Klaas, B. S., McClendon, J., & Gainey, T. (2000). Managing HR in the small and medium enterprise: The impact of professional employer organizations. *Entrepreneurship Theory and Practice, 25,* 107-124.

Klaas, B. S., McClendon, J., Gainey, T., & Yang, H. (2003). *Technical report: PEOs and their impact on the small and medium enterprise.* SHRM Foundation, Alexandria, VA.

LePak, D. P., & Snell, S. A. (1999). Virtual HR: Strategic human resources in the 21st century. *Human Resource Management Review, 8,* 215-234.

NAPEO. (1993). *The business of employee leasing,* Alexandria, VA: Author.

Nooteboom, B., Berger, H., & Noorderhaven, N. G. (1997). Effects of trust and governance on relational risk. *Academy of Management Journal, 40,* 308-338.

Ring, P. S., & Van de Ven, A. (1992). Structuring cooperative relations between organizations. *Strategic Management Journal, 12,* 483-498.

Sexton, D. L., Upton, N. B., Wacholtz, L. E., & McDougall, P. P. (1997). Learning needs of growth-oriented entrepreneurs. *Journal of Business Venturing, 12,* 1-8.

Shelanski, H. A., & Klein, P. G. (1995). Empirical work in transaction cost economics. *Journal of Law, Economics, and Organization, 11,* 335-361.

Ulrich, D. (1996). *Human resource champions.* Boston: Harvard University Press.

Walker, G., & Weber, D. (1984). A transaction cost approach to make or buy decisions. *Administrative Science Quarterly, 29,* 373-391.

Welbourne, T. A., & Cyr, L. A. (1999). The human resource executive effect in initial public offering firms. *Academy of Management Journal, 42,* 616-632.

Williamson, O. E. (1996). *The mechanisms of governance.* New York: Oxford University Press.

Wright, P. M., Smart, D. L., & McMahan, G C. (1995). Matches between human resources and strategy among NCAA basketball teams. *Academy of Management Journal, 38,* 1052-1074.

CHAPTER 9

MINORITY AND MAJORITY TRUCK OWNER-OPERATORS

Entrepreneur or Galvanized Employees

Dale Belman and Ellen Ernst Kossek

By examining a group of self-employed truck driver owner-operators, the authors examine the following question: Are owner-operators "entrepreneurs" and do they accrue personal benefits of entrepreneurship? Results indicate that even though they are not more economically successful than other truck drivers, owner-operators may choose their positions for superior working conditions, greater control over their lives, and to improve their longevity in their chosen profession. Thus, quality of life issues may pay a role in decisions to become an entrepreneur. Individual entrepreneurial behavior must be understood as an interaction with the institutional context in which it is embedded.

INTRODUCTION

This chapter focuses on a modest corner of entrepreneurship in the context of self-employed truck driver owner-operators, which offers an inter-

Human Resource Strategies for the High Growth Entrepreneurial Firm, 189–222
Copyright © 2006 by Information Age Publishing
All rights of reproduction in any form reserved.

esting opportunity for exploring HRM and labor issues in small, emerging or entrepreneurial ventures. Our chapter examines the profession of over-the-road truck drivers as a lens to raise and understand key issues for managing entrepreneurship and diversity in established businesses. We address two main research questions. The first is: "Are truck driver owner-operators 'Entrepreneurs' as typically conceived and according to these criteria, do they accrue any personal benefits of entrepreneurship compared to employee drivers?" The second is: "What is the effect of race on this situation?" These are important issues to address, as there are relatively low barriers to entry to the over-the-road operator market, which means this type of self-employed profession is one that is within reach of many individuals throughout the United States.

Minorities comprise a greater portion of the low income strata of the U.S. population so examining the intersection of ethnic background with entrepreneurship allows for examination of whether entrepreneurship is a strategy that benefits increased well-being and benefits to minority members of society. It is particularly important to understand linkages between race and the experiences of owner-operators, since minorities typically have less ready access to financial capital and education—predictors of successful entrepreneurship—than other ethnic groups. Fairlie (1999) reports that 11.6% of white men are self-employed compared to 3.8% of black men. Although minorities are less likely to be self-employed or have access to requisite resources, if they do get access to human & financial capital, their success rate is equal (Fairlie, 1999). In sum, this chapter will shed light on the consequences for employees of taking on greater risk while being employed for large organizations, and how these outcomes vary with race, a key issue as the workforce shifts toward greater diversity.

We begin this chapter with a brief discussion of the definition of entrepreneurship used in our analysis. We apply this definition to Owner-Operators in the development of our hypotheses and also look at relationship of entrepreneurial behavior with minority ethnic status, before moving to methodology, and discussing our findings.

MOVING AWAY FROM PERSON-CENTERED DEFINITIONS OF ENTREPRENEURS

The entrepreneurship field is entering into the mainstream of the U.S. business world (Kautz, 1999), as the number of self-employed individuals is increasing annually and employment relationships are shifting toward greater use of employer driven contingent and flexible arrangements. Venkataraman (1997) notes that most researchers to date have defined entrepreneurship in terms of whom the entrepreneur is and what the individual does. An example of this approach to defining entrepreneurship is provided by Carton, Hofer, and Meeks (1998), who state an entrepreneur is someone who identifies the opportunity, gathers resources, creates, and is responsible for ensuring performance outcomes. However, in their review, Shane and Venkataraman (2000) point to the need for new scholarship to move away from focusing on person-centered definitions of entrepreneurship, which have the limitations of confounding individual characteristics with the quality of opportunities identified and available. They suggest entrepreneurship involves the intersection of BOTH enterprising individuals and the existence of financially attractive opportunities. We draw on their approach in this chapter's examination of truck owner-operators as a case of entrepreneurship in small business.

Entrepreneurship research entails scholarly inquiry into "how, by whom, and with what effects opportunities to create future goods and services, are discovered, evaluated, and exploited" (p. 218). To have entrepreneurship, Shane and Venkataraman, (2000) argue that you must have a number of existing conditions. These include the existence of entrepreneurial opportunities for new goods or services, raw materials or organizing mechanisms that can be sold at a higher rate than currently done, and variation in beliefs among individuals in the value of and incentives for exploiting these opportunities for profit. Such variation results in the discovery of these opportunities by some individuals and not others due to differences in one or more of the following: cognitive or personal properties, information, or access to capital. These approaches suggest that it is unlikely that entrepreneurship can be understood solely on the basis of stable individual characteristics independent of situations, but rather the tendency of some individuals to respond to situational cues or available opportunities over others (Shane & Venkataraman, 2000). Thus, the self-employed may or may not be entrepreneurial depending on whether opportunities for profit are being identified.

Entrepreneurialism, in theory suggests that owner-operators perceive greater market opportunities from taking on greater economic risks than other drivers, and they should receive higher return than employees in similar positions. Besides the greater opportunities for reward, they also may choose to do so more out of personal preference than economic necessity as evidence suggests that many factors ranging from gender, family characteristics, or personal proclivities are relevant (Dennis, 1996; Gatewood, Shaver, & Gartner, 1995; Honig, 1998; Mathews & Mosier, 1995).

Before proceeding, we also should note that there is variation internationally regarding whether owner-operator truckers are viewed as self-employed. Although this debate has not yet affected policy in the United

States, the European Union is currently studying whether Owner-Operators should be classified as or whether they are, de facto, employees.[1] As employment relations moves toward greater subcontracting and more contingent employment, this issue of defining entrepreneurship and self-employment becomes increasingly important not only in the United States but abroad and in global enterprises.

TRUCK DRIVER OWNER-OPERATORS: SELF-EMPLOYMENT RISKS AND REWARDS

Truck driver owner-operators can be viewed as a Schumpeterian (1951) form of routine as opposed to New (N form) entrepreneurship (Leibenstein, 1968), as this form involves well-understood parameters for business. They are common form of a small-scale entrepreneur. Truck driver owner-operators are self-employed. Their capital is typically limited to a tractor (the cab or power unit of a tractor-trailer) typically valued at $75,000 to $100,000, not allowing for the debt incurred in its purchase. They are an extremely small business as 84% own only one truck. Truck driver owner-operators are typically paid for their work within 1 week of completing a haul. As there are low capitalization barriers to entry, it is easy for many individuals to enter this business.

There are approximately 360,000 owner-operators currently operating in the United States with notable stories of individual success among the self-employed. The second largest trucking company in the United States, J. B. Hunt, was begun by the owner-operator after whom the company is named. Given that entrepreneurship is defined as involving the intersection of BOTH enterprising individuals and the existence of financially attractive opportunities, we assume that owner-operators fit the criteria of an entrepreneur. It is useful here, to examine the pros and cons of being self-employed as distinct from being an employee driver.

The difference between employees and the self-employed is, at its core, a legal distinction. Prior to the beginning of social regulation of the employment relationship in the 1890s, the legal distinction in the relationship between employee and employer and that between contractor and self-employed worker was not great. The regulation of the employment relationship through social insurance programs, protective labor legislation and tax treatment of retirement and other insurance programs has, over the last century, defined the difference between self-employed workers and employees. The duties and obligations of the parties to the employment relationship are legally defined. Starting with federal law, where an employment relationship exists, employers are required to pay their share and withhold the employee share of social security taxes pursuant to the Federal Income Contributions Act, as well as collect payroll taxes from employees. They are additionally liable for taxes under the Federal Unemployment Tax Act as well as state income, unemployment, and workers' compensation acts. The Fair Labor Standards Act establishes a minimum wage and overtime pay for employees, Title VII of the Civil Rights Act of 1964 prohibits discrimination against employees on the basis of color, religion, gender, national origin or race, while the Age Discrimination in Employment Act prohibits discrimination on the basis of age. The Employment Retirement Security Act establishes the rules of qualified benefit plans for employees. The Americans with Disability Act prohibits discrimination against employees based on disabilities. The Family Medical Leave Act requires employers provide qualified employees with up to 12 weeks of leave annually in certain life situations. The National Labor Relations Act provides for the right to organize and governs labor management relations, while the Davis-Bacon Act and the Service Contracts Act require that employees of government contractors be paid the wage rate prevailing in comparable private sector occupations. The employment relationship is also being subject to state and local laws.

In contrast, the relationship between a contractor and the self-employed worker is typically governed by business law and the self-employed are exempted from the protections afforded by the protective labor legislation noted in the preceding paragraph. For example, contractors are not required to withhold payroll or social security taxes from the payments to self-employed workers and the self-employed are not covered by the minimum wage or overtime of the Fair Labor Standards Act or, in most states, by Workers' Compensation Acts.[2]

Why then would workers choose to be self-employed? The positive reasons for self-employment align closely with those often cited as reasons for becoming an entrepreneur. The self-employed have more *control* over their work, making decisions about what to do and when and how to do it and their job demands, which is more frequently denied to most employees. In trucking, control over loads and hours of work are central to one's quality of life. For example, owner-operators have greater latitude than do employees over adhering to legal limits on maximum working hours. The self-employed are also typically expected to *earn more for their efforts* both because they accept more risk than employees and because there are stronger incentives to apply abilities and creativity to a task than exist for employees.[3] There may also be cultural reasons for self-employment, being an entrepreneur may have positive value to the employee even absent economic rewards, as one's own boss and controlling one's own destiny is glorified in U.S. society. Although there is no large study of whether owner-operators tend to cluster in families or by other kinship structure, we did find evidence collected by the first author suggesting that owner-operators often involve family members in their work. Twelve percent of drivers were taught to drive by a family member or neighbor (Belman, Monaco, & Brooks, 2005).

Yet there are also negative incentives to entrepreneurship and some tendency for employers to prefer to use self-employed workers rather than employees. First, there is typically a shift of risk from the firm to the self-employed worker. In the case of trucking, the firm no longer supplies capital, a tractor, to the employee. The self-employed worker provides their own capital and incurs expenses for that capital. In trucking, return on capital is at risk during slack seasons, when there is delay between loads and in back hauls. Negative incentives to entrepreneurship also result as self-employed workers are exempt from most protective labor legislation. Use of self-employed workers reduce firms' payments of these expenses. Firms may also reduce employment costs by avoiding payments into health care plans and retirement plans which they would make for employees. In a perfectly functioning market, firms would not benefit from these differences between employees and the self-employed as the self-employed would receive implicit compensating payments for added risk and exemption from protective labor legislation.[4]

HYPOTHESES

We now turn to our hypotheses. Recently, theory from human resource management and organizational behavior literatures has begun to have greater integration with the entrepreneurship literature (cf. Heneman, Wang, Tansky, & Wang, 2002; Heneman, Tansky, & Camp (2000). Building on this tradition, we draw from total compensation theory and diversity and discrimination theory in the development of our hypotheses. Total compensation theory holds that individuals are motivated to perform on the job by both extrinsic and intrinsic rewards (Milkovich & Newman, 2005). Extrinsic rewards relate to monetary economic rewards from employment. Intrinsic rewards are noneconomic and might include job autonomy, job control, and personal achievement (Stroh, Northcraft, & Neale, 2002). Given the assumption that being an owner operator has greater extrinsic reward opportunities than employee truckers, our first hypothesis is as follows:

Hypothesis 1: Owner-operators should, on average, be *better rewarded* than employees doing similar work.

Further, as total compensation theory suggests that being an owner oper-ator is likely to be both extrinsically (i.e., greater opportunity to make more money) and intrinsically (i.e., more job control and autonomy) rewarding, we theorize Hypotheses 2a and 2b:

Hypothesis 2a: Owner-operators work effort (hours worked and miles driven) will be higher than employees.

Hypothesis 2b: Owner-operators should have more *control* over their work than employees.

We also examined linkages whether minorities are more likely to be owner-operators than employees. Becker's seminal work on discrimina-tion suggested three sources of discrimination in the employment rela-tionship: discrimination originating in the preferences of employers, of employees, and of customers (Becker, 1957). Becker has also suggested that the self-employed are less likely to be subject to discrimination. He surmised that although still subject to customer discrimination, they are not subject to discrimination by an employer or co-workers. Diversity research also suggests that minorities are more likely to be attracted to employment contexts that they perceive are likely to be more welcoming to minorities and people of color (Heneman, Waldeck, & Cushnie, 1996). This leads to our next hypothesis:

Hypothesis 3:   Owner-operators should be more diverse than employees since this employment relationship will be more attractive to minorities as it will be less subject to employment discrimination.

Last, the theory of the learning curve in the training and performance literature suggests that as entrepreneurs, owner-operators should, over time, be able to accumulate more wealth than otherwise similar employ-ees (Goldstein & Ford, 2002). This theory that suggests that more senior workers tend to perform better due to greater familiarity with job require-ments, greater learning on how to do the job well, and the ability to build on the job resources they have accumulated due to greater experience. We will conduct multivariate analysis to examine:

Hypothesis 4:   Older owner-operators should perform better than younger owner-operators as they have accumulated more physical and human capital.

THE DRIVER SURVEY: BACKGROUND
AND METHODOLOGY

National data sets are not rich sources of information on truck drivers. The questions on compensation and hours of work do not conform well to employment systems used in the motor freight industry and there is little work related data beyond hours and earnings. We are fortunate to have data from a survey of over-the-road and local drivers in the motor freight industry conducted by the Sloan Foundation Trucking Industry Program (TIP) in cooperation with the Institute of Social Research at the University of Michigan. The analysis in this chapter compares the entrepreneurial characteristics and business performance drawing on interviews with more than one thousand truck drivers interviewed mostly face to face at truck stops in 1997-1999. The survey used a two-stage stratified sampling procedure in which interview sites, truck stops, were randomly selected within state and establishment size categories. Interviewers approached entrants to the selected truck stops using a random selection scheme. Sixty-three percent of eligible participants, 1,007 drivers, agreed to take the survey, which took forty minutes. Of these 27% were owner-operators and the remaining were employee drivers. Only truck drivers holding a class C Commercial Drivers License who were currently employed as drivers and were driving a truck at the time of the interview were eligible for the survey. Surveys were only conducted on weekdays with the exception of followup telephone interviews, which collected information on the last full day of work (potentially a weekend).

This survey collected unique, rich, and detailed information on the structure of owner-operators' business, on sources of capital and of work. In addition, it also solicited information on income, benefits, work history, education and job training, job characteristics, working and resting time, technology uses, future opportunities in the industry, service regulations, and decision-making, which allows meaningful comparison between owner-operators and employee drivers. A complete summary of the survey and description of the methodology can be found in Belman et al. (2005). Before making comparisons between drivers and owner-operators, it is useful to first briefly provide background on truck drivers in general.

THE TRUCKER DRIVER'S BUSINESS LIFE

Drivers are typical blue-collar workers. They are somewhat older than a national sample of blue-collar workers, a result of the twenty-one-year legal minimum age for obtaining a Commercial Drivers License. Consistent with their greater age, drivers are somewhat more likely to be married and have children than other blue-collar males. Although women make up a smaller proportion of the driver workforce than they do of the blue-collar labor force, the racial and ethnic composition of the driver labor force is comparable to that of other blue-collar workers. The educational attainment of drivers is also similar to that of other blue-collar workers: 43.7% of drivers have a high school degree, 22.7% have some college courses, 4.8% have a college degree.

Judged by their annual income, motor freight drivers are solidly middle class. The median annual income of drivers in 1996 was $35,000, slightly above the $34,522 median family income for families with a wife who is not in the paid labor force (for more background, see Mishel, Bernstein, & Schmitt, 1998, Table 1.5). However, they seem less middle class when rates of pay, hours of work and working conditions are considered.

The median respondent drove approximately 110,000 miles per year. How long does it take to drive these miles? Drivers' hours are set by the Hours of Service Regulations administered by the U.S. Department of Transportation. Prior to the 2004 revisions, drivers were limited to fifteen hours of total working time prior to taking a mandatory eight-hour break. The fifteen hours could comprise up to ten hours of driving time with the balance accounted for by nondriving on duty time. Effective working time could be extended by inserting off duty breaks during working time as these did not count against the fifteen-hour limit. The Hours of Service Regulations also limited drivers to 60 hours of total work time in a 7-day period, and 70 hours of working time in an 8-day period. The TIP survey found that drivers worked an average of 11.4 hours with 8.5 hours of driving time and 2.0 hours on duty not driving in the day prior to the interview. Drivers also have long work weeks: 20% of drivers reported working 6 days in the last 7, and 19% reported working 7 of the last 7 days.

How many hours do drivers work in 7 days? When asked about hours of work in the last week, the median driver reported working exactly 60 hours, but 25% reported working at least 75 hours and 10% reported working at least 90 hours. Using data on the last pay period, the median respondent worked 62 hours in 7 days. The mean working time was 65.7 hours. In combination with data on time taken off work in the previous year, we calculate that the typical driver works 3000 hours per year, one and one half times the full time work year of 2080 hours established by the Fair Labor Standard Act.[5]

How much do drivers earn per hour? The answer is less straightforward than it would be for most employees as hourly pay is rare (10.0% of the sample). Pay by mileage (55.8% of the sample) or as a percentage of revenue (29.9% of the sample) is more common. An hourly rate can be constructed as the ratio of reported annual income to estimated annual hours of work. (For more information on the methodology of hourly wage construction, see Belman et al., 2005.)

The mean rate for drivers was $11.67. Union drivers earned the top rate of $14.68 per hour, while nonunion drivers averaged $10.75 and nonunion owner-operators earned $12.03. Using these figures to recalculate annual earnings on a standard work year, drivers would be expected to earn $23,340 annually, with union drivers earning $29,360 and nonunion employees earning $21,500. Benefit coverage is also limited. Only half of the drivers (46.6%) reported participation in a deferred compensation plan such as a 401(K). Conventional pension plans are rare outside of the organized sector; 77% of union members report having a conventional pension, but only 21.4% of nonunion employee drivers and 15.4% of owner-operators have pensions from any source including military pensions. Medical insurance is more common among employees; 100% of union members and 87.4% of nonunion employees reported some form of medical insurance, but only 66% of owner-operators carry such plans. Most medical plans are contributory. Only 27.4% are fully funded by the employer, and most of these are in the organized sector. Time off from work, much less paid time off, is rare. The median driver took 5 days of vacation, 4 days of holiday time, and no sick leave in 1996. Only the vacation days were compensated.

The dynamics of the occupation, in which drivers compensate for low rates by driving long hours and working as many days as possible, leads to habitual violation of the hours of service rules, lack of sleep and drowsiness while on duty, and job instability. Drivers' gaming of the hours of service rules is well established. The typical driver worked up to and often beyond the legal hours of work. Some drivers refer to their logs as "comic books," many carry multiple logbooks (DiSalvatore, 1988). Survey respondents often distinguished between their actual hours of work and the hours recorded in their logs, only 16.1% of drivers believed that logbooks accurately reflected drivers' hours of work. Fifty-six percent reported that they had worked more than they had logged in the last 30 days, and 55% reported that they had driven more than 10 hours without an 8-hour break in the last 30 days. Sixteen percent of drivers reported violating the 10-hour rule more than fifteen times over that period.

Long hours of work may affect drivers' quality of life and their performance on the job. Over-the-road drivers spend several days to several weeks away from home. The median driver had last been home for 24 hours 4 days prior to the interview, and the mean time since being home was 8.3 days. Seventy percent of drivers slept in a bunk in their truck on the previous night. Only 24% had slept at home. Problems of dozing and lack of sleep while driving are relatively common; 35% of drivers reported dozing while driving at least once in the last 30 days, and 15% reported dozing at least three times over that period. Lack of sleep is most pronounced on the last day of work before returning home, when 15% of drivers reported not sleeping in the last 24 hours. Taken as a whole, these figures suggest that control over work is central to the quality of drivers' work experience.

BUSINESS CHARACTERISTICS OF OWNER-OPERATORS: DESCRIPTIVE STATISTICS

We turn next to the characteristics of owner-operators as business owners. In this section we consider the size and nature of owner-operators operations (i.e., number of trucks, whether they own or lease), their sources and form of financing, and their sources of shipments. In addition, we make some initial comparisons of owner-operators operations across racial groupings. In all, 274 of the 1,007 survey respondents, approximately one fourth (27%) were owner-operators.

Number of Trucks

Although owner-operators may own or lease multiple trucks, the typical driver own or lease only the tractor he or she is driving (Table 9.1). Eighty-four percent of drivers have a single truck, an additional 9.1% have two trucks and 3.8% have three trucks. Only 2.5% of the sample has four or more trucks. How does the number of trucks operated vary by race? Although the percentage of Black owner-operators with a single truck is substantially lower than that for the White respondents, 71.3 versus 85.9%; the difference is not statistically significant in a two tailed 5% test for a difference in means (t = 1.52). Pearson's Chi-square for independence of outcomes does not reject the hypothesis that the number of trucks operated does not vary by race. The lack of statistical significance may be a consequence of the relatively small number of non-White owner-operators. While there are 191 White owner-operators, there are only 24 Black owner-operators and 27 owner-operators of Asian, American-Indian or Other racial origin. Based on this data, we conclude that most owner-operators are running very small businesses, essentially employing only themselves. We also surmise that there is no immediate evidence of a difference in business size by race. It should be noted that there is a pre-sample selection process at work. Successful owner-operators who go on to create a large business, such as J. B. Hunt, are unlikely to spend much time in their truck or in truck stops. Their success takes them out of the sample. One owner-operator in our sample reports owning 75 trucks, so

Table 9.1.   Number of Trucks Owned or Leased

# Trucks	# In Sample (weighted)	% of Sample	White	Black	Other
1	230.34	84.38%	85.87%	71.33%	83.37%
2	24.92	9.13%	6.76%	22.93%	16.63%
3	10.40	3.81%	4.07%	5.75%	0.00%
4	.813	.30%	0.00%	0.00%	0.00%
5-8	5.88	2.17%	2.66%	0.00%	0.00%
75	.624	.23%	.28%	0.00%	0.00%

perhaps the occasional successful owner-operator is taken with a desire to throw himself back behind the wheel. We also lose the failures, those who go out of business and either leave the industry or migrate back into being an employee driver.

Own or Lease

We next consider whether the owner-operator owns or leases their truck(s) (Table 9.2). The own-lease distinction is important as leasing provides a means of becoming an owner-operator for those without the capital to purchase a tractor. At the same time, it limits the opportunities for capital accumulation by the owner-operator and hence their ability to grow the business. The overwhelming majority of owner-operators with a single truck, 82.9%, own their tractor, only 17.1% lease. Leasing is more common among those with multiple trucks: 73.7% own all of their trucks, an additional 20.8% both own and lease, while 5.5% of those with multiple trucks lease all of their trucks. As numbers with multiple trucks are small, some caution about the own/lease pattern is needed. Pearson's chi-square test for the independence of outcomes indicates that the hypothesis that own/lease patterns do not vary by the number of trucks cannot be rejected in even a 10% test. However, this finding again possibly results from the small number of owner-operators with multiple trucks in the sample.

The pattern in truck ownership/leasing arrangements varies by racial group. Among those with one truck, 84% of White Owner-operators and 96.6% of Other owner-operators own their truck, but only 47% Black owner-operators own their trucks. The difference between White and Black proportions is statistically significant in a 1% two-tailed test for a difference in proportions ($t = 3.01$). This is consistent with Black owner-operators having more limited access to capital markets. We do not dis-

Table 9.2. Own or Lease Truck

	Single Truck				Two or More Trucks			
	Total	White	Black	Other	Total	White	Black	Other
Own	82.89%	84.37%	47.07%	96.64%	73.73%	66.15%	91.55%	100%
Lease	17.11%	15.63%	52.93%	3.36%	5.50%	5.65%	8.45%	0.00%
Both	X	X	X	X	20.78%	28.20%	0.00%	0.00%
Total (weighted)	230.3	191.1	16.7	22.5	42.7	30.4	6.8	4.5

cuss the differences in racial patterns of ownership for the multiple truck sample as the number of individuals is too small to provide meaningful results.

Sources of Financing: General Background and Patterns by Race

Where do those who own their trucks obtain financing? The most common source is a bank, as 54.8% of respondents had bank financing (Table 9.3). The next most common was a truck dealer (21.4%), followed by self-financing (12.5%) and financing from the shipper, which the owner-operator works for (11.2%).

For financing, white owner-operators are most likely to use a bank (58.0%). However, black owner-operators are more likely to use a truck dealer (63.4%). Those in the Other category are equally likely to use a bank (40.1%) or the company for whom they work (37.8%). Again, the small number of observations on non-White owner-operators limits the predictive power of the sample. With the exception of the distribution of lease patterns by race, it is not possible to reject the hypothesis that sources of funding do not vary by race in a 5% Pearson chi-square test.

Table 9.3. Sources of Financing

	% of Sources			
	Total	White	Black	Other
Self	12.51%	12.07%	15.42%	14.27%
Bank	54.82%	58.00%	38.08%	40.10%
Dealer	21.44%	19.17%	63.39%	14.38%
Leasing Firm	11.19%	8.37%	0.00%	37.79%
Other	5.04%	5.04%	14.63%	0.00%

Table 9.4.   How Do Owner-Operators Get Shipments?

	Total	White	Black	Other	Weighted Number of Observations
Permanent lease	62.6%	64.4%	57.6%	52.9%	171.7
Broker	14.9%	14.0%	25.2%	13.1%	40.8
Contract with shipper	15.2%	13.4%	15.8%	29.9%	41.6
Other	7.3%	8.3%	1.5%	4.0%	19.9
Total	100%	100%	100%	100%	
Weighted number of observations	274	223.4	23.5	28.0	

Sources of Shipments

Owner-operators obtain their shipments by three means: brokers, permanent leases and other means such as directly contracting with shippers (Table 9.4). Some owner-operators operate in spot markets through brokers. Shortly before becoming available to take a shipment they call a freight broker and the broker offers them one or more shipments. Others establish permanent leases with shippers. These leases, which vary considerably in complexity, commit the owner-operator to work for the company for a fixed period of time, usually a minimum of 30 days. During this period they will take the shipments the leaseholder offers and will not take shipments from other firms. Permanent leases restrict, at least temporarily, owner-operators range of decision-making. These leases are often held by firms which offer trucking services to shippers and many larger trucking companies "employ" a mixture of employee drivers and owner-operators under permanent lease. Permanent leases are the method of obtaining shipments, which most restricts the latitude of decision making of owner-operators and is least consistent with owner-operators as entrepreneurs. Owner-operators may also contract directly with a shipper, offering to carry the shippers loads with an agreed upon system of payment but not agreeing to limit their work to that shipper.

In our sample, 62.6% of owner-operators operate under permanent leases. Almost equal numbers, 14.9% and 15.2% operate through brokers and under a contract with one or more shippers. An additional 7% operate under some other relationship. There is little difference in the proportion of the driver workforce that permanently leased to a firm by race: 64.4% of the White owner-operators, 57.6% of Black owner-operators and 52.9% of Other owner-operators holding permanent leases; Pearson's chi-square test for differences in the means of obtaining shipments by race cannot reject a null of no difference in even a 10% test.

Hypothesis 3 suggests that, as permanent leases are the most "employment like" arrangements through which owner-operators obtain shipments, minorities should be less likely use permanent leases as their means of obtaining shipments. This hypothesis is not supported by the small and statistically nonsignificant difference by race in the proportion of owner-operators under permanent leases. It may be that the factors driving differences in minority representation between employees and owner-operators do not apply within varying types of arrangements among owner-operators, but it may also be that the hypothesis does not characterize relationships in the trucking industry.

OWNER-OPERATORS AND EMPLOYEES: AN INITIAL COMPARISON

We turn next to the comparison between owner-operators and employees. We first compare their age and experience before investigating our four hypotheses that owner-operators should: be better rewarded (H1) than employee counterparts, have higher work effort and more control over their work than employees than employees (H2a & b), be more racially diverse than employee drivers (H3), and, after accounting for physical and human capital, and perform better (H4).

The Distribution of Age and Occupational Experience

We would expect that Owner-Operators would be older and more experienced than employee drivers, because they either need to accumulate capital or convince a lender that they have sufficient knowledge of the job to make a success of their business. Lenders may also be concerned about maturity, stability and noncapital asset accumulation, all of which suggest older and more experienced drivers will have more ready access to capital. Finally, drivers themselves may be unwilling to become owner-operators until they understand the job and the industry. Running counter to these factors are the relatively brief time needed to obtain the skills required to be a successful driver. Formal training takes 5 weeks. It also takes only two to three months of on-the-job experience to provide the driver with sufficient knowledge to work alone.

Comparison of occupational experience finds that owner-operators are moderately older and have more experience with commercial driving than employee drivers (Table 9.5). The mean age of owner-operators is

Table 9.5.   Driving Experience & Time As Owner-Operator

	Owner-Operator			Employee	
	Years as Driver	Years as Owner-Operator	Age	Years as Driver	Age
Mean	16.4	7.9	43.4	12.9	41.1
10%	4.0	1.0	30.0	2.0	27.0
25%	8.0	1.0	37.0	4.0	34.0
50%	15.0	4.0	42.0	10.0	41.0
75%	22.0	13.0	50.0	20.0	48.0
90%	30.0	20.0	58.0	28.0	54.0

43.4. They average 16.4 years of commercial driving experience and 7.9 years as an owner operator. In contrast, the average age of employee drivers is 41.1 and they have, on average, 12.9 years of commercial driving experience. Median experience is 15 years for owner-operators and 10 years for employee drivers. The difference in years of driving experience narrows to close to two years at the 75th and 90th percentiles and at the 10th but not the 25th percentile. Although the differences in age and experience are usually not great, the gap in experience at the median provides some evidence for our hypotheses.

Annual Earnings

Our first hypothesis is that owner-operators will be better off financially than employee counterparts. We examine this issue by comparing annual earnings (Table 9.6) and benefit coverage (Table 9.7) by employ-

Table 9.6.   Annual Income

		Employee		Owener-Operator			
	Average	Union	Nonunion	Nonunion	White	Black	Other
Mean		$42,842	$35,294	$37,133	$37,366	$31,968	$40,104
10%	$18,000	$24,000	$20,000	$15,000	$15,000	$10,000	$18,000
25%	$27,000	$35,000	$27,000	$25,000	$26,000	$25,000	$25,000
50%	$36,000	$42,000	$35,000	$37,000	$40,000	$32,000	$38,000
75%	$45,000	$52,000	$42,000	$50,000	$50,000	$35,000	$60,000
90%	$53,000	$62,000	$50,000	$60,000	$57,000	$45,000	$62,000
99%	$78,000	$78,000	$70,000	$76,000	$76,000	$67,000	$85,000

Table 9.7.   Benefit Coverage

	Employee		Owner-Operator
	Union	Nonunion	Nonunion
		401(k)	
All	54.11%	49.25%	15.01%
White	51.03%	54.67%	15.27%
Black	57.19%	56.51%	18.26%
Other	N/A	36.58%	11.51%
		Pension	
All	72.13%	19.87%	15.14%
White	72.51%	21.23%	19.67%
Black	71.74%	30.80%	15.76%
Other	N/A	7.58%	10.01%
		IRA	
All	27.76%	9.95%	29.59%
White	41.32%	14.55%	34.58%
Black	14.20%	1.87%	26.72%
Other	N/A	13.42%	27.46%
		Health Insurance	
All	100.00%	85.72%	70.84%
White	100.00%	87.25%	64.96%
Black	100.00%	95.03%	75.91%
Other	100.00%	74.89%	71.65%

ment status. Examination of annual earnings is complex because, with the exception of those who belong to the Teamster's union, owner-operators receive a single payment covering their labor and use of their truck. For example, the typical employee driver is paid 34 cents per mile for their work while the typical owner-operator will earn $1.03 per mile for their work and use of their truck. We construct our comparison of earnings from two questions: owner-operators were asked about their earnings after truck expenses including interest in the last year, employee drivers were asked about their last years' earnings from driving. Although imperfect, these comparisons provide a first cut at comparability.

To facilitate comparison, we subdivide our employee sample into employees who are covered by collective bargaining (i.e., individuals who are union members or whose earnings are established by a collective agreement) and those who are not. We also limit our sample of owner-operators to those who are not members of a union by removing the eight union owner-operators from the sample. These steps help avoid conflating the owner-operator comparison with the effects of collective bargaining.

Our estimates suggest that owner-operators annual earnings after truck expenses are modestly greater than those of nonunion employees, but substantially less than the earnings of employees who are union members. Mean and median earnings for nonunion owner-operators were $37,133 and $37,000 respectively, while those of nonunion employees were $35,294 and $35,000 respectively. The dispersion of owner-operators earnings was substantially larger than that of employees. Employee earnings were above those of owner-operators at the 25th and 10th percentile, but owner-operator earnings were $8,000 to $10,000 above those of employees at the 75% and 90th percentile. The earnings of union employees were above those of owner-operators throughout the earnings distribution, but owner-operators earnings approach those of union employees at the 75% percentile.

The distribution of earnings suggests that, although the typical owner-operator is only doing moderately better than the typical nonunion employee, there is a substantial tail in the earnings distribution, encompassing from 25 to 35% of owner-operators, who are earning substantially more than their employee counterparts.

Benefits

We next turn to whether owner-operators are better off, not only in terms of salary but also benefits (indirect compensation). Federal regulations have been structured to encourage firms to provide employees with retirement plans and health insurance coverage. For example, the deductibility of managerial retirement expenses is contingent on adequate coverage of the work force. It is typically less expensive for employees to obtain health care coverage through their employer than through private purchase.

The same incentives do not apply to owner-operators. Owner-operators are not included among employees for IRS calculations of retirement coverage. Similarly, firms seldom extend employee health plans to self-employed contractors. These factors will increase the cost of obtaining benefits for owner-operators and may act to reduce their participation in benefits.

We compare owner-operators and employees participation in health insurance, pension, and deferred compensation plans and IRAs. In this analysis, we consider whether they participate in some form of each type of plan without attention to its source (Table 9.7). For example, we treat obtaining health insurance through an employers, through a spouse's employer or through direct purchase as having health insurance coverage. We also do not investigate the generosity or cost of the insurance.

Turning first to health insurance, 82.8% of the sample is covered by some form of health insurance. Not surprisingly, unionized employees have the highest coverage rate, 100%. Nonunion employees rank second with 86.7% reporting health insurance coverage. Owner-operators have the lowest coverage rate, 66.5% report having health insurance from some source. Although non-White employees and owner-operators in our sample, are more likely to be covered by health insurance than their White counterparts, the sample is not sufficiently large to be able to reject the null of no difference by race in even a 10% χ^2 test. The second category of benefit is deferred compensation plans such as 401(k) and Keogh plans. Approximately 56.6% of the sample reports having such plans. They are most common among nonunion employees, 53.0% of these employees report having such a plan. Union employees rank second with 51.2% reporting participation. Participation among nonunion owner-operators is substantially lower, at 15.1%. There is no evidence of differential participation by race within the owner-operator or nonunion employee category.

The third category is pension plan. This includes both defined benefit and defined contribution plans, although the latter are most common in trucking. Almost one quarter of the respondents to the survey report participating in a pension plan, most of these were union members. Divided by driver type, 72.7% of union employees reported participating in a pension plan, 20.8% of nonunion employees reported participating in such a plan, while 18.4% of nonunion owner-operators reported participating in a pension plan. Most of the nonunion employees who reported participation were employed by firms whose primary activity was not trucking (e.g., a supermarket which had its own trucks to move goods from warehouses to their stores); most of the owner-operators who reported participation were referencing a plan from a previous employer.

The final category of benefit plan is IRA, another type of tax deferred saving account. IRAs are not typically included in discussions of benefits as they are not sponsored by employers but established by individuals. The simplicity of IRAs may recommend them to owner-operators over other retirement savings plans; omitting IRAs would neglect a potentially important element in owner-operators retirement savings. Overall 20.4% of respondents reported having an IRA. One third of owner-operators, 33.2%, reported having an IRA. This was slightly below the rate reported by unionized employees (38.0%), but substantially above their prevalence among nonunion employees, 13.5%. Despite their imperfections, particularly the cap on annual on contributions, IRAs seem to be an important component in owner-operator retirement savings that partially redresses their low rates of participation in other savings schemes.

Considering compensation and benefits as a whole, owner-operators earn somewhat more than nonunion employee drivers, but are less likely to have health insurance or participate in retirement savings programs. The lack of participation in retirement savings would be less of a concern if the owner-operators were building substantial capital value in their business. This however, is not the case as their major asset, the tractor, depreciates rapidly in use. Taken together, the compensation and benefit estimates suggest that the typical owner-operator is better off in terms of immediate compensation but, when benefits are considered, is unlikely to be better off and may be worse off than the typical employee driver. There is, however, a group of owner-operators who are doing better than their nonunion employee counterparts. Many of the owner-operators in the upper part of the owner-operator earnings distribution have both health insurance plans and one or more retirement plans. This group better conforms to our expectations about owner-operators as entrepreneurs than does the owner-operator labor force as a whole.

Work Effort and Control over Work

Hypothesis 2 suggested that drivers become owner-operators not to improve their financial position but rather to gain control over their work and work effort. One important element in work effort is working time. As discussed in Truck Driver's Business Lives, work time is regulated by the Hours of Service regulations of the Department of Transportation. Under these regulations, drivers are limited to 10 hours of driving and 5 hours of additional work before a mandatory 8-hour break. They are also limited to no more than 60 hours of work in 7 days. Although, if enforced, these regulations would obviate most of the advantages owner-operators might have in controlling work time and effort, violations of the hours of service rules are ubiquitous. For example, driver survey data suggests that half of the drivers violated the 60-hour rule in the last 7 days. Given the de facto weakness of regulation, owner-operators may be better able to control working time and effort. We investigate this by considering annual mileage (Table 9.8) and work time (Table 9.9).

Mileage is closely related to drivers work effort and pay. Most pay systems are directly or indirectly linked to mileage. While there is considerable work associated with nondriving time (loading and unloading and waiting time), the majority of work time is spent driving. Turning first to miles driven in the last week, nonunion employees reported the greatest weekly mileage, 2,251 miles per week. Nonunion owner-operators ranked

Table 9.8.   Mileage

	Type of Driver		
	Employee		Owner-Operator
	Union	Nonunion	Nonunion
	Last 7 Days		
All	1,991.0	2,251.4	2,109.9
White	1,978.0	2,255.3	2,080.3
Black	2,096.1	2,062.6	2,284.8
Other	2,000.0	2,394.4	2,210.1

Table 9.9.   Work Time

	Employee				Owner-Operator	
	Union		Nonunion		Nonunion	
	Hours Last 7 Days					
	Mean	Median	Mean	Median	Mean	Median
All	57.5	54	61.1	58.7	52.5	48.3
White	64.7	60	64.6	60.0	56.9	57.0
Black	47.7	42	55.0	56.0	54.3	50.0
Other	60.0	60	63.6	60.0	46.2	38.0
	Days Worked In Last 7					
0	0.00%		0.94%		1.68%	
1	6.06%		0.48%		1.09%	
2	0.00%		2.29%		2.96%	
3	1.06%		4.84%		7.31%	
4	12.34%		10.09%		13.88%	
5	57.74%		39.98%		32.91%	
6	16.16%		23.27%		20.62%	
7	6.66%		18.10%		19.54%	

second, with 2,110 miles in the previous week while union employees reported 1,991 miles. Owner-operators drive about 6% fewer miles per week than do nonunion employee drivers. Calculated on a 50-week work year, owner-operators would drive about 7,000 fewer miles annually than nonunion employees.

Working Time: Hours and Days Worked in the Last 7 Days

Paralleling the mileage data, owner-operators work fewer hours than do employee drivers. Driver survey data suggests that nonunion employees worked an average of 63.6 hours in the previous week (with a median of 60), union employees worked an average 62.8 hours (with a median of 60) while nonunion owner-operators reported working 55.7 hours (with a median of 55 hours) (Table 9.9). Owner-operators then work between 9 and 14% fewer hours than nonunion employee drivers.

There is however, no difference between owner-operators and non-union employee drivers in the number of days worked over the last 7 days. Union status seems to be a more important predictor of the number of days worked than owner operator status. Almost 60% (59.8%) of non-union owner-operators reported working 5 or fewer days in the prior week, an additional 20% reported working 6 days, and 20% reported working 7 days. This distribution is similar to that of nonunion employees of whom 58.6% reported working 5 days, 22% reported working 6 days, and 18% reported working 7 days. Union employees had a more favorable distribution of working days with 76% reporting working 5 or fewer days, 18% reported working 6 days and 7% reported working 7 days. Owner-operators have a higher probability of working 1 or 2 days in the previous week than do union or nonunion employees. They are however no more likely than nonunion employees to take holiday, vacation or sick days.

Days Since Last Home

Another measure of the nature of work, quality of life, and control over work is how long it has been since a driver returned home. Drivers place considerable value on returning home regularly and perceived job quality is closely related to firm's commitment to returning drivers home on schedule. Other research from the driver survey suggests that driver retention rises by 1.5 months for each additional day home in a month (Belman & Monaco, 2004). Owner-operators do not however return home as regularly as employee drivers. Union drivers return home after 3 days on average, nonunion employees return home after 4.1 days on average, while nonunion owner-operators average 5 days before returning home.

The evidence on mileage and working time is then mixed. Owner-operators drive somewhat fewer miles and work 10% fewer hours than employees for a package of compensation that is similar, on average, to that of nonunion employee drivers. This contradicts our Hypothesis 2a, which argues owner-operators will work harder than employee drivers. An alternative view is that the self-employed may use their added control over their work to improve their working conditions. This would suggest that owner-operators may be taking the gains associated with self-employment in the form of better working conditions rather than as compensation. However, the similarity in the distribution of days of work per week between nonunion employee drivers and owner-operators, and owner-operators longer absence from home is not consistent with this explanation. It is a conundrum why owner-operators would voluntarily forgo income by working less than 60 hours per week, but work as many days per week as nonunion employees while spending additional days away from home if they were spending the gains of self-employment in the form of improved working conditions.

Response to Job Pressures and Violations of Hours of Service

As we have suggested in Hypothesis 2b, the gain to being an owner-operator may be in added control over work rather than monetary compensation. We examine this further by considering how drivers respond to unrealistic schedules for shipments and how often drivers violate the hours of service regulation's 10-hour rule.

Drivers often complain about being given unrealistic schedules, schedules that provide too little time to pick up, move and deliver single or multiple loads. For example, a schedule might provide realistic times for the long distance part of the trip, but be unrealistic with regard to time involved in moving across a metropolitan area between dropping one load and picking up another. Or it might not allow sufficient time to enter a loading dock and load the trailer.

One measure of a driver's control over their work is how they respond to unrealistic schedules. The survey provided drivers with four possible responses to being offered an unrealistic schedule: refusing the load, renegotiating the time, taking the load but not changing their behavior, and driving faster. Drivers indicated any of the methods they used when given an unrealistic schedules (Table 9.10). The first response is to refuse the load. Owner-operators are more likely to indicate that they would refuse a load with an unrealistic schedule (19.5%) than either unionized employees (15.9%) or nonunion employees (11.3%). The null of no difference in response between types of drivers is rejected in a 1% chi-square test. This pattern is not unexpected as employees are potentially subject to discipline for refusing work, union drivers can be disciplined up to termination for refusing work. Although some owner-operators are in a similar position, those on permanent leases can be required to take loads. In contrast, those who obtain loads from brokers would find it relatively easy to refuse a particular undesirable load. The owner-operator would not have to tell the broker, they were refusing the load because of scheduling, as there are always good reasons not to take a particular load. Given the institutional position of owner-operators and employees, the difference in

Table 9.10.   What do you do when offered an unreasonable schedule?

	Employee		Owner-Operator
% Anserwing	Union	Nonunion	Nonunion
Refuse load	15.9%	11.3%	19.4%
Renegotiate	48.6%	59.6%	59.5%
Drive faster	10.0%	15.4%	19.9%
Don't change anything	33.0%	35.5%	27.6%

the proportion who report refusing a load is moderate in magnitude. It is consistent with owner-operators having more control over their work.

Owner-operators and nonunion employees are equally likely to respond to an unrealistic schedule by renegotiation of that schedule, 59.5% of owner-operators and 59.6% of nonunion employees indicate they would renegotiate. Union drivers are less likely (48.7%) to renegotiate. This lower propensity to renegotiate reflects both the type of work union drivers engage in, largely fixed routes with known schedules, and a system in which the response to managerial action is to "obey and grieve." A null hypothesis of no difference in response by driver type cannot however be rejected in even a 10% chi-square test.

A third option for drivers is to take the load and drive according to their usual procedures. This response is more common between union and nonunion employees (35.6% and 33.0% respectively) than among nonunion owner-operators (27.7%) but the differences are not large. Again, the difference in response may reflect the different situation of employees and owner-operators. It is difficult to penalize an employee if they conform to firm and government policies, but easier to penalize a self-employed driver by giving them less work, and less desirable routes in the future. A null of no difference in response by type of driver cannot be rejected in even a 10% chi-square test.

A final option was to drive faster. Owner-operators are more likely to choose this approach (19.9%) than nonunion employees (15.4%) and union employees (10.0%). The null of no difference in response by type of driver can be rejected in a 10%, but not a 5% chi-square test. This pattern is consistent with the immediacy of risks of economic loss for the three types of drivers.

A second measure of response to unrealistic schedules is how often a driver violates the 10-hour rule. As discussed previously in this paper, the 10-hour rule is most honored in its breech. Drivers are, nevertheless, responsible for obeying the rule and are subject to fines when they are caught violating that rule. We use the number of violations of the 10-

hour rule as a measure of how drivers handle schedules which either begin as or evolve into requiring driving beyond 10 hours before a break.

Data from the driver survey suggest there is no difference in the number of violations in the last 30 days between owner-operators and non-union employee drivers. Both groups average 7.5 violations with a median of 3 violations. Union employees averaged 3.3 violations with a median of 1 violation. This suggests no great difference in driver behavior between owner-operators and nonunion employees with regard to working hours beyond those legally permitted.

We also provide some data on hours of service violations by race and type of driver. Although the samples of non-White drivers are not large, it is apparent that non-White drivers are less likely to violate the 10-hour rule. The difference by race may reflect non-White drivers being more subject to inspections and reviews or receiving higher penalties when found in violation than White drivers. The similarity of the response by race across types of drivers suggests that discrimination of this type, if it indeed exists, does not vary between owner-operators and employees, which brings us to Hypothesis 3.

Racial Diversity

We turn to the issue of differential racial diversity for employees and owner-operators. The Midwestern sample for the driver labor force was 82.8% White, 8.4% Black, 0.1% Asian, 3.7% Native American and 5.0% Other. We believe that the large number of drivers indicating that they were Native American is accurate. There is a significant Native American population in the Midwest, particularly in the northern tier of states from Michigan across to Minnesota and beyond.

Hypothesis 3 asked whether the division between owner-operators and employees differs along racial lines. Table 9.11 suggests not. Here we divided the labor force into three groupings: employees, owner-operators

Table 9.11.   Racial Composition of the Labor Force

	Total		Owner-Operator	Both	Employee
	#	%			
White	834	82.83%	24.48%	0.67%	74.85%
Black	84	8.39%	26.16%	0.00%	73.84%
Other	88	8.79%	28.28%	0.50%	71.21%

and both. The latter are members of the Teamster's union who are paid as employees, but receive separate payments for their truck. There is virtually no difference in the distribution of driver type across the races. Between 71% and 75% of drivers are employees, between 24% and 28% are owner-operators, and a small fraction fall into both categories. The small differences in the distribution of owner-operators by race do not support the hypothesis that self-employment is supportive of racial diversity among truck drivers.[6]

A MULTIVARIATE COMPARISON OF OWNER-OPERATORS AND EMPLOYEES PERFORMANCE

Although the proceeding comparison is suggestive of only modest differences between owner-operators and employees, the apparent similarity could be caused by conflation with other factors. For example, the higher annual earnings of owner-operators may be due to their greater age and occupational experience rather than representing a return to risk or to the superior human capital of the self-employed. We examine this (Hypothesis 4) by estimating regression models of annual earnings, annual mileage, hours worked in the last 7 days and the number of violations of the 10-hour rule. The models draw on the work of Belman and Monaco (2001) and include controls for firm and industry characteristics, individual characteristics including human capital (age, experience, education), unionization, type of work (over-the-road vs. local driver), and use of technology. Descriptive statistics for the sample used to estimate these models are found in Table 9.12; estimates of the models of annual earnings, mileage, hours and violations are found in Table 9.13. We include a dummy variable to indicate whether an individual is an owner-operator, the base group is employee drivers. Only the first wave of the driver survey was used in this research and equations were estimated with 420 observations. We focus narrowly on the estimates of the effect of being an owner-operator on these various outcomes, but an extensive discussion of this model and the full set of estimates is provided in Belman and Monaco (2001). The hypothesis that the coefficients on the explanatory variables were uniformly zero could be rejected in better than a 1% F test for each of the five models.

The evidence on the performance of owner-operators relative to employee drivers is mixed. The dependent variable for the annual earnings model is, for employee drivers, the log of annual earnings from driving in the previous year. For owner-operators it is the log of annual earnings after truck expenses but before taxes. Applying the Palmer-Lundquivst correction, our sample estimate indicate that owner-operators

Table 9.12.   Descriptive Statistics on the UMTIP Driver Survey Sample Used for Estimation

Communications Technologies	fax	30.5%
	beeper	27.0%
	two way radio	6.8%
	cellular phone	29.8%
	e-mail	2.3%
	satellite based system	28.6%
Computing Technologies	laptop computer	4.3%
Routing Technologies	dispatcher	31.4%
	cb radio	63.9%
	on-board computer with maps	7.7%
	laptop with maps	3.6%
Collective Bargaining	union member	12.2%
Human Capital	age	42.4 years
	occupational experience	15.3 years
	less than high school education	20.1%
	high school diploma	47.0%
	vocational or technical degree	3.4%
	some college	21.1%
	associate of arts	4.3%
	college degree or higher	4.1%
Other Characteristics	local driver	12.1%
	owner operator	25.9%
	private carriage	18.3%
	paid by the hour	15.3%
	paid percent of revenue	34.2%

earned 9.4% less than otherwise similar employee drivers in 1996, but this estimates is not close to significance in even a 10% two-tailed t-test.

Annual earnings are affected by factors such as how many months one has driven, use of a measure which standardizes pay for effort may provide different estimates than annual earnings. Creating such a measure for truck drivers is more difficult than for most occupations as base pay can be calculated by mileage, as a percent of revenue or by the hour. Each of these systems is further complicated by the presence of bonuses and, for some owner-operators, penalties. Our approach to constructing a standardized metric of pay has been to divide the prior year's income from trucking by the prior year's mileage. In the case of owner-operators, we use income less truck expenses but before taxes as

**Table 9.13.   Effects of Self-Employment and Race
on Performance Outcomes of Truck Drivers**

Variable	Annual Earnings	Mileage Rates	Annual Mileage (1996)	Hours Worked in Last Seven Days	Violations of 10 Hour Rule
			Characteristics of Work		
owner-operator	-.0993277 (-1.121)	.03843 (1.249)	-12882.5 (-2.275)	-12.50988 (-3.658)	1.357145 (0.932)
local driver	-.0012475 (-0.020)	.2190202 (3.197)	-20497.79 (-4.023)	3.217044 (1.005)	.6002021 (0.437)
private carriage	.1040398 (1.465)	.0414804 (1.040)	3603.242 (0.500)	-.1268981 (-0.043)	-1.808616 (-1.844)
			Communications Technology		
fax	-.0073582 (-0.221)	-.0730204 (-1.739)	6056.952 (1.565)	.8017403 (0.251)	.4351484 (0.502)
beeper	.0711955 (1.589)	.0860227 (1.619)	418.7865 (0.089)	3.621275 (1.290)	.1051567 (0.093)
radio	-.1508661 (-0.924)	.148308 (1.965)	-22567.91 (-3.689)	-4.417602 (-0.681)	-2.779379 (-1.856)
cell phone	.1007267 (1.439)	.0644686 (2.043)	2150.976 (0.392)	1.861068 (0.896)	-.7714342 (-0.685)
e-mail	.0961504 (0.661)	-.0390344 (-0.739)	10215.61 (1.002)	-3.044983 (-0.341)	.0023664 (0.001)
satellite based system	.1496488 (2.399)	-.0759707 (-1.563)	21264.86 (4.090)	7.637126 (1.767)	-1.02786 (-0.831)
			Computing Technologies		
laptop Computer	-.0378838 (-0.214)	-.0238097 (-0.502)	6947.18 (0.637)	-2.544288 (-0.495)	1.511284 (0.772)
			Routing Technologies		
use dispatcher	-.0723803 (-1.889)	.0739097 (1.991)	-9053.825 (-2.021)	2.801391 (0.750)	1.131983 (0.960)
cb radio	-.0034539 (-0.061)	-.057279 (-1.714)	9858.524 (3.583)	.3394181 (0.092)	2.690801 (3.695)
on-board computer w/ maps	-.0377493 (-0.473)	-.0379909 (-1.190)	-3017.065 (-0.462)	-8.765722 (-2.342)	-1.049796 (-0.512)
laptop with maps	-.2156378 (-1.494)	-.1010211 (-1.851)	9970.109 (1.154)	-7.764447 (-1.112)	-.4609609 (-0.197)
			Collective Bargaining		
union member	.191998 (2.442)	.0675854 (2.029)	-3041.434 (-0.436)	.166194 (0.048)	.0858031 (0.062)
Less than High School	-.0664492 (-1.254)	-.0470559 (-2.099)	4901.058 (1.492)	-.4728194 (-0.137)	.0071913 (0.006)

(tables continues)

Table 9.13.   Continued

Variable	Annual Earnings	Mileage Rates	Annual Mileage (1996)	Hours Worked in Last Seven Days	Violations of 10 Hour Rule
	Human Capital (continued)				
Less than	-.0664492	-.0470559	4901.058	-.4728194	.0071913
High School	(-1.254)	(-2.099)	(1.492)	(-0.137)	(0.006)
Vocational	-.0823517	.1389289	-5876.541	12.42526	5.501158
Degree	(-0.604)	(0.930)	(-0.482)	(1.506)	(1.266)
Some College	-.0744796	.0183911	-9229.401	.9770617	1.104912
	(-0.794)	(0.495)	(-2.458)	(0.228)	(0.877)
Associate of	.0801656	-.0107187	-1521.463	2.54517	.0373074
Arts	(0.530)	(-0.169)	(-0.241)	(0.289)	(0.012)
College or	-.1399572	-.0486968	-7383.482	15.40994	5.536212
more	(-1.239)	(-0.784)	(-0.710)	(2.652)	(2.186)
	Pay Systems				
Paid by hour	-.0077003	.0667675	-12192.55	-4.112222	-.6630246
	(-0.096)	(1.166)	(-2.589)	(-1.427)	(-0.361)
Paid as % of	.0112605	.0091269	3052.709	-1.941254	1.33657
revenue	(0.221)	(0.298)	(0.614)	(-0.866)	(1.335)
	Additional Controls				
Annual miles	no	no	no	no	.0000452
					(2.824)
Annual wage	no	no	no	no	.000015
					(-0.545)
Race/Ethnic-ity/Gender	yes	yes	yes	yes	yes
Region	yes	yes	yes	yes	yes
Industry Segment	yes	yes	yes	yes	yes
Firm Size	yes	yes	yes	yes	yes
r-square	.2546	..3423	.3131	.2741	.3131

our measure of income. The resulting, measure, one we call the effective mileage rate, is the driver's payment in cents per mile. This measure is regressed on the same explanatory variables as was annual income. Although the sample estimate for the owner-operator dummy suggests owner-operators earn 3.84 cents more per mile than otherwise similar employee drivers, the estimate is again, far from significant in even a one-tailed 10% t-test.

Although our estimates indicate that owner-operators are not paid and do not earn more than employee drivers, the regressions indicate that owner-operators are working less than employee drivers. The third equation regresses 1996 annual mileage on the set of explanatory variables, including age and occupational experience, used in the annual income and effective mileage rate models. Owner-operators are indicated to drive 12,288 fewer miles annually than employee drivers, the coefficient is significant in a 5% two-tailed test against a null of no difference between employees and owner-operators. The results for hours worked are, if anything, stronger than those for annual mileage. Owner-operators are estimated to work 12.5 fewer hours per week than otherwise similar employee drivers, the null of no difference between owner-operators and employee drivers is easily rejected in a 1% two-tailed test.

The last model takes the number of reported violations of the 10-hour rule as the dependent variable. The specification is similar to that of the other models, but adds controls for annual miles and income in the previous year. The estimated coefficient for owner-operators is very small, .007 and far from being statistically significant in any conventional test. There appears to be no difference in the behavior of owner-operators and employee drivers with regard to the 10-hour rule.

Taken together, these estimates suggest that once we control for human capital, as measured by age and experience, owner-operators differ from employee drivers in important ways. Although they are not paid more or earn more than employee drivers, they do not work as hard for their income as they drive fewer miles and work fewer hours. They are also no more likely to violate the 10-hour rule than are employee drivers. These results are consistent with the view that owner-operators take the gains from self-employment in better working conditions rather than as direct income. Although we cannot determine whether this gain comes from ownership of capital, the superior skills and knowledge of owner-operators or some combination of the two, owner-operators appear to have better working conditions than otherwise similar employee drivers, at least with regard to these two aspects of their work life.

CONCLUSIONS

In summary, the analysis in this chapter suggests that owner-operators are not more economically successful than employee drivers particularly when benefits and other nonsalaried forms of compensation are considered. However, although they may be less economically successful, their working conditions are considerably superior to those of otherwise similar drivers. It may then be that owner-operators choose their positions for superior working conditions, the ability to have greater control over their

working lives, and possibly to improve their longevity in their chosen profession.

While in general, our chapter suggests that the majority of owner-operators are not distinct from employees drivers in terms of garnering higher
reward for taking on higher risk; there is, however, a substantial tail in the
distribution of owner-operators, who appear to lead successful small businesses. These owner-operators not only have higher income than their
nonunion employee driver counterparts, their benefit coverage is similar
to or better than that of such employee drivers. Interviews with these drivers suggest that this group has found niches which demand skills not possessed by many drivers and they take advantage of these skills to earn
both higher incomes and obtain better working conditions. For example,
one driver in this group worked for a firm that specialized in oversized
loads. The driver was expected, as part of his duties, to determine appropriate routes, obtain certificates from state police, make arrangements for
escorts when needed, and take particular care to assure that these loads,
which included objects such as the rollers for paper mills, arrived at their
final destination unmarked. The reward for these activities was not just
high pay and good benefits, but a short work day—oversized loads can
only be moved during daylight hours—and considerable freedom with
regard to scheduling.

Future research should examine the conditions that lead to extremely
successful owner-operators and nonsuccessful owner-operators. We know
little about what factors predict these outliers. More important, entrepreneurial research might need to be revised to not only consider the ability
to accrue wealth as the main outcome of interest, but also to have
increased emphasis on other key outcomes such as the ability to control
one's work effort, hours of work, and quality of live. With the shift in the
U.S. and global workforce to more women with children working changing family structures of support at home and more men interested in family life, greater consideration needs to be given to these nonfinancial
outcomes in conventional entrepreneurship theory. Our review of the
entrepreneurship literature showed little or no discussion of quality of life
issues. Future research should delve more in these issues.

In addition, more work is needed on linkages between diversity and
employee and self-employed status. We were surprised to not find more
minorities who were owner-operators. It could be that civil rights legislation has had a greater impact on the employment practices of large firms
than on structural changes affecting minorities' access to human and
financial capital enabling them to become owner-operators. More
research should be done on how to increase minority access to owner
operator status and the barriers that exist. One limitation of this study is
that it is only conducted on one industry. While on the one hand it is

helpful to focus analysis on one industry in order to make sure industry differences are controlled for. On the other hand, it would be helpful to collect data such as those in this paper on earnings, benefits, control over work hours, work effort, diversity and employment status, use of technology, and quality of life for entrepreneurs across a variety of industries at one time.

Overall, the evidence presented in this chapter suggests that it is not so much opportunities for profit that drive the truckers' behavior toward self-ownership, as much as the result of institutional competitive forces pushing trucking firms to be more flexible and responsive. Owner-operators are truck drivers who are more likely to perceive this increased flexibility and responsiveness over company employed truckers. Thus, our chapter adds to the field by underscoring the value of Shane and Venkataraman's (2000) definition that shows us that individual entrepreneurial behavior must be understood as an interaction with the institutional context in which it is embedded. Our discussion of owner-operator truck drivers also has provided a useful means for understanding whether individuals employed by large organizations can be viewed as Entrepreneurs. We also have demonstrated the importance for future research on entrepreneurship to draw from human resource and organizational behavior research and theory on total compensation and job motivation and performance, diversity, and the learning curve. We also hope our chapter encourages entrepreneurial researchers to look creatively at many work fields in their studies in order to better generalize entrepreneurial theory to the wide spectrum of jobs and careers across the economic and class strata.

NOTES

1. See Thill (2002, pp. 7-10). Additional discussion of the issue may be found at http://www.europarl.org.uk/news/infocus/R3oadTransportSocialLegislation2005.htm while the current directive can be found at http://europa.eu.int/eur-lex/pri/en/oj/dat/2002/1_080/1_08020020323en00350039.pdf

2. We draw heavily on Muhl (2002) for this discussion.

3. See Taylor (1996) and Bernhardt (1994).

4. See Smith and Ehrenberg (2000).

5. There are many possible definition of full time work. The overtime provisions of the Fair Labor Standards Act establishes a full time work week of 40 hours, or 2080 hours per year. If we consider those working 30 hours per week or more as full time employees, the average full time employee worked 39.88 hours per week, if we move the dividing line for full time employment up to 35 hours per week, the average full time employee

worked 40.6 hours in 2000 (authors analysis of the Outgoing Rotation Files of the of the 2000 Current Population Survey).

6. We do not consider diversity by gender in this paper because women are such small proportion of truck drivers, about 2% nationwide, and of the sample, 1.8%, that it is difficult to develop meaningful analyses so small a proportion of this sample.

REFERENCES

Becker, G. (1957). *The economics of discrimination*. Chicago: University of Chicago Press.

Belman, D., & Monaco, K. (2001, March). The consequences of deregulation, deunionization, technology and human capital on the work and work lives of truck drivers. *Industrial and Labor Relations Review*, 502-524.

Belman, D., & Monaco, K. (2004). Voice effects in trucking. Working paper.

Belman, D., Monaco, K., & Brooks, T. (2005). *Sailors of the concrete sea: The work and life of truck drivers*. East Lansing: Michigan State University Press.

Bernhardt, I. (1994, May). Comparative advantage in self-employment and paid work. *Canadian Journal of Economics, XXVII*(2), 273-289.

Carton, R. B, Hofer, C. W., & Meeks, M. D. (1998). *The entrepreneur and entrepreneurship—Operational definitions of their role in society*. Paper presented at the annual International Council for Small Business conference, Singapore. Retrieved January 16, 2003: http://www.sbaer.uca.edu/Research/1998/ICSB/k004.htm

Dennis, W. (1996). Self-employment: When nothing else is available? *Journal of Labor Research, 17*(4), 645-661.

DiSalvatore, R. (1988, Sept. 12 & 19). Large cars. *The New Yorker*, pp. 39-77 & pp. 63-84, respectively.

Fairlie, R. (1999). The absence of African-owned business: An analysis of the dynamics of self-employment. *Journal of Labor Economics, 17*(1), 80-108.

Gatewood, E., Shaver, K., & Gartner, W. (1995). A longitudinal study of cognitive factors influencing start-up behaviors and success at venture creation. *Journal of Business Venturing, 10*, 371-391.

Goldstein, I., & Ford, J. (2002). *Training in organizations: Needs assessment, development and evaluation* (4th ed.). Belmont, CA: Wadsworth.

Heneman, R., Tansky, J., & Camp, S. (2000). Human resource management practices in small and medium enterprises: Unanswered questions and future research perspectives. *Entrepreneurship Theory and Practice, 25*, 11-26.

Heneman, R., Wang, S., Tansky, J., & Wang, Z. (2002). Compensation practices in small entrepreneurial and high growth companies in the U.S. and China. *Compensation and Benefits Review, 34*(4), 13-22.

Heneman, R., Waldeck, N., & Cushnie, M. (1996). Diversity considerations in staffing decision-making. In E. Kossek & S. Lobel (Eds.), *Managing diversity: Human resource strategies for transforming the workplace* (pp 74-102). Oxford: Blackwell.

Honig, B. (1998). What determines success? Examining the human financial and social capital of Jamacian microentrepreneurs. *Journal of Business Venturing, 13*, 371-394.

Kautz, J. (1999). What is an entrepreneur, *About.com*. Retrieved April 19, 2002: http://entrepreneurs.about.com/ (c20021301)

Leibenstein, H. (1968). Entrepreneurship and development. *The American Economic Review, 58*(2), 72-83.

Mathews., C., & Mosier, S. (1995). Family background and gender: Implications for interest in small firm ownership. *Entrepreneurship and Regional Development, 7*, 365-377.

Milkovich, G., & Newman, J. (2005). *Compensation management* (8th ed.). Burr Ridge, IL: McGraw Hill.

Mishel, L., Bernstein, J., & Schmitt, J. (1998). *The state of working America*. Ithaca, NY: Cornell University Press.

Muhl, C. J. (2002, January). What is an employee? The answer depends on federal labor law. *Monthly Labor Review, 125*(1), 3-11.

Schumpeter, J. A. (1951). *Theory of economic development*. Cambridge, MA: Harvard University Press.

Shane, S., & Venkataraman, S. (2000). The promise of entrepreneurship as a field of research. *Academy of Management Review, 25*(1), 217-226.

Smith, R. S., & Ehrenberg, R. G. (2000). *Modern labor economics* (7th ed., pp. 251-284). Reading, MA: Addison-Wesley Longman.

Stroh, L., Northcraft, G., & Neale, M. (2002). *Organizational behavior: A management challenge*. Chicago: Dryden Press.

Taylor, M. P. (1996). Earnings, independence, or unemployment: Why become self-employed? *Oxford Bulletin of Economics and Statistics, 58*(2), 253-66.

Thill, Y. (2002). Brief study of the European Road Transportation Sector and the situation of the owner-driver in Europe, MBA paper for Professor Francine Lafontaine, Fisher School of Business, University of Michigan.

Venkataraman, S. (1997). The distinctive domain of entrepreneurship research: An editor's perspective. In J. Katz & R. Brockhaus (Eds.), *Advances in entrepreneurship, firm emergence, and growth* (Vol. 3, pp. 119-138). Greenwich, CT: JAI Press.

CHAPTER 10

HUMAN RESOURCE MANAGEMENT IN SMALL FIRMS

Evidence From Growing Small Firms in Australia

Susan Mayson and Rowena Barrett

Human resource management (HRM) is important in developing a firm's ability to adjust to their competitive environment, while poor "fit" between business strategy and HRM may hinder firm growth. Research shows HRM in small firms is informal, which is problematic for firm success and survival. In growth-oriented small firms effective deployment of people is vital for continued growth. In this paper we examine whether formalized HRM practices are used in growth-oriented small firms. We use data from CPA Australia's 2002 small business employment survey where small firms employ less that 20 people and growth-oriented ones had employed new staff because of expansion or diversification. Our analysis shows growth-oriented small firms are more likely than nongrowing ones to use formalized HRM practices. However, whether this is evidence of a distinct competence

Human Resource Strategies for the High Growth Entrepreneurial Firm, 223–243
Copyright © 2006 by Information Age Publishing
All rights of reproduction in any form reserved.
223

in aligning HRM with business strategy cannot be determined from this data. In conclusion therefore future research ideas are proposed.

INTRODUCTION

In Australia there are some 1.16 million private sector firms employing just over 6.9 million people in a population of about 20 million (Australian Bureau Statistics [ABS], 2002). Small firms or firms that employ less than 20 people make up 97% or 1.23 million firms in the private sector while in agriculture, fishing and forestry there are another 111,200 small firms (those firms with an estimated value of operations of between A$22,500 and A$400,000) (ABS, 2002). Nearly 3.6 million people work in these private sector nonagricultural small firms: 30% are owner-managers or self-employed and 70% as employees (ABS, 2002). Small firms dominate all private sector industries and they play a significant role in rural and regional economies and communities. Recognition of the significance of small firms in the Australian economy has seen a consistency across the political spectrum in recent times with small firms being said to be the "engine room" of the economy in general and job generation in particular.

However a recent Australian federal government report shows that small firms face difficulties finding and keeping 'good' staff and this has an impact on their ability to grow (Senate Employment, Workplace Relations, and Education References Committee [Senate EWRERC], 2003). The few Australian studies of HRM in small firms (see, e.g., Kotey & Sheridan, 2001; Mazzarol, 2003; Weisner & McDonald, 2001) also point to this problem and at the same time support the general conclusion of international studies (see, e.g., Benmore & Palmer, 1996; Heneman & Berkley, 1999; Hornsby & Kuratko, 1990, 2003; Marlow & Patton, 1993; McEvoy, 1984; Ram, 1999), which is that informality characterizes HRM in small firms. Given the threats in small firms' regulatory and external environments which should see a greater emphasis on HRM, Hornsby and Kuratko (2003) argue that HRM practices in smaller ventures (firms with less than 150 employees) have stagnated or even regressed over the last decade.

A number of writers argue that a strategic approach to managing employees is vital for the success of all firms (Dyer, 1993; Pfeffer, 1994, 1998), including small ones (Deshpande & Golhar, 1994; Heneman, Tansky, & Camp, 2000; Hornsby & Kuratko, 2003; Marlow, 2000). Similarly, a number of writers argue that a strategic approach to planning and decision making in small firms can contribute to firm survival and growth (Gibb & Scott, 1985; Hannon & Atherton, 1998). This is particularly the case in growth-oriented small firms as these will make significant contributions to economic performance.

In this context, our chapter aims to further understanding about the nature and type of HRM practices in Australian small firms. Small firms in Australia are an interesting case in point because they are considerably smaller than those in Europe and the United States (less than 20 people compared with less than 200 or 500). Hence the firms we discuss in this chapter are very small, small firms. More important, our chapter addresses an emerging area in the literature and that is the intersection of the HRM, small firm and entrepreneurship literatures (see overviews by Baron, 2003; Cardon & Stevens, 2004; Katz, Aldrich, Welbourne, & Williams, 2000). We do this by taking the approach that growth is sometimes entrepreneurship and vice versa (Davidsson, Delman, & Wiklund, 2002) when entrepreneurship is accepted to be the creation of new economic activity (e.g., Shane & Venkataraman, 2000; Stevenson & Jarillo, 1990; Venkataraman, 1997). The focus in this chapter is therefore on the HRM practices in growing small firms compared to those in nongrowing small firms.

Drawing on theory and concepts from the strategic HRM literature, in this chapter we argue that taking a strategic approach to managing employees in a small firm—that is aligning HRM practices to business strategy (Delaney & Huselid, 1996) or using environmental information to make business decisions (Hannon & Atherton, 1998)—could be evidenced by formalization in HRM practices and procedures. "Formal" HRM can mean that the procedure or practice is (a) written down (e.g., a list of skills and qualifications for jobs); (b) regularly applied within an organization (e.g., yearly performance reviews); or (c) assured to take place (e.g., employer-sponsored training) (de Kok & Uhlaner, 2001). We investigate this argument using data collected by CPA Australia in their Small Business Survey Program in March 2002.[1] In the next section of the chapter we address the literature on the nature of HRM in small firms and identify key HRM issues for growing small firms. This is followed by an analysis and discussion of the CPA Australia data. We conclude with suggestions for future research in this important area of study.

Small Firms, Growth and HRM Theory, and Practice

The resource-based view of the firm suggests that human resources can be a source of competitive advantage (Barney, 1991). Writers argue that a firm's ability to develop distinct and unique "bundles" of interlinked HRM practices aligned with business strategy are a source of sustainable competitive advantage (Boxall, 1996; Delaney & Huselid, 1996; Dyer & Reeves, 1995; Huselid, Jackson, & Schuler, 1997; Lado & Wilson, 1994). However, HRM in small firms is commonly found to reflect operational needs and pragmatic concerns of small firms: record keeping; staffing activities, such as recruiting and selecting staff; and, to a lesser extent, motivation and retention activities such as compensation and reward practices (Deshpande & Golhar, 1994; Duberley & Walley, 1995; Heneman & Berkley, 1999; Hornsby & Kuratko, 2003; Kotey & Sheridan, 2001; McEvoy, 1984) and as suggested earlier there is a range of studies indicating small firms are characterized by informal HRM practices (see, e.g., Benmore & Palmer, 1996; Heneman & Berkley, 1999; Hornsby & Kuratko, 1990; Marlow, 2000; Marlow & Patton, 1993; McEvoy, 1984; Ram 1999).

The literature on strategic HRM, while more commonly associated with the study of HRM in large firms, deals with how firms develop the internal capacity to adapt and adjust to their competitive environments by aligning HRM policies and practices with business strategies (see, e.g., Delery & Doty, 1996; Lengnick-Hall & Lengnick-Hall, 1988; Wright & Snell, 1998; Wright, Dunford, & Snell, 2001). This literature contains important insights for growing firms which face problems caused by the complexity associated with resource (including human resource) acquisition, allocation and development (e.g., Arthur, 1995). The application of strategic thinking and the implementation of appropriate HRM policies and procedures can have a considerable impact on the speed and direction of growth in high growth firms (Baron, 2003; Chaganti, Cook, & Smeltz, 2002; Heneman et al., 2000; Katz et al., 2000; Morris, 2001; Williamson, 2000) and whether that growth is sustainable.

The role of the owner/manager may influence the take up and formalization of HR practices and hence firm effectiveness. Heneman et al. (2000) argue that in growing small firms there is a pressure on the small business owner/manager to delegate responsibility for HRM although Matlay (1999) and Mazzarol (2003) suggests this will depend on the owner/manager's management style and personality. Gibb and Scott (1985) argue that the strategic awareness and personal commitment of owner/managers contribute to goal achievement in firms that seek to expand their markets. Indeed Scase (1995) argues that those small business owners who are unable to change their style act as a barrier to firm growth (see Penrose, 1959).

As such there is consistency here with the ideas underpinning the staged growth models of small firms which concentrate on the stages through which small firms transition (see, Churchill & Lewis, 1983; Scott & Bruce, 1987, for example), which suggest that transitioning depends on internal capabilities and managerial capacity (see also, Gibb & Scott,

1985; Hannon & Atherton, 1998). The ability to overcome the "managerial capacity problem" (Barringer, Jones, & Lewis, 1998) depends in part on the owner/manager's recognition of the importance of HRM to the firm's performance. Ardichivili et al. (1998) study of 576 U.S. startups over a 10-year period showed the delegation of HRM issues lagged well behind the delegation of accounting, production and information systems. Hornsby and Kuratko (2003) argue that managerial incompetence in handling HRM issues is a major source of firm failure. While Cassell, Nadin, Gray, & Clegg (2002) found in their study of SMEs that having an internal "HR champion" contributes an HRM approach to solving business problems.

In comparison to larger firms, implementing HRM is costly in terms of time and money for small firms (McEvoy, 1984; Reid, Morrow, Kelly, & McCartan, 2002). Their idiosyncratic needs mean that they are unable to achieve economies of scale and they rarely have the managerial resources and expertise in the area (Chandler & McEvoy, 2000; Hornsby & Kuratko, 1990; Klaas, McClendon, & Gainey, 2000; Kotey & Sheridan, 2001; McEvoy, 1984; McLarty, 1999). Small firms typically do not have a designated HRM (or employment) specialist and access to specialist HRM advice are costly (Gilbert & Jones, 2000; Kotey & Sheridan, 2001). In the absence of dedicated and qualified HR professionals, research (e.g., Hornsby & Kuratko, 2003; Marlow, 2000) suggests there is considerable scope for appropriately skilled external advisors to help small business with HRM matters. For example, small business operators tend to turn to those they trust for this: usually their accountant or lawyer (Harris, 2000; Jay & Schaper, 2003). While advice from external professionals can be expensive, the outsourcing of HRM can be an investment against the cost of HRM recruitment and selection "mistakes" or defending an unfair dismissal case arising from poor HRM practices and policies (Heneman et al., 2000).

So while the formalization of HRM policies becomes desirable as firms grow, the ability for this to occur in small firms depends on the recognition of the owner/manager to act strategically and/ or take an HRM approach to business problems. In addition if they have decided on the importance of strategic action, can the owner/manager delegate responsibility for HRM tasks? Moreover the formalization of HRM is also dependent on the awareness of legislation and legal requirements on HRM and employment matters (e.g., payroll tax level, unfair dismissal, occupational health and safety, workcover insurance, superannuation etc.) and recognition of the impact on their business should they not be compliant.[2] However as the section below indicates, small firms' HRM are characterized by informality.

Small Firm HRM

Small firm HRM practices are commonly examined in the literature in terms of traditional HR activities such as recruitment and selection, training, performance appraisal and compensation. As Cassell et al. (2002) argue these traditional activities are often used because owner/managers are most familiar with these basic activities. They are also commonly recognized as key operational HR functions in the broader HRM literature. Drawing on the small firm HRM literature, this section identifies recruitment and selection, training, and attraction, motivation and retention as HR activities commonly found in small firms.

Recruitment and Selection

In Australia one of the main problems faced by small firms is said to be their ability to recruit "good" staff. The government's *Small Business Employment* report summarizes a range of industry surveys showing this to be the case (Senate EWRERC, 2003), while the unfair dismissal legislative regime has come under a great deal of criticism as the main reason for inhibiting small firms employing new staff. Arguably recourse to unfair dismissal provisions is an outcome of the larger problem of ineffective recruitment, selection and retention strategies in small firms.

Studies of small firm recruitment support this argument and point to a reliance on informal, word-of-mouth methods. This increases as firm size decreases, to the point where recruitment in the smallest firms can be conditional on the availability of a known individual. For example, Heneman and Berkley (1999) found that firms in their study (n = 117) used attraction practices that were convenient, inexpensive and directly controllable by the firm, while others found a reliance on word of mouth and other informal recruitment processes are frequently used in small firms (see, e.g., Carroll, Marchington, Earnshaw, & Taylor, 1999; Gilbert & Jones, 2000; Kotey & Sheridan, 2001; Marchington, Carroll, & Boxall, 2003).

McEvoy's (1984) study of 84 small businesses with an average of 75 employees, showed that while employers identified finding competent workers a major problem, their recruitment practices were "unimaginative" (newspaper ads, and walk-ins) and their selection techniques were confined to application blanks and face to face interviews. Marlow and Patton (1993) suggest small firm employers believe these informal recruitment and selection methods are an effective means of ensuring new recruits "fit in." Others found that selection procedures such as face to face interviews, reference checks, job try outs and application blanks were chosen for ease of use and convenience (see also, Deshpande & Golhar, 1994; Gilbert & Jones, 2000; Kotey & Sheridan, 2001; McEvoy, 1984).

However, as small firms grow, managers exhaust their informal staffing contacts (e.g., family members, referrals and "walk ins") and need to develop more formal methods to recruit employees to sustain growth (Williams, 2000). The result of employing informal recruitment and selection practices can be the employment of the "wrong" or "not quite right" person, as the pool of suitable recruits is potentially untapped. Additionally these methods could leave the firm open to accusations of indirect discrimination (Carroll et al., 1999).

Training and Development

If the "not quite right" person is employed, all is not lost as training can fill the gap between the recruit's skills and knowledge and what they need for the job. To reduce costs this can be done in-house or on-the-job: maybe as simply as having an employee work alongside the new one until they've "got the hang of the job." Unfortunately research tells us that small firms are less likely than large firms to invest in training (see, e.g., Storey, 2004). Storey and Westhead (1997) provide two explanations for this: first the "ignorance" explanation where training is not provided because the benefit of training is underestimated by the small firm employer/manager; and second, the "market" explanation where the cost of training is too high for small firms (Storey, 2004; Storey & Westhead, 1997).

In other studies, Kotey and Sheridan (2001) and Gilbert and Jones (2000) found that induction training was implemented on an informal basis and internal and external training was not linked to employee performance appraisals (see also, Marlow, 2000). Cassell et al. (2002) found in their study of SMEs that staff training and retention were closely linked but not in a way commonly thought about. Training was considered an important investment in growing the skills base of the firm but it also made staff more mobile and marketable. In the absence of other factors to encourage retention, trained staff were often poached by other small firms.

Attraction, Motivation and Retention

Small firms' ability to attract, motivate and retain employees by offering competitive salaries and appropriate rewards is linked to firm performance and growth. The fact that small firms tend to opt for informal practices is not surprising. McEvoy (1984) found that only 29% of his sample used salary surveys to set compensation levels and 33% used job evaluation as a basis of determining compensation. He also found that recognition and reinforcement, pay rises or job security were commonly used reward systems (McEvoy, 1984). More recently, Hornsby and

Kuratko (2003) found that the availability of quality staff and the provision of employee benefits remain important staffing issues for small firms.

Performance appraisal practices in small firms tended to be informal and continuous and often used for monitoring and control rather than development purposes (Gilbert & Jones, 2000). Cassell et al. (2002) found in their study of SMEs ($n = 100$) that half of the respondents used some form of appraisal but there was a diversity of approaches and formal systems were rare. However, in a much earlier study, McEvoy (1984) found that performance review meetings in his sample served the dual purpose of providing feedback for developmental purposes as well as a forum for discussing compensation matters, that is evaluation or monitoring of performance.

CPA Australia's Small Business Survey Program on Employment Issues

The findings outlined above are consistent with those of the CPA Australia survey of small firm employment practices. By telephone, CPA Australia surveyed a random sample of 600 small firms (defined as independently owned and employing less than 20 people). Key findings from the survey in relation to HRM practices are shown in Table 10.1.

In particular CPA Australia reported that while 48% of respondents who employed staff ($n = 461$) had employed a new staff member (either full-time or part-time) in the previous 12 months, the use of outside help for recruitment was not widespread (21% used outside help) however some 53% used a written job description and 75% listed the skills and qualifications sought. In terms of HRM practices in the small firms employing staff: 59% offered flexible hours; 45% paid for off-site training or work-related education; 35% had an incentive scheme and 57% used incentive schemes or bonuses to reward performance; 32% offered job sharing or part-time work; 28% had salary packaging: and 20% allowed staff to work from home. Employee performance was primarily rewarded by praise and recognition (82%), bonus or incentives (57%), a salary increase (51%), additional time off (27%), promotion (24%) or a special training seminar, workshop or conference (22%).

In general HRM in small firms tends to be informal and this can contribute to the inability to find and keep the "right" staff and therefore on the ability for firms to grow and that growth be sustainable. The implementation of formal HRM practices is an important contributor to small business success but as Heneman and Berkley (1999, p. 53) indicate the "liability of smallness" presents unique challenges for HRM in small firms

Table 10.1.   HRM Practices in the Small Firms Surveyed by CPA Australia

	All Small Firms (Percent)
Reward performance by praise and recognition	82
Have a list of skills and qualifications being sought	75
Offer flexible working hours	59
Offer bonuses or incentives to reward performance	57
Offer bonus or incentives to reward performance	57
Have a written job description for the position being filled	53
Offer increases to salary to reward performance	51
Pay for off-site training or work-related education	45
Have an incentive scheme	35
Offer job-sharing or part-time work	32
Offer salary packaging	28
Offer additional time off to reward performance	27
Offer promotions to reward performance	24
Offer special training, seminars or conferences to reward performance	22
Have a succession plan	21
Get outside help with recruitment	21
Allow staff to work from home	20
Have an employee share plan	1

$n = 461$.

(see also, Deshpande & Golhar, 1994; Klaas et al., 2000). In the next section of the chapter we outline the details of the CPA Australia data on which we base our analysis of HRM practices in growing and nongrowing small firms. In particular the question we are interested in answering is "do growth-oriented small firms use formal HRM practices?"

DO GROWTH-ORIENTED SMALL FIRMS USE FORMAL HRM PRACTICES?

Data and Methodology

The data in this paper was gathered in March 2002 by CPA Australia as part of their small business survey program. Questions focused on attitudes to employment and sought to gain information about the motivating factors behind employment decisions in small firms. The full report of the telephone survey with 600 small firms (defined as independently

owned and employing less than 20 people) is available at http://
www.cpaaustralia.com.au.[3]

The 600 small firms were drawn from across the Australian states and
metro/rural and regional locations. Eighty-five percent of the small firms
employed staff, although 49% of the small firms surveyed employed one
or two people in total (including owners/managers). The mean number
per employing business of full-time staff was 3.16; 0.97 for part-time staff,
1.82 for casuals, 0.56 for contractors and 0.03 for labor hire staff. Quite
clearly the firms we are dealing with in this paper are predominantly very
small.

HRM in Growth-Oriented Small Firms

In the previous section of the paper we argued that growing small firms
should exhibit greater formalization in their HRM practices than nongrowing small firms. Using the CPA Australia data we identified growing
small firms by the owner/manager's positive response to the following
question "Have you employed any new permanent full-time or part-time
staff in the last 12 months?" and then their reason for doing so as either
being "Because your business expanded?" or "You decided to diversify the
business?"[4] Some 98 small firms were categorized as growing small firms
compared to 238 nongrowing small firms. The 159 respondents who did
not employ anyone were not asked these questions in the telephone survey.

Key characteristics of the growing and nongrowing small firms are
shown in Table 10.2. In terms of their location, years of establishment,
ownership characteristics (gender, age and education) and industry sector,
the data indicate that growing small firms were more likely to be metro-
based (70%) than rural (30%) and they were also more likely to operate in
the services sector. Unsurprisingly, growing small firms were significantly
more likely to operate from more than one location ($p < .01$) than nongrowing small firms.

Statistically significant differences in ownership characteristics existed
between growing small firms and nongrowing small firms in terms of the
age of the owner ($p < .05$). Specifically, owners of nongrowing small firms
were more likely to be more than 60 years of age than owners of growing
small firms (10% compared to 5%), whereas the owners of growing small
firms were more likely than nongrowing small firms to be less than 40
years (49% compared to 31% were under 40 years of age, Furthermore the
owners of growing small firms were more likely than the owners of nongrowing small firms to have trade and/or tertiary qualifications (74% compared to 53%) ($p < .01$). There were no statistically significant differences

**Table 10.2.   Key Characteristics of Growing
and Non-Growing Small Firms**

		Growing Small Firms (Percent)	Nongrowing Small Firms (Percent)
Location	Metro	70.4	61.8
	Rural	29.6	38.2
Sector	Services	71.4	63.4
	Manufacturing	28.6	36.1
Years established	<5 years	21.4	18.3
	5-10 years	24.5	28.9
	11-20 years	24.5	23.0
	21+ years	29.6	29.8
No. locations	One	68.4	81.4
	Two	14.3	14.0
	Three+	17.3	4.7
Owner's gender	Male	66.3	67.6
	Female	33.7	32.4
Owner's age	Under 40 years	49.0	31.2
	40-49 years	35.7	35.9
	50-59 years	11.2	22.6
	60+ years	4.1	10.3
Family business	Yes	52.0	57.1
	No	48.0	42.9
Owner's Education	Secondary School	25.8	46.7
	Trade/Tertiary	74.2	53.3

Note: Growing small firms n = 98. Nongrowing small firms n = 235-238.

in the time the firms had been running, the owner's gender, or whether family members were employed in the firm.

In terms of the HRM practices in these small firms our analysis of the CPA Australia data shows that in growing small firms more formalized methods of recruitment and selection were more likely to be used than in nongrowing small firms (See Table 10.3). However, there was no statistically significant difference in terms of satisfaction with the last person employed: 83% of nongrowing small firms were satisfied with that person as were 93% of growing small firms.

Other HRM practices are shown in Table 10.4. Statistically significant differences between growing and nongrowing small firms primarily occurred in the areas of rewards and training.

The survey also asked a series of questions about the perceived barriers to employing people. There were no significant differences between growing and nongrowing small firms about their perception of

Table 10.3.   The Last Time You Employed New Full-Time or Part-Time Staff, did you...

	Growing Small Firms (Percent)	Nongrowing Small Firms (Percent)
Have a list of skills and qualifications being sought	80.6*	67.8
Have a written job description for the position being filled	59.2*	42.6
Get outside help with recruitment	23.5*	15.2

*$p < .01$.

Table 10.4.   As an Employer, do you...

	Growing small firms (percent)	Nongrowing small firms (percent)
Offer bonuses or incentives to reward performance	72.5**	48.7
Pay for off-site training or work-related education	69.4**	31.1
Offer increases to salary to reward performance	66.3**	42.4
Have an incentive scheme	49.0**	29.8
Offer salary packaging	46.9**	18.9
Offer job-sharing or part-time work	43.9**	25.1
Offer additional time off to reward performance	35.7*	22.7
Offer promotions to reward performance	34.7**	14.3
Offer special training, seminars or conferences to reward performance	31.6*	18.1
Have a succession plan	26.9*	16.3
Have an employee share plan	3.1*	0

*$p < .05$. **$p < .01$.

whether the payment of superannuation, workcover or payroll tax acted as a barrier to employment. In all cases more than 50% of both growing and nongrowing firms did not see these as barriers to employment.

Five questions addressed the issue of unfair dismissal legislation. These questions used a 5-point Likert scale where 1 = Strongly Agree and 5 = Strongly Disagree. F-tests and ANOVAs were used to assess the differences between the responses for growing and nongrowing small firms. The CPA Australia report shows that 53% of small firms disagreed with the statement about their ability to dismiss employees even if their business was struggling. Our analysis showed that nongrowing small firms disagreed with the statement to a significantly lesser extent than growing small firms. Moreover, the CPA Australia report also

Table 10.5.   Unfair Dismissal

	Growing Small Firms M (SD) n	Nongrowing Small Firms M (SD) n
1. I am not able to dismiss my employees even if my business is struggling	3.83 (1.29)** 90	3.32 (1.44) 210
2. The unfair dismissal laws require me to follow a complex process to dismiss staff	2.39 (1.27) 92	2.23 (1.26) 212
3. The employer always loses unfair dismissal cases	3.34 (1.33) 80	2.97 (1.32) 184
4. You can't dismiss a person even if they are stealing from you	3.74 (1.42) 93	3.46 (1.45) 214
5. I'm confident I know how to dismiss staff in line with the unfair dismissal laws	2.09 (1.32)*96	2.62 (1.42) 219

*$p < 0.005$. **$p < 0.05$.

Table 10.6.   Total Sales in Growing and Nongrowing Small Firms

	Growing Small Firms (Percent)	Nongrowing Small Firms (Percent)
Under A$200,000	20.7	38.0
A$200,000 – A$500,000	20.7	26.3
A$500,000 – A$1 million	23.2	16.1
A$1 million – A$2 million	15.9	9.3
A$2 million – A$5 million	9.8	9.8
A$5 million+	9.8	0.5

Note: Growing small firms $n = 82$. Nongrowing small firms $n = 205$

showed that 58% of small businesses were confident they understood how to dismiss staff correctly, while our analysis showed that growing small firms agreed they understood the correct process to a significantly greater extent than nongrowing small firms. There were no significant differences between growing and nongrowing firms on the other three statements (see Table 10.5).

The CPA Australia survey did not collect data on HRM outcomes such as absenteeism or staff turnover. One question addressed total sales and our analysis showed that nongrowing small firms were more likely to have lower total sales than growing small firms (see Table 10.6). Specifically, t-tests revealed that nongrowing small firms were significantly more likely than growing small firms to have total sales of under A$200,000 (38% compared to 21%) while growing small firms were more likely than nongrowing small firms to have total sales of more than $5 million (10% compared to 0.5%) ($p < .001$).

DISCUSSION

The argument is that growing small firms will begin to experience problems with HRM due to the complexity increasing size imposes. As a means of dealing with this complexity our argument in this chapter is that growing small firms should begin to exhibit more formalized HRM practices as this could be indicative of a strategic approach to managing staff. Our analysis of the CPA Australia small firm employment data shows that this is the case. The growing small firms, where growth is defined as employing new staff because of expansion or diversification, rather than simply replacement of staff, were more likely to use formal recruitment practices than nongrowing small firms. Further growing small firms were also more likely than nongrowing small firms to use formal selection practices: a list of skills and qualifications desired and a job description.

The literature suggests there is a need for growth oriented small firms to more carefully recruit, select, motivate and retain employees if firm growth is to be sustained. Our analysis shows that growing small firms are more likely than nongrowing small firms to use a range of rewards for performance to engender employee commitment including: additional time-off; bonuses and incentives; training; and promotions. In particular the use of promotions suggests growing small firms have some sort of formalized organizational structure enabling promotions. Growing small firms are also more likely than nongrowing small firms to pay for off-site training or work-related education for employees. The use of training and promotions are indicative of more formalized HRM in growing small firms.

While growing small firms are more likely than nongrowing ones to have an employee share plan, the incidence of such is very low. Similarly the number of small firms with a succession plan is also low (21%), however growing small firms are more likely than nongrowing ones to have such a plan in place, indicating some thought for the future of the firm. Again, although the incidence of both types of plans is low, our analysis does suggest that growing small firms have more formalized planning practices than nongrowing small firms.

Finally the issue of unfair dismissal as a barrier to employment in small firms was comprehensively addressed in the CPA Australia survey. While some 62% of all small firms agreed the unfair dismissal process was complex, some 58% were confident they knew how to dismiss staff correctly. Our analysis showed that growing small firms were more likely to agree they understood this complex process than nongrowing small firms, which suggests some level of competence or confidence with procedural formality.

The CPA Australia survey did not ask questions about the incidence of a business or strategic plan and therefore we could not examine whether the HRM practices in growing small firms were the result of a strategic approach to HRM or not. In de Kok and Uhlaner's (2001) study of HRM in 16 small Dutch companies (with an average employment of 17.6 persons), weak support was found for the relationship between formalized HRM practices in growth firms. They concluded that while there was a presumption that formal HRM policies are beneficial to firms there is a need to more fully "test" this connection. Our analysis of the CPA Australia data tells us that growing small firms are more likely than nongrowing small firms to have higher total sales, and while we might like to attribute that better performance to a more careful approach to managing HR, we are unable to do so statistically.

CONCLUSION AND SUGGESTIONS FOR FUTURE RESEARCH

Recently there have been calls for more research at the intersection of HRM and entrepreneurship. Katz et al. (2000) noted this as did Baron (2003) more recently in a special edition of *Human Resources Management Review* on entrepreneurship and HRM. There is some considerable debate about the meaning of entrepreneurship and the term is often abused by equating all small firm activity with entrepreneurial activity. Moreover, as Cardon and Steven (2004) point out while a range of "problems" relate to the presence and contribution of HRM to small firm effectiveness and sustainability, issues of size, newness and entrepreneurial activity are not clearly articulated and theorized in the literature. However in this chapter we have followed Davidsson et al.'s (2002) argument and focused on growing small firms as these are more likely to be entrepreneurial than nongrowing small firms. As a result our chapter makes a contribution to understanding whether more formal organizational systems and routines are more likely to be used (or not) to nurture human capital in entrepreneurial firms.

Our analysis of the CPA Australia data indicates that growing small firms are more likely than nongrowing small firms to have formal HRM practices where that means they are either written down, regularly applied or assured to take place (de Kok & Uhlaner, 2001). Our analysis indicated formal practices of each sort were more likely to be used by growing small firms.

The data used in this chapter did pose limitations on the form of analysis that could be undertaken and the relationships that could be explored. In particular the cutoff for data collection is limited to small firms with less than 20 employees, and this is a size barrier which growth oriented small firms will rapidly breach. Moreover the firms in this sample had an average size of 6.54 people and therefore we are dealing with very small, small firms. Further, the data is a single snapshot of small firms in time (CPA Australia, , 2002). While we are able to identify non-growing small firms among the sample, it is not correct to assume that they have neither grown in the past to reach their current size (with the exception of the single person firms) nor that they will not grow in the future. Moreover we do not know whether the growth, which the growing small firms indicate they undertook, was or is sustained.

Despite the smallness of the firms in this sample our analysis of the data does support the argument that growing small firms are more likely than nongrowing small firms to use formalized HRM practices. However, we do not know the causal order of this relationship. Further, we are unable to determine, using this data, whether these firms have a distinct competence in aligning HRM systems and practices with business strategy to enable superior organizational performance, despite the fact that the growing small firms were more likely to have higher total sales. In depth qualitative research could be fruitfully undertaken to explore these issues.

Our analysis also suggests that growing small firms are more likely to operate in the services sector and in metropolitan locations, (which is not surprising given the structure of the Australian economy) and that the owners of growing small firms are more likely to be less than 40 years of age and have trade and/or tertiary qualifications.

In a related project we have begun the process of case studying small firms based in Victoria, Australia. In that project, which was grew out of an online survey of HRM in small firms funded by CPA Australia, we have sufficient cases to differentiate between small firms, and for example, to consider the results for particular sectors (services vs. manufacturing), locations (rural vs. metro), and firms owned and operated by particular groups of people. This is important as small firms, and growing small firms are not a homogeneous group. In so doing we hope to develop a greater understanding of how growth oriented small firms handle HRM.

ACKNOWLEDGMENT

The authors would like to acknowledge CPA Australia's generosity is providing us with the data as well as the valuable assistance provided by Anne-Marie Gut with the statistical analysis.

NOTES

1. CPA Australia is one of the two peak bodies that accredits and represents the accounting profession is Australia. The other organization is the Institute of Chartered Accountants. CPA Australia's interest in small firms and particularly HRM in small firms derives from the fact that their members are often called upon to advise small business clients about employment in addition to providing financial and accounting advice.

2. In Australia there are a complex set of arrangements governing employment matters that arise from the federal and state government jurisdictional limits. For example, the payment of superannuation (or employer-sponsored pensions) is a compulsory requirement set by federal government legislation. The current rate of employer-sponsored superannuation is 9%. Occupational health and safety requirements and workcover insurance levels are determined in the state government jurisdictions and different markedly across the six state jurisdictions. In some states discounted premiums are offered to reward businesses with appropriate occupational health and safety risk management plans and this can lead to firms registering in a jurisdiction where there is a favorable regime rather than in the state where they operate. Payroll tax is also a state government (rather than federal government) concern and is paid once a certain level of wages is paid by the small firm. Unfair dismissal provisions are contained within industrial relations legislation and there are five state jurisdictions (New South Wales, Queensland, Western Australia, South Australia and Tasmania) and one federal jurisdiction (which also covers Victoria and the Australian territories) in this area. This is an area where there is much confusion and the federal government is currently proposing to harmonize the unfair dismissal regimes as well as exempt small business from unfair dismissal (see, Barrett, 2003 on this issue).

3. The report uses the term "small business," for simplicity and consistency we use the term "small firm" in this chapter. In addition to the telephone survey of a random sample of 600 small firms, CPA Australia also contacted a random sample of 105 CPA accountants on a range of employment issues. Only the small firm data is analyzed in this chapter.

4. These questions were the best available proxies for defining growth in the survey.

REFERENCES

Ardichvili, A., Harmon, B., Cardozo, R., Reynolds, P., & Williams, M. (1998). The new venture growth: Functional differentiation and the need for human resource development interventions. *Human Resource Development Quarterly,* 9(1), 55-70.

Arthur, D. (1995). *Managing human resources in small and mid-sized companies*. New York: American Association of Management.

Australian Bureau of Statistics (ABS). (2002). *Small business in Australia 2000-2001*. Catalogue Number 1321.0. Canberra: Australian Government Printing Service.

Barney, J. (1991). Firm resources and sustained competitive advantage. *Journal of Management, 17*(1), 99-120.

Baron, R. (2003). Editorial: Human resource management and entrepreneurship: Some reciprocal benefits of closer links. *Human Resource Management Review, 13,* 253-256.

Barrett, R. (2003). Small business and unfair dismissal. *Journal of Industrial Relations, 45*(1), 87-93.

Barringer, B., Jones, F., & Lewis, P. (1998). A qualitative study of the management practices of rapid-growth firms and how rapid growth firms mitigate the managerial capacity problem. *Journal of Developmental Entrepreneurship, 3*(2), 97-122.

Benmore, G., & Palmer, A. (1996). Human resource management in small business: Keeping it strictly informal. *Journal of Small Business and Enterprise Development, 3,* 109-118.

Boxall, P. (1996). The strategic HRM debate and the resource-based view of the firm. *Human Resource Management Journal, 6*(3), 59-75.

Cardon, M., & Stevens, C. (2004). Managing human resources in small organizations: What do we know? *Human Resource Management Review, 14,* 295-323.

Carroll, M., Marchington, M., Earnshaw, J., & Taylor, S. (1999). Recruitment in small firms: Processes, methods, and problems. *Employee Relations, 21*(3), 236-250.

Cassell, C., Nadin, S., Gray, M., & Clegg, C. (2002). Exploring human resource management practices in small and medium sized enterprises. *Personnel Review, 31*(6), 671-692.

Chaganti, R., Cook, R., & Smeltz, W. (2002). Effects of styles, strategies, and systems on the growth of small businesses. *Journal of Developmental Entrepreneurship, 7*(2), 175-192.

Chandler, G., & McEvoy, G. (2000). Human resource management, TQM, and firm performance in small and medium-sized enterprises. *Entrepreneurship Theory and Practice, 25*(1), 43-58.

Churchill, N., & Lewis, V. (1983). The five stages of small business growth. *Harvard Business Review, 61*(3), 30-50.

CPA Australia. (2002, March). *Small business survey program: Employment issues.* Melbourne: Author.

Davidsson, P., Delmar, F., & Wiklund, J. (2002). Entrepreneurship as growth: Growth as entrepreneurship. In M. Hitt, R. D. Ireland, S. M. Camp & D. Sexton (Eds.), *Strategic entrepreneurship: Creating a new mindset.* Oxford: Blackwell.

de Kok, J., & Uhlaner, L. (2001). Organisation context and human resource management in the small firm. *Small Business Economics, 17*(4), 273-291.

Delaney, J., & Huselid, M. (1996). The impact of human resource management practices on perceptions of organisational performance. *Academy of Management Journal, 39*(4), 949-969.

Delery, J., & Doty, D. (1996). Modes of theorizing in human resource management: Tests of universalistic, contingency and configurational performance indicators. *Academy of Management Journal, 39*(4), 802–835.

Deshpande, S., & Golhar, D. (1994). HRM practices in large and small manufacturing firms: A comparative study. *Journal of Small Business Management, 32*(2), 49-56.

Duberley, J., & Walley, P. (1995). Assessing the adoption of HRM by small and medium sized manufacturing organizations. *International Journal of Human Resource Management, 6*(4), 891-909.

Dyer, L. (1993). *Human resources as a source of competitive advantage.* Ontario: IRC Press.

Dyer, L., & Reeves, T. (1995). Human resource strategies and firm performance: What do we know and where do we need to go? *The International Journal of Human Resource Management, 6*(3), 656-670.

Gibb, A., & Scott, M. (1985). Strategic awareness, personal commitment and the process of planning in small business. *Journal of Management Studies, 22*(6), 597-631.

Gilbert, J., & Jones, G. (2000). Managing human resources in New Zealand small business. *Asia Pacific Journal of Human Resources, 38*(2), 55-68.

Hannon, P., & Atherton, A. (1998). Small firm success and the art of orienteering: The value of plans, planning, and strategic awareness in the competitive small firm. *Journal of Small Business and Enterprise Development, 5*(2), 102-119.

Harris, L. (2000). Employment regulation and owner-managers in small firms: Seeking support and guidance. *Journal of Small Business and Enterprise Development, 7*(4), 352-362.

Heneman, H., & Berkely, R. (1999). Applicant attraction practices and outcomes among small businesses. *Journal of Small Business Management, 37*(1), 53-74.

Heneman, R., Tansky, J., & Camp, S. (2000). Human resource management practices in small and medium-sized enterprises: Unanswered questions and future research perspectives. *Entrepreneurship Theory and Practice, 25*(1), 11-26.

Hornsby, J., & Kuratko, D. (1990). Human resource management in small business: Critical issues for the 1990s. *Journal of Small Business Management, 28*(3), 9-18.

Hornsby, J., & Kuratko, D. (2003). Human resource management in U.S. small business: A replication and extension. *Journal of Developmental Entrepreneurship, 8*(1), 73-92.

Huselid, M., Jackson, S., & Schuler, R. (1997). Technical and strategic human resource management effectiveness as determinants of firm performance. *Academy of Management Journal, 40*(1), 171-88.

Jay, L., & Schaper, M. (2003). Which advisors do micro-firms use? Some Australian evidence. *Journal of Small Business and Enterprise Development, 10*(2), 136-143.

Katz, J., Aldrich, H., Welbourne, T., & Williams, P. (2000). Guest editors' comments. Special Issue on "Human resource management and the SME: Towards a new synthesis." *Entrepreneurship Theory and Practice, 25*(1), 7-10.

Klaas, B., McClendon, J., & Gainey, T. (2000). Managing HR in the small and medium enterprise: The impact of professional employer organisations. *Entrepreneurship Theory and Practice, 25*(1), 107-123.

Kotey, B., & Sheridan, A. (2001). Gender and the practice of HRM in small business. *Asia Pacific Journal of Human Resources, 39*(3), 23-40.

Lado, A., & Wilson, M. (1994). Human resource systems and sustained competitive advantage: A competency based perspective. *Academy of Management Review, 19*(4), 699-727.

Lengnick-Hall, C., & Lengnick-Hall, M. (1988). Strategic human resources management: A review of the literature and a proposed typology. *Academy of Management Review, 13*, 454-470.

Marchington, M., Carroll, M., & Boxall, P. (2003). Labour scarcity and the survival of small firms: A resource-based view of the road haulage industry. *Human Resource Management Journal, 13*(4), 5-22.

Marlow, S. (2000). Investigating the use of emergent strategic human resource management activity in the small firm. *Journal of Small Business and Enterprise Development, 7*(2), 135-148.

Marlow, S., & Patton, D. (1993). Managing the employment relationship in the smaller firm: Possibilities for human resource management. *International Small Business Journal, 11*(4), 57-64.

Matlay, H. (1999). Employee relations in small firms. *Employee Relations, 21*(3), 285-296.

Mazzarol, T. (2003). A model of small business HR growth management. *International Journal of Entrepreneurial Behaviour and Research, 9*(1), 27-49.

McEvoy, G. (1984). Small business personnel practices. *Journal of Small Business Management, 22*(4), 1-8.

McLarty, R. (1999). The skills development needs of SMEs and focus on graduate skills application. *Journal of Applied Management Studies, 8*(1), 103-112.

Morris, M. (2001). From the editor: The critical role of resources. *Journal of Developmental Entrepreneurship, 6*(2), v-vii.

Penrose, E. (1959). *The theory of growth of the firm.* New York: John Wiley.

Pfeffer, J. (1994). *Competitive advantage through people.* Boston: Harvard Business School.

Pfeffer, J. (1998). *The human equation.* Boston: Harvard University Press.

Ram, M. (1999). Managing autonomy: Employment relations in small professional services firms. *International Small Business Journal, 17*(2), 13-30.

Reid, R., Morrow, T., Kelly, B., & McCartan, P. (2002). People management in SMEs: An analysis of human resource strategies in non-family business. *Journal of Small Business and Enterprise Development, 9*(3), 245-259.

Scase, R. (1995). Employment relations in small firms. In P. Edwards (Ed.), *Industrial relations: Theory and practice in Britain.* Oxford: Blackwell.

Scott, M., & Bruce, R. (1987). Five stages of growth in small business. *Long Range Planning, 20*(3), 45-52.

Senate Employment, Workplace Relations, and Education References Committee. (2003). *Small business employment.* Canberra, Australia: Senate Printing Unit.

Shane, S., & Venkataraman, S. (2000). The promise of entrepreneurship as a field of research. *Academy of Management Review, 25*(1), 217-226.

Stevenson, H., & Jarillo, J. (1990). A paradigm of entrepreneurship: Entrepreneurial management. *Strategic Management Journal, 11*, 17-27.

Storey, D. (2004). Exploring the link among small firms, between training and firm performance: A comparison between UK and other OECD countries. *International Journal of Human Resource Management, 15*(1), 112-130.

Storey, D., & Westhead, P. (1997). Management training in small firms: A case of market failure? *Human Resource Management Journal, 7*(2), 61-71.

Venkataraman, S. (1997). The distinctive domain of entrepreneurship research: An editor's perspective. In J. Katz & J. Brockhaus (Eds.), *Advances in entrepreneurship, firm emergence and growth.* Greenwich, CT: JAI Press.

Weisner, R., & McDonald, J. (2001). Bleak house or bright prospect? Human resource management in Australian SMEs. *Asia Pacific Journal of Human Resources, 39*(2), 31-53.

Williamson, I. (2000). Employer legitimacy and recruitment success in small businesses. *Entrepreneurship Theory and Practice, 25*(1), 27-42.

Wright, P., & Snell, S. (1998). Towards a unifying framework for exploring fit and flexibility in strategic human resource management. *Academy of Management Review, 23*(4), 756-772.

Wright, P., Dunford, B., & Snell, S. (2001). Human resources and the resource based view of the firm. *Journal of Management, 27*(6), 701–721.

CHAPTER 11

ENTREPRENEURSHIP AND HUMAN RESOURCES

Directions for Future Research

Brian S. Klaas and Malayka Klimchak

The chapters in this volume have provided ample evidence as to the importance of human resources to the success or failure of entrepreneurial ventures. The chapters in this volume also have emphasized the need for scholarly research examining how human resources should be managed within the context of the high growth entrepreneurial firm. In this chapter, we addressed how future research might help us better understand when entrepreneurial firms would be most likely to benefit from investing in HR, what kind of HR practices and programs are likely to be most critical to entrepreneurial firms, and how such practices should be implemented and delivered.

INTRODUCTION

The chapters in this book have clearly demonstrated the important role the management of human resources plays within the entrepreneurial

Human Resource Strategies for the High Growth Entrepreneurial Firm, 245–258
Copyright © 2006 by Information Age Publishing
All rights of reproduction in any form reserved.

firm. As has been argued in the preceding chapters, high growth ventures depend heavily on being able to recruit and hire the right kind of employees, on being able to train and develop these new hires, and on being able to manage and motivate a workforce within the context of substantial change and uncertainty. However, as the preceding chapters suggest, many entrepreneurs feel ill-equipped to manage their human resources and often are frustrated by questions about how they should manage their people.

But is there actually a need for scholarly research that focuses on human resources within the entrepreneurial context? In the broader HR literature, extensive research has examined any number of questions that should be fundamental to entrepreneurs wanting to maximize the effectiveness of their human resource practices. For example, doesn't the voluminous literature on selection (Heneman & Judge, 2005) offer some very useful insights regarding how employees should be hired? Doesn't the literature on procedural justice in human resource practices (Greenberg & Colquitt, 2005) offer keen insights regarding how entrepreneurs should evaluate and manage their staff? And doesn't the literature on pay and rewards (Milkovich & Newman, 2004) provide useful information regarding how entrepreneurs should structure their pay system? Indeed, given the vast amount of human resources research, some might argue that there is little reason for entrepreneurs to be frustrated by uncertainty regarding how to manage people. Furthermore, the abundant literature on human resources may raise questions about whether there is a critical need for academic research to specifically address how human resources should be managed within entrepreneurial organizations.

This volume, however, is premised on the assumption that context matters. The papers presented throughout the book suggest that size, instability, uncertainty, and growth orientation are all key distinctive contextual elements associated with the entrepreneurial organization. Accordingly, the assumption here is that findings from research conducted within the context of larger, more stable organizations may not necessarily be relevant for entrepreneurial organizations. If this assumption is valid, then, questions might legitimately be raised about the applicability of the existing body of research in human resources for entrepreneurial organizations (Heneman & Berkley, 1999; Heneman, Tansky, & Camp, 2000; Leung, 2003). To this end, this volume offers many insightful contributions regarding the role of human resources within the entrepreneurial firm and it highlights how the contextual environment for entrepreneurial organizations may affect how human resource practices should be designed and delivered. In closing, then, it is appropriate to discuss possible directions for research in this important area.

In thinking about where research on human resources in the entrepreneurial organization should go in the future, it might be argued that theory and practice might benefit from examining how the distinctive contextual elements associated with the entrepreneurial firm might affect the impact associated with HR systems and with specific HR practices (Hayton, 2003). The goal of such research would be to highlight when entrepreneurial organizations would be most likely to benefit from investing in HR. Such research should also lend insight into what kind of HR practices are likely to be most critical to entrepreneurial organizations and how such practices should be implemented and delivered. In the sections that follow, we highlight several critical questions for scholars examining the role of human resources in entrepreneurial organizations.

WHICH TYPES OF HR PRACTICES MATTER IN THE ENTREPRENEURIAL ORGANIZATION

The research in the strategic HR literature has documented the impact of the HR system on overall firm performance within large firms (Harris & Ogbonna, 2001; Richard & Johnson, 2001) and, further, it has documented when different kinds of HR systems are most likely to have the desired effect (Delery & Doty, 1996). Much of this work has focused on HR systems that have been referred to as high commitment practices or high performance work organizations. It should be noted that in the normative literature discussing the value of high performance organizations, emphasis is given to addressing a number of organizational pathologies that are likely to emerge in large, stable, and complex organizations. The normative literature on high performance organizations offers prescriptions for addressing these organizational pathologies and managerial challenges. Large, stable, and complex organizations have a tendency to ossify, making it unlikely that the firm will be sufficiently responsive to environmental change. Similarly, large and complex firms often suffer from an inadequate flow of information across the firm, a lack of social capital, and insufficient learning across organizational units (Snell & Wright, 1999). Large, complex organizations also create managerial challenges relating to how the firm can identify and manage talent flows across multiple units that often are geographically dispersed and involved in disparate activities. Also, because large organizations have numerous managers with substantial decision-making authority, challenges exist relating to the potential for conflict resulting from a lack of consistency across diverse units (Wright, Gardner, & Moynihan, 2003). Advocates of high performance work organizations argue that a number of initiatives are needed to counter these challenges and pathologies. And indeed, many of these initiatives relate to human resource practices and programs (Richard & Johnson, 2004).

Scholars within the strategic HR literature, then, have examined the impact of a set of HR practices that, collectively, are thought to help firms address the pathologies and challenges associated with large, stable, and complex organizations. But small firms face very different challenges and likely have different organizational pathologies. It is unclear whether the same set of reinforcing HR practices that have been studied within the strategic HR literature would function to contain the typical challenges and organizational pathologies likely to emerge within entrepreneurial firms. If scholars are to examine the impact of HR practices on firm-level outcomes within smaller organizations, efforts must first be made to address questions about what set of reinforcing HR practices are relevant for entrepreneurial firms.

One area where research might contribute to our understanding of the role of HR in the entrepreneurial firms relates to theory regarding organizational pathologies for the entrepreneurial organization. The normative literature on high performance organizations is premised on the idea that, left to their own devices, large, stable, and complex organizations will experience problems that stem from rigidity and the lack of information flow. Thus, positive effects are likely to be observed among firms that develop HR programs that counter these classic problems (Lepak, Takeuchi, & Snell, 2003; Youndt & Snell, 2004). Entrepreneurial firms are likely to be susceptible to a very different set of problems. While organizational sociologists have offered much insight into pathologies within large, complex organizations, there is less work that simply documents such pathologies within entrepreneurial firms. To the extent that researchers can develop a conceptual framework for identifying the organizational pathologies to which small and medium enterprises are likely to be susceptible, it then becomes possible to think about the HR systems that might lead to competitive advantage.

Such a conceptual framework might well give emphasis to the fact that small firms often must depend on ad-hoc decision-making, largely because precedents often do not exist (Leung, 2003). Very much related to this, large firms often have established processes and procedures that rationalize highly subjective decisions and offer highly systematic mechanisms for making assessments. By contrast, the ad-hoc nature of decision-making within small and medium enterprises suggests that little is likely to be done in terms of rationalizing subjective processes. Emphasis might also be given to the lack of structure in terms of job expectations and in terms formal processes within the firm. Another key component might relate to uncertainty that small firms face and the effect this has on the ability of managers to provide structure or make commitments (Cardon,

2003). Because these organizational characteristics have the potential to affect the motivation and commitment of employees, one might argue that key characteristics of a HR system for the small and medium enterprise would involve practices that counter these tendencies—but in a way that is compatible with the dynamic nature of the small and medium enterprise. Many of the papers in this volume give attention to the distinctive nature of the organizational problems faced by small and medium enterprises. This distinctive nature suggests that an important contribution for researchers involves fully developing a conceptual framework that identifies common organizational pathologies within the entrepreneurial firm. Such a framework might then allow for greater insight into the components of the HR system that is likely to address those pathologies.

WHICH EMPLOYEE RELATIONS NORMS TRANSLATE?

Within many large firms, norms have emerged regarding how employees should be treated in order to ensure the commitment and motivation of employees while at the same time avoiding workplace conflict via fair and consistent treatment. These norms affect how employees are managed even though they are not formal or explicit HR practices. Instead, these norms allow for HR practices to be implemented in different ways and are part of the workplace culture. These norms represent unwritten rules about how organizations should balance the need for productivity and managerial discretion with the need for fair and consistent treatment of employees. Just as we are uncertain about how specific HR practices affect behavior and outcomes within entrepreneurial organizations, we also are uncertain about the impact in entrepreneurial firms of many of the employee relations norms that have emerged within many large organizations. Thus, the need exists for research to examine the impact of employee relations norms within entrepreneurial firms.

For example, consider norms that have emerged relating to progressive discipline that are designed to ensure the problem employees are treated fairly while still protecting the employer's need for productivity. With progressive discipline systems, employees who commit minor infractions are warned and given the opportunity to improve. Second offenses (and perhaps even third offenses) result in an additional warning or a suspension. Termination is not permitted until repeated offenses are observed. Further, emphasis is given to written disciplinary rules that identify what behavior is unacceptable. Such norms within progressive discipline models ensure that employees are protected from arbitrary treatment and they provide the employee with an opportunity to comply with organizational norms (Greenberg & Colquitt, 2005). But should small and medium enterprises adhere to the same norms regarding employee relations issues like progressive discipline? To what extent can smaller organizations at critical stages in their development be patient with employees who exhibit some form of deficiency? Is it more important for small and medium enterprises to foster a sense of urgency, even if it means that an employee is terminated without providing him/her with opportunity to develop into an acceptable employee? Similar questions could be raised about other employee relations issues as well. For researchers, then, it may well be beneficial to explore what employee relations norms are most appropriate for small and medium enterprises.

WHEN DOES THE ENTREPRENEURIAL FIRM BENEFIT FROM HR?

This volume argues that there are conditions under which entrepreneurial firms are likely to benefit from investing in HR programs and systems. But this volume also highlights conditions that might affect when entrepreneurial firms are most likely to benefit from investing in HR. Clearly, a need exists for future research to explore when investing in HR is most likely to generate benefits. Ownership structure, size, growth rate, occupational characteristics, and uncertainty may all affect the need for investment in HR. For example, consider a family-owned firm with several long-term employees and strong interpersonal ties within the firm. Assume also that it is believed that any anticipated growth in sales can be managed with the existing workforce. In such an environment, would significant opportunities exist for HR programs to affect outcomes? The lack of turnover among employees reduces the need for HR programs in such areas as staffing and training. Additionally, with long-established relationships, there may be less need to programs designed to promote coordination and information flow among employees. Finally, feedback may be more readily accomplished via informal means due to the nature of family relationships.

At the opposite end of the spectrum, one can envision how investing in HR programs and services would be critical to an individually-owned firm with 200 recently hired employees that expects to grow rapidly over the next several years. Firm size and the management structure make it difficult to rely on personal relationships to ensure effective communication and feedback within the organization. Moreover, rapid growth means that there will be opportunities to affect workforce quality through recruiting and staffing as well as through training and development (Hillidge, 1990;

Leung, 2003). Also, the firm is at a stage in the growth process where it is more feasible to establish organizational norms and develop a cohesive organizational culture.

But at what point within this spectrum is it critical to invest in HR services and programs? Will a five-person firm that plans to double in size over the next year benefit from investing in HR? What about a firm with 40 employees that anticipates 10% annual growth? Among small and medium sized enterprises, there is likely to be substantial variation in the degree to which investment in human resource practices and services yield benefits. While personal relationships and ad-hoc decision-making may be viable options for many smaller firms, there is likely to be a point as firms grow where it is preferable to employ different approaches to managing human resources. But it is unclear when firms need to invest in human resource practices and services. Thus, research examining how size and growth affect the need for investment in human resource services and programs is clearly needed.

Related to this, research is needed that examines how industry and occupational characteristics affect the need for human resource programs and services in entrepreneurial firms. Research in the strategic HR literature has shown that among larger firms, industry moderates the impact of HR systems on productivity (Datta, Guthrie, & Wright, 2005). Where higher levels of human capital are required, investing in HR programs and services has been found to generate greater returns (Lepak et al., 2003). Where jobs require higher education and training and involve more complexity, the returns from improved selection processes are likely to be greater than in situations where jobs are more routine and standardized. The impact and value associated with the job in such situations are likely to be greater, which makes it more likely that HR programs that affect employee motivation and quality will yield greater returns for the organization.

While industry and occupation have been found to moderate the impact of HR programs within larger organizations, it is unclear whether this finding would also be observed in entrepreneurial organizations. Many entrepreneurial firms are in the service sector, where the firm's success depends on the employee's ability to ensure high levels of customer satisfaction. And within smaller firms, one or two employees can sour a firm's customer service climate. Moreover, in smaller firms, it may not be feasible to standardize the process by which customer satisfaction is ensured. For such firms, even where the jobs themselves may not involve great complexity or require high levels of human capital, HR programs that affect employee ability and motivation may yield substantial benefits. Given the composition of entrepreneurial firms, it is unclear, then, whether human capital intensity would moderate the impact of HR practices. Thus, research is needed that explores how occupational and industry variables moderate the impact associated with the use of HR programs and services within entrepreneurial firms.

Another key variable that may affect the utility associated with investment in HR practices and systems relates to financial stability and uncertainty regarding the firm's viability. Investing in HR practices might well be viewed as a long-term investment. While some benefits may be observed immediately, it may be years before the full returns from the building a culture and developing systems and procedures are observed. However, for many entrepreneurial firms, uncertainty exists regarding their long-term prospects. But what does this mean for investing in HR practices and programs? Does this mean that only those small and medium enterprises that have achieved some stability with regard to their financial prospects should invest the resources required for an effective HR system? Conversely, is the development of an effective HR system a prerequisite for gaining financial stability? Clearly, there is a need for research to examine how financial stability affects the utility of investing in HR systems by entrepreneurial firms.

In examining this issue, it seems appropriate for researchers to explore whether the utility of investing in HR systems prior to gaining financial stability depends on the firm's strategy as well as key drivers for success within the firm. For example, in service businesses where long-term success depends on slowly building a reputation within the community for quality service, it may well be that firms benefit from investing in HR even before they have achieved financial stability. By contrast, in technology firms, business prospects often hinge on the ability of key stakeholders to develop products or applications that distinguish the firm's offerings from that of competitors. In such settings, it may well be that there is less utility associated with investing in HR systems prior to the point where stakeholder contributions have reduced uncertainty regarding the firm's prospects.

WHAT ROLE DOES THE CEO PLAY?

In small and medium enterprises, most critical HR decisions must be made by the CEO. Further, the CEO is likely to often be personally involved in the implementation of many HR policies and programs. Because the HR function is often relatively limited within smaller organizations, the CEO plays a critical role in forming and implementing HR policy. Indeed, in the absence of formal processes and procedures, the management of human resources is determined by the day-to-day behavior and decisions of the CEO. Furthermore, many of the more strategic

HR policies and programs are strongly linked to issues of managerial style and philosophy. Thus, it may be difficult to separate questions about the personality and style of the CEO from issues about how HR should be managed in a small and medium enterprise.

Given that the CEO plays such a dominant role in determining how human resources are managed within the entrepreneurial firm, it is likely that—within such firms—the CEO's leadership style is likely to play a more significant role in determining HR outcomes. This then raises questions about whether the impact of HR practices and policies depends on the personality and style of the CEO. Where the CEO's interpersonal style naturally leads to increased trust within the organization, regular communication and feedback, and strong interpersonal connections, it may well be that formal HR practices will have less of an impact on key HR outcomes. The CEO's style and personality may serve as a substitute for formal HR practices and, thus, reduce the impact associated with formal HR practices. Alternatively, it may be that the impact of formal HR practices may actually increase when the CEO has strong interpersonal and leadership skills. It may well be that trust, communication, and strong interpersonal connections serve as the foundation for formal HR practices. For example, where trust exists between employees and the management team, reward systems may be perceived more favorably and employees may be more likely to see a link between effort and rewards (Ramaswami & Singh, 2003).

Clearly, the CEO's leadership and interpersonal skills have the potential to moderate the relationship between formal HR systems and HR outcomes. However, it is unclear how leadership style and personality will moderate the impact of formal HR practices and procedures. Since this issue has significant implications for when entrepreneurial firms should invest in formal HR systems, there is a need for research to address these issues.

Questions also exist about whether different types of HR practices and programs should be used for CEOs with different leadership styles. If the leader of the entrepreneurial firm plays a more significant role in determining the impact associated with HR practices, it may well be that there is a need for HR systems to be tailored to reflect the CEO's personality and style. For example, some CEOs may be less interested in obtaining input from employees regarding the direction of the firm and less interested in building consensus regarding how to proceed. Given the dominant role of the CEO in entrepreneurial firms, should HR practices be designed to allow the CEO to function within his/her comfort zone and to compensate for the personal style of the CEO? Alternately, should CEOs implement what might be viewed as HR best practices and then attempt to change his/her personal style to fit within the HR system? Again, given the central role of the CEO in determining HR decisions and as well as HR outcomes, it is important for research to examine the link between leadership style and how organizations should implement different kinds of HR practices.

HOW SHOULD HR PRACTICES BE DELIVERED?

Large organizations have traditionally depended on an internal HR function for the delivery of HR services and programs. However, there is increasing debate about how much of the HR function should be outsourced (Lilly, Gray, & Virick, 2005). Similar questions exist for entrepreneurial firms with regard to the delivery of HR programs and services (Klaas, Gainey, McClendon, & Yang, 2005). To what extent should entrepreneurial firms rely on internal staff members versus an outsourcing firm to deliver HR services and programs? For smaller firms, hiring a full time staff member for HR services would be cost-prohibitive. For these firms, then, the choice is between giving responsibility for HR activities to line managers and relying on an outsourcing firm. However, as firms grow, they increasingly have a choice about whether they should rely on an internal HR person or whether they should contract with an outside vendor.

These governance choices raise important questions for future research. For firms that are approaching the size where it might be feasible to have an internal HR staff person, questions remain about whether the firm will benefit more from adding a HR professional versus affiliating with an external vendor. Internal staff members may be able to gain familiarity with the firm's culture and business strategy and, thus, work to ensure that HR programs and policies meet the needs of the business. However, relying on an internal staff member would require that the firm, in essence, pay for the development of programs and policies across a wide variety of HR areas that would then apply across a limited numbers of employees. Relying on an external vendor would clearly offer cost advantages resulting from greater economies of scale. But, this would potentially come at the expense of having programs and services that reflect the firm's culture and strategy.

In terms of directions for future research, there is a need for studies that examine the actual tradeoffs involved when choosing to rely on an external vendor versus relying on internal staff. Do the tradeoffs depend on characteristics of the firm, the nature of the relationship that a firm has with the external vendor or on the way in which services are provided? For example, do the tradeoffs differ when the firm has 150 employees versus 500 employees? Instead, do the tradeoffs change when a vendor is used that allows for services to change depending on the unique needs of the firm? Or, do the tradeoffs change when a vendor is used that specializes by focusing on firms that are in the same industry or that share similar strategic objectives?

With regard to firms that lack the size to make it feasible to hire an internal HR person, there is also a need for research examining the tradeoffs between relying on the CEO, or some other line manager, to direct basic HR policies and programs versus utilizing a Professional Employer Organization or some other type of vendor. And do the tradeoffs depend on characteristics of the CEO or of the vendor? For example, do CEOs with substantial experience in dealing with HR issues have less need to rely on an external vendor for advice and counsel regarding more strategic HR issues or does their experience enable them to better take advantage of the expertise residing within the vendor?

INVESTMENTS IN HR: WHY IS THERE VARIATION AMONG ENTREPRENEURIAL FIRMS?

Implicit in the preceding discussion is the assumption that entrepreneurial firms will differ in the degree to which they will benefit from investing in HR. Because of differences in the expected utility of investing in HR, differences might be expected in the degree to which firms actually invest in HR. However, differences may also exist because of factors that have little to do with the likely utility associated with investing in HR. Factors relating to beliefs, values, and the managerial style of the leadership of the entrepreneurial firm may also play an important role in explaining why there is variation in investment in HR activities. These factors may have little to do with whether an entrepreneurial firm actually should invest in HR programs and services and more to do with the preferences and biases of the leader. Why might some SME leaders be willing to invest in HR while others are not? For some, there may well be a belief that they are fully capable of making decisions about issues such as rewards, employee development, and selection by relying on instinct and subjective assessments. They may feel little need to introduce systematic procedures or processes to guide decision-making and structure subjective evaluations. The concept of hubris has been used within the strategic management literature to explain differences in decision-making across executives (Schwartz, 1991). Hubris (and related constructs) may prove relevant here in that many human resource procedures and processes are designed to guide managers through subjective assessments and limit the options available when managing people. Hubris may well affect the perceived need for such guidance and constraints and, thus, may affect the desire to make use of many human resource procedures and programs.

Other characteristics of the leader of the entrepreneurial firm may also affect the willingness to invest in human resource activities. While frustration with human resource issues is common within smaller organizations, familiarity with the tools and procedures available when making human resource decisions is less common. This suggests that one possible explanation for variation in the willingness to invest in human resource activities relates to the experience and background of the CEO. Where past experiences have exposed the CEO to the range of tools available within well-developed HR systems, entrepreneurial firms may be more likely to appreciate the value of investing in HR activities. Those with little exposure to HR systems may be unfamiliar with the tools and mechanisms available to them. As such, prior exposure to HR systems may also explain why variation is seen in the willingness to invest in HR among entrepreneurial firms.

This section has suggested that there is likely to be much variation in the willingness of entrepreneurial firms to invest in human resource activities. Furthermore, this paper has suggested that at least some of this variation may be due to differences in the expected utility associated with investing in HR. However, as suggested in this section, some of this variation may be due to biases and preferences that flow from differences in the personality and background of the leadership within the entrepreneurial firm. Our understanding of investment in HR among entrepreneurial firms would, therefore, benefit from research that explores these different sources of variation in investment in HR.

CONCLUSION

This volume has shown how human resources can play an important role in determining the success or failure of entrepreneurial ventures. Further, this volume has shown where academic research might help identify how an entrepreneurial organization could make more effective use of its human resources. In closing, this chapter has attempted to highlight some key areas where researchers might focus their attention to further advance our understanding of the critical link between human resource management and entrepreneurship.

REFERENCES

Cardon, M. S. (2003). Contingent labor as an enabler of entrepreneurial growth. *Human Resource Management, 42,* 357-373.

Datta, D. K., Guthrie, J. P., & Wright, P. M. (2005). Human resource management and labor productivity: Does industry matter? *Academy of Management Journal, 48,* 135-145.

Delery, J. E., & Doty, D. H. (1996). Modes of theorizing in strategic human resource management: Tests of universalistic, contingency, and configurational performance predictions. *Academy of Management Journal, 39,* 802-835.

Greenberg, J. S., & Colquitt, J. (Eds.). (2005). *Handbook of organizational justice.* Mahwah, NJ: Lawrence Erlbaum.

Harris, L. C., & Ogbonna, E. (2001). Strategic human resource management, market orientation, and organizational performance. *Journal of Business Research, 51,* 157-166.

Hayton, J. C. (2003). Strategic human capital management in SMEs: An empirical study of entrepreneurial performance. *Human Resource Management, 42,* 375-391.

Heneman, H. G., III, & Berkley, R. A. (1999). Applicant attraction practices and outcomes among small businesses. *Journal of Small Business Management, 37,* 53-74.

Heneman, H. G., III, & Judge, T. A. (2005). *Staffing organizations.* New York: McGraw-Hill/Irwin.

Heneman, R. L., Tansky, J. W., & Camp, S. M. (2000). Human resource management practices in small and medium-sized enterprises: Unanswered questions and future research perspectives. *Entrepreneurship: Theory & Practice, 25,* 11-26.

Hillidge, J. (1990). Planning for growth in a small company. *Long Range Planning, 23,* 76-81.

Klaas, B. S., Gainey, T. W., McClendon, J. A., & Yang, H. (2005). Professional employer organizations and their impact on client satisfaction with human resource outcomes: A field study of human resource outsourcing in small and medium enterprises. *Journal of Management, 31,* 234-254.

Lepak, D. P., Takeuchi, R., & Snell, S. A. (2003). Employment flexibility and firm performance: Examining the interaction effects of employment mode, environmental dynamism, and technological intensity. *Journal of Management, 29,* 681-702.

Leung, A. (2003). Different ties for different needs: Recruitment practices of entrepreneurial firms at different developmental phases. *Human Resource Management, 42,* 303-320.

Lilly, J. D., Gray, D. A., & Virick, M. (2005). Outsourcing the human resource function: Environmental and organizational characteristics that affect performance. *Journal of Business Strategies, 22,* 55-73.

Milkovich, G., & Newman, J. (2004). *Compensation.* New York: McGraw-Hill/Irwin.

Ramaswami, S. N., & Singh, J. (2003). Antecedents and consequences of merit pay fairness for industrial salespeople. *Journal of Marketing, 67,* 46-66.

Richard, O. C., & Johnson, N. B. (2001). Strategic human resource management effectiveness and firm performance. *International Journal of Human Resource Management, 12*, 299-310.

Richard, O. C., & Johnson, N. B. (2004). High performance work practices and human resource management effectiveness: Substitutes or complements? *Journal of Business Strategies, 21*, 133-148.

Schwartz, H. S. (1991). Narcissism project and corporate decay: The case of general motors. *Business Ethics Quarterly, 1*, 249-268

Snell, S. A., & Wright, P. M. (1999). Social capital and strategic HRM: It's who you know. *Human Resource Planning, 22*, 62-65.

Wright, P. M., Gardner, T., & Moynihan, L. M. (2003). The impact of HR practices on the performance of business units. *Human Resource Management Journal, 13*, 21-36.

Youndt, M.A., & Snell, S.A. (2004). Human resource configurations, intellectual capital, and organizational performance. *Journal of Managerial Issues, 16*, 337-360.

ABOUT THE AUTHORS

Sharon Alvarez is an assistant professor of entrepreneurship at the Max M. Fisher College of Business, The Ohio State University and a Max Planck Scholar at the Max Planck Institute for Entrepreneurship and Economic Systems Research. She received her PhD from the University of Colorado in Entrepreneurship and Strategy. She has published in *Academy of Management Executive, Journal of Business Venturing, Journal of Management, and Human Resource Management Journal.* Her current research includes entrepreneurship and theory of the firm, and high technology alliances between entrepreneurship firms and larger established firms.

David B. Balkin is professor and chair of the management division at the Leeds School of Business at the University of Colorado at Boulder. He received his PhD from the University of Minnesota. His research focuses on the management of innovation and compensation strategy.

Alison E. Barber is secretary of the board of trustees and executive assistant to the president of Michigan State University. She is also associate professor of management at The Eli Broad College of Business. Her teaching and research focus on employee recruitment and compensation. Dr. Barber is the author of *Recruiting Employees: Individual and Organizational Perspectives* (1998, Sage Publications). She earned her doctoral degree at the University of Wisconsin in Madison and has been on the Michigan State faculty since 1990. Prior to that date, she was employed in the field of human resource management.

Rowena Barrett (PhD Melbourne) is an associate professor in the Department of Management, Monash University and director of the Family and Small Business Research Unit (FSBRU) in the Faculty of Business and Economics, Monash University. Rowena's research on small business, particularly with respect to employment relations, has resulted in a number of journal articles in international and domestic refereed journals and a reputation as one of Australia's only academic specialists on small business employment/industrial relations.

Dale Belman is Professor and associate director for graduate studies in the School of Labor and Industrial Relations at Michigan State University. He received his PhD from the University of Wisconsin-Madison. He is an associate director of the Trucking Industry Program, academic chair of the Construction Industry Council of the Labor and Employment Relations Association, and facilitates the Construction Economics Research Network of the CPWR.

Melissa S. Cardon is an assistant professor of management at Pace University's Lubin School of Business. Her research focuses on unleashing human potential within entrepreneurial firms, including a dual interest in HR practices that maximize employee potential, especially for nontraditional employees such as contingent workers, and the emotional, relational, and cognitive aspects of entrepreneurs that contribute to optimizing their behavior and performance.

Bob Cardy is a professor of management at Arizona State University. He has teaching and research interests in human resource management, particularly in the areas of performance appraisal and the design of effective management systems. His work on management focuses on merging human resource management practices with the contemporary organizational environment.

Thomas W. Gainey is an associate professor in the Richards College of Business at the State University of West Georgia. He received his PhD from the University of South Carolina. His research interests include HR outsourcing, E-HR, and alternative work systems. His research has appeared in such journals as *Personnel Psychology, Industrial Relations, and Human Resource Management Journal.*

Roshni M. Goswami is a doctoral candidate and graduate teaching assistant at The University of Texas at Arlington. Her research interests include strategic human resource management, social capital, work-family conflict, and diversity. Her research has been published in the *Academy* *of Management Proceedings, Southern Management Association Proceedings* and *Proceedings of the Institute of Behavioral and Applied Management.* She holds a master's degree from Illinois State University and a bachelor's degree from the University of Mumbai in Bombay, India.

James C. Hayton (PhD Georgia State) is an assistant professor of HRM at Bocconi University. His research, which focuses upon linkages among HRM, organizational learning and corporate entrepreneurship, has been published in *Human Resource Management Journal, Organizational Research Methods, Entrepreneurship Theory & Practice, Human Resource Management Review, European Management Journal, International Journal of Technology Management, R&D Management, Journal of Management Education,* and numerous book chapters.

Robert L. Heneman if a professor of management and human resources and director of graduate programs in labor and human resources in the Max M. Fisher College of Business at The Ohio State University. Rob's primary areas of research, teaching, and consulting are in performance management, compensation, staffing, and works design. He has worked with business organizations and universities in North America, Europe, Russia, Asia, and Africa.

Brian S. Klaas is a professor of management and chair of the Management Department at the Moore School of Business, University of South Carolina. His research interests include HR outsourcing, workplace dispute resolution and employee relations, compensation, and HR in the entrepreneurial firm. He received his PhD from the University of Wisconsin-Madison.

Malayka Klimchak is a doctoral candidate in the Management Department of the Moore School of Business at the University of South Carolina. Prior to pursuing her doctoral degree, she was an HR technology and transformation consultant for PricewaterhouseCoopers. Her research interests include eHR, HR outsourcing and alternate forms of HR service delivery.

Ellen Ernst Kossek (PhD, Yale University—organizational behavior) is a leading award-winning U.S. researcher on employer support of work and family policies. She is an elected fellow of the American Psychological Association (2002) and the Society for Industrial Organizational Psychology (2001) for her contributions to work and family research. She recently co-edited two major work and family books: *Work and Life Integration: Organizational, Cultural and Individual Perspectives* (Erlbaum, 2005) and *The*

Handbook Of Work-Family: Multi-Disciplinary Perspectives and Approaches (Erlbaum 2005). She recently has been invited to present her work and family research at conferences sponsored by the National Institute of Health (2003, 2004), the Alfred P. Sloan Foundation (2003), the Conference Board of Europe (2004), the Boston College Work and Family Roundtable, and the Rockefeller Foundation (2001).

Susan Mayson (PhD, Swinburne, Grad Dip Org Beh, Swinburne) is a lecturer and director of undergraduate studies with the Department of Management, Monash University, Melbourne, Australia. She teaches and publishes in human resource management and her areas of research include HRM and small firms with a particular focus on the formalization of HR in small firms and the contribution of HRM to growth oriented small firms. Along with colleague Rowena Barrett, her next research project will be a series of small firm case studies designed to gather data on the nature and bases of HR practices in small firms.

John McClendon joined the Fox School of Business, Temple University after 25 years of demonstrated excellence in a broad array of human resource management activities. His research activities focus on HR outsourcing, compensation strategies, and labor-management relations. Since 1993, his publications have appeared in *Journal of Labor Research, Industrial and Labor Relations Review, Employee Rights and Responsibilities Journal, Journal of Management, Human Resource Management Journal*, and *Personnel Psychology*, among several others.

Gary C. McMahan is an associate professor of management and coordinator of the PhD program in management at The University of Texas at Arlington. His primary research interest is on the strategic role of human resources in organizations. He has published over 32 articles, monographs, and book chapters. Gary serves on the editorial board of the *Journal of Applied Behavioral Science*. His research has been published in premier management journals including: *The Academy of Management Journal, Journal of Management, Journal of Applied Psychology, Personnel Psychology, Human Resource Management Journal, International Journal of Human Resource Management, Human Resource Planning Journal*, and *Organizational Behavior and Human Decision Processes*.

Janice S. Miller conducts research in human resource management, with primary interests in compensation and performance management. Her recent work includes the study of HR practices that motivate part-time and seasonal workers. She received her PhD from Arizona State

University and is an associate professor at the University of Wisconsin-Milwaukee.

Janice C. Molloy is a doctoral student in labor and human resource management at The Ohio State University. Her research interests are talent attraction and strategic human resource management in entrepreneurial firms.

Michele Swift is a doctoral candidate in management at the Leeds School of Business at the University of Colorado at Boulder. Her research focuses on knowledge management and strategic human resource management.

Judith W. Tansky is a senior lecturer in labor and human resources in the Max M. Fisher College of Business at The Ohio State University. Judy has a PhD in labor and human resources from The Ohio State University. Judy's primary areas of research, teaching, and consulting are compensation, employee development and human resources in small and entrepreneurial firms.

Paul D. Tolchinsky is the managing partner of Performance Development Associates and senior lecturer at Weatherhead School of Management, Case Western Reserve University. Paul's particular expertise is in the design of organizations, applying sociotechnical principles and whole-scale approaches to the process of change in organizations.

Patrick M. Wright is professor of human resource studies and director of the Center for Advanced Human Resource Studies in the School of Industrial and Labor Relations, Cornell University. He holds a PhD in organizational behavior/human resource management from Michigan State University. Professor Wright teaches, conducts research, and consults in the area of strategic human resource management (SHRM), particularly focusing on how firms use people as a source of competitive advantage. He has published over 50 research articles in journals such as *Academy of Management Journal, Academy of Management Review, Strategic Management Journal, Organizational Behavior and Human Decision Processes, Journal of Applied Psychology, Personnel Psychology,* and *Journal of Management* as well as over 20 chapters in books and edited volumes such as *Research in P/HRM* and *Handbook of I/O Psychology.*

Hyuckseung Yang is associate professor of management at Yonsei University in Korea. He received his PhD from the Industrial Relations Center at the University of Minnesota in 1998. He also served as an assistant professor at the University of South Carolina. His research has been published in such journals as *Journal of Applied Psychology* and *Personnel Psychology.*

Printed in the United States
87615LV00001B/235/A